بِسْمِ اللهِ الرَّحْمٰنِ الرَّحِيْمِ

﴾تذکرہ سلطانیہ﴿

First published 2012 by Fast-Print Publishing of Peterborough, England.

www.fast-print.net/store.php

Biography of Qibla Alam, His Ancestors, Descendants and Devotees
Copyright © Dr Mu'in Nizami 2012
Translation copyright © Muhammad Muzamil Khan (Bawa) 2012

ISBN: 978-178035-415-6

An environmentally friendly book printed and bound in England
by www.printondemand-worldwide.com

This book is made entirely of chain-of-custody materials

بِسْمِ اللهِ الرَّحْمٰنِ الرَّحِيْمِ

﴿ تذکرہ سلطانیہ ﴾

Tazkira-e Sultaniyya: Biography of Qibla Alam, His Ancestors, Descendants and Devotees Raḥmatullāh ʿAlayhim

<u>Revised Edition</u> (2012)

Compiled by Dr Mu'in Nizami

Translation by Muhammad Muzamil Khan (Bawa)

Contents Page

Dedication

This work is humbly dedicated to the great mystic and ascetic, Hadrat Qibla Mai Sahiba *Rahmatullah Alayha,* the noble mother of Hadrat Sahib *Rahmatullah Alayhi* who not only fulfilled the rights of companionship with her husband Qibla Alam *Rahmatullah Alayhi,* but also provided spiritual training to her biological and spiritual children. *"Surely Allah does not discard the good deeds of the righteous,"* (12:90).

Preface

Hadrat Khwaja Qadi Muhammad Sadiq Naqshbandi Mujaddidi 'Hadrat Sahib' [1] *Rahmatullah Alayhi* would often relate recollections of his father, Hadrat Khwaja Qadi Muhammad Sultan Alam 'Qibla Alam' *Rahmatullah Alayhi*. These memoirs consist of the life and teachings of his noble father and spiritual guide.

In 2004 for the benefit of the *Sangis* (companions), it was decided to have these recollections published as a book. Hadrat Sahib's intuitive vision chose Professor Mu'in Nizami Sahib for this task. In 2007 Nizami Sahib sent the draft of the book *Tazkira-e Sultaniyya* to Hadrat Sahib *Rahmatullah Alayhi* and after approving the draft, he wondered, "Who knows when it shall be published?"

Praise be to Allah and with Hadrat Sahib's blessing and spiritual gaze the publication process was completed in May 2009. May Allah the Majestic make this book a source of guidance for both the elite and the masses.

Insignificant slave of God,

Muhammad Aqsad Tabi

---

[1] Custodian and Guide of the Naqshbandiyya Mujaddidiyya Sultaniyya spiritual legacy

IV

Introduction

Hadrat Khwaja Qadi Muhammad Sultan Alam *Rahmatullah Alayhi* was the spiritual master of the Naqshbandiyya Mujaddidiyya order. This Sufi order is well established in the Kashmir region. He successfully guided thousands of people in both religious and secular matters. Some of his followers completed their spiritual training with him and were then authorised to lead their own respective communities. As a result of his extensive spiritual influence he became known as 'Qibla Alam' *Rahmatullah Alayhi*.

Qibla Alam *Rahmatullah Alayhi* was born into the noble and learned al-Bakri al-Siddiqi family circa 1870/1871 in old Mirpur in a village called 'Checheyan Sharif.'[2] He passed away on 9th May 1934/23rd Muharram 1352, AH and was buried in the same village. Due to the construction of the Mangla Dam this area was submerged, therefore in 1967 his blessed body was transferred to Khanqah-e Sultaniyya, Kaladeo, Jhelum, where his shrine is now a major attraction. The present work, *Tazkira-e Sultaniyya* is based upon his noble life and personality. It also contains accounts of his *khulafa* (deputies) and some of his sincere *Sangis*.

Tazkira-e Sultaniyya is divided into three chapters:

The first chapter consists of Qibla Alam's life and teachings. The second chapter examines the life and teachings of Qibla Alam *Rahmatullah Alayhi*, his Deputies and *Sangis*. These recollections of Hadrat Sahib's are full of wisdom and contain valuable information about the local history of Azad Kashmir. Chapter Three focuses on the biographies of Twenty Seven Deputies of Qibla Alam *Rahmatullah Alayhi*.

Indeed, this book is an attempt to document and preserve the wide-ranging historical and spiritual influence of the blessed al-Bakri al-Siddiqi family of Kashmir. The main aim is to provide guidance for the devotees of this noble family. It is hoped that this account might serve as a reliable source of information for future generations.

Arguably, *Tazkira-e Sultaniyya* is a unique account as it contains the history of the Naqshbandiyya Mujaddidiyya masters of the al-Bakri al-

---

[2] Located around 5 kilometres north-west of Old Mirpur

Siddiqi family of Checheyan Sharif; their lives, the establishment of their lodges and their services to society. In addition it provides an account of the devotees of the noble al-Bakri al-Siddiqi family. Indeed, *Tazkira-e Sultaniyya* is also an account of the Kashmir region, its religion, culture and society. It contains many local customs and preserves local dialects; particular attention is given to the mosques and shrines of the region. Apart from the spiritual masters many other personalities including intoxicated mystics, memorisers and the Qur'an reciters, poets, calligraphers, teachers and people from other professions can be found throughout the book. Although it contains many Sufi and spiritual terms, one may also find many other specialised terms as well; words for different weapons, clothes and foods are mentioned which enhances its cultural importance.

I was given the task of re-arranging and finalising the composition of *Tazkira-e Sultaniyya*. I received two handwritten documents containing the recollections of Hadrat Sahib but later further information was made available to me. In this regard there was written communication between me and the Khanqah-e Fathiyya. In order to make the manuscript suitable for publication my aim has been to:

Provide all the accounts in a chronological order, whereas in the original manuscripts the accounts were not arranged in such a manner. Some comments have been omitted and new information added. Every possible effort has been made to gather only authentic accounts, and to provide the account in the style that is consistent with the tradition of the al-Bakri al-Siddiqi family.

The prose is kept simple so that ordinary Urdu readers can understand the text. I have tried to avoid difficult and complex sentence structures. Urdu translation is provided for the Persian couplets and also for expressions in the local dialects.

Despite all efforts, ultimately this remains a humble human endeavour and is not free from error. Due to various reasons this work took longer than originally anticipated and therefore publication was delayed. To all the people who were eagerly awaiting its publication, I sincerely offer my apologies and seek their forgiveness for the delay.

And finally some words of appreciation:

First and foremost I would like to thank Hadrat Sahib, who chose this sinner for this important task. Despite constant delays on my part, due to his kind nature, he never expressed any displeasure. This level of tolerance and resolve is in itself not short of a miracle. During this period Hadrat Sahib was seriously ill and could not even go to the mosque. Yet even in that poor health he remembered this humble person several times in the early hours of dawn and also enquired about the *Sangis* and blessed us with his supplications.

I was first introduced to Hadrat Sahib about nine or ten years ago. During all this time I have been blessed by his help, kindness and supplications. For me this link is a valuable source of support in this life and in the hereafter. Although the honourable Shaykh was not my spiritual master, but the love and affection that I have for him and his family means that he is equally important to me. I have only met him personally on one brief occasion; however I have had the opportunity to see him on numerous occasions.

In Hadrat Sahib's personality, I saw qualities of the great spiritual masters, whom I have admired since my childhood. It is a source of a great comfort that he is my benefactor, a considerate and compassionate guide, and one who remembers me in his supplications and gives me special attention of which I am not worthy. It is my firm belief that for this sinner to even enter his blessed thoughts is in itself similar to a supplication. May Allah protect him, preserve his spiritual blessings and bless his *Sangis* and grant him the best reward for his unique service to *din*.

I am indebted to the esteemed Munir Husayn Mujaddidi Sahib who compiled the original manuscript of *Tazkira-e Sultaniyya* with the utmost care. He gathered the recollections of his noble master with great precision and trust. Munir Mujaddidi Sahib's effort is the basis of this book. May Allah grant him what is befitting.

It is an obligation upon me to thank Hadrat Sahibzada Muhammad Aqsad Tabi who continuously supported me throughout this task and read the final draft of the book. It is his supplications and supervision that has led to the completion of *Tazkira-e Sultaniyya*, May Allah always keep him under His Grace.

During this time, Professor Muhammad Habib Allah Shah Sahib displayed exemplary patience. I was greatly impressed by his sincerity and steadfastness. I sincerely pray that may Allah keep his noble master and his descendents pleased with him as this is the key to success in both worlds.

And to all those people that I have met and those I have not, who due to instructions from their master played any part in this noble effort. Praise be to Allah in the Beginning and in the End.

14th Dhul hijjah 1428/25th December 2007,

Mu'in Nizami,

Lahore

NB: *Tazkira-e Sultaniyya* had not completed the publication process when on 31st December 2008 on Wednesday night around 11.15 pm Hadrat Sahib *Rahmatullah Alayhi* passed away, (2nd Muharram 1430). His funeral prayer was read after *dhur* on 1st January 2009. He was buried next to his great ancestor Hadrat Qadi Fath Allah Siddiqi Shattari *Rahmatullah Alayhi*. His physical separation was nothing short of the lesser doomsday. May Allah continue his spiritual legacy by the honour of His Beloved ﷺ, (*Amin*).

Translator's Note

This is not a literal translation of the Urdu book *Tazkira-e Sultaniyya* (2009) although every attempt has been made to stay faithful to the text. As the main aim is to provide a simple account of Qibla Alam's life, for sake of clarity some alterations and corrections had to be made. It would be incorrect to assume that the book merely narrates simple accounts of Qibla Alam's life, in reality it discusses many complex spiritual issues which may not be understood by the English readers. So despite all efforts to make the text simple and clear for the English readers, there remain a number of passages where a mere translation is insufficient and which require commentary. Hopefully someone will provide such a commentary in the future.

Following the publication of the English translation of *Tazkira-e Sultaniyya* entitled *Biography of Qibla Alam* (2012), it emerged that parts of the book needed further clarification. The main aim of the Revised Edition is to make the narrative simpler and also to correct minor typing errors. To achieve the aforementioned aim, most of the place names have now been moved to the footnote.

4

Chapter One

Life of Qibla Alam *Rahmatullah Alayhi*

Preamble

The land of the Indo-Pak subcontinent has the special distinction that Islam was spread in this region by the simple clothed mystics who were the upholders of the virtues of both the Islamic law and the mystical path. These holy people built their lodges throughout the land which provided practical training in both religious and mystical matters. Allah accepted their sincerity and blessed their activities and made it possible for their spiritual legacy to continue until the Day of Judgement. Consequently both Islam and Islamic culture have become an integral part for the inhabitants of this land. God willing, the glory of His name and that of His Messenger ﷺ shall continue until the Day of Judgement and from the light of which the seekers of truth shall be able to find their way.

The heavenly valley of Kashmir in the subcontinent has always been a focal point of saints. Throughout Islamic history this region has produced such pious souls whose very existence acted as a source of guidance for the heedless. Qibla Alam *Rahmatullah Alayhi* was one such holy figure, who can rightly be regarded as one of the architects of the nation.

Blessed Name

This book is written in honour of 'Hadrat Qadi Muhammad Sultan Alam' *Rahmatullah Alayhi* known to his devotees as 'Qibla Alam' and to the local people as *'Masiti Wallay Qazi Sahib'*. He often spent his time in the mosque and became known the 'Qadi Sahib of the mosque', what greater honour can there be for a Muslim?

Birth

As yet the actual date of birth of Qibla Alam *Rahmatullah Alayhi* is unknown. It would have been possible to determine his date of birth if we had the official records; unfortunately those records were burnt during the Independence Movement in 1947. A possibility still exists that those records might be amongst the few documents that are still preserved in the Jammu Audit Office. As that area is presently occupied by India and partly due to the political tension it is not possible to have access to those records. In light of these documents one could determine his actual date of birth. Presently one has to rely on two sources of data to establish his date of birth: a) family account and b) the 1931 Census. According to the family narrative he lived for sixty three years and passed away on 9th May 1934, so one could speculate that he was born in 1871. The second source is the 1931 Census, this written record is important as Qibla Alam *Rahmatullah Alayhi* personally had his age registered at sixty years, in view of which 1871 is considered his birth date.

Another factor that supports this is the external evidence which suggests that according to the family account Qibla Alam *Rahmatullah Alayhi* went to Bawali Sharif at the age of twelve where he served and gained spiritual training from his complete master for around twelve years. Shortly after Qibla Alam *Rahmatullah Alayhi* departed from Bawali Sharif, his noble master passed away. Qibla Alam *Rahmatullah Alayhi* passed away in 1934 and at that time the noble wife of his master, Hadrat Mai Sahiba *Rahmatullah Alayha* (Bawali Sharif) wrote a letter of condolence to Qibla Alam's wife, Qibla Mai Sahiba *Rahmatullah Alayha* in which she stated that she had been a widow for forty years and during all this time she had been totally dependent upon Allah and she advised her to do the same. By joining these pieces of information together one could surmise that Qibla Alam's total age was sixty three years and his birth date can either be 1870 or 1871.

Appearance

Qibla Alam's complexion was brown and he was of medium height. His chest was wide, his shoulders were broad and his forehead was wide. His eyes had a sparkle in them and were very alluring. His face showed signs of majesty. He had shoulder length hair; his beard was thick and longer than a hand span. He used Henna. He had a good physique. He was the epitome of love and kindness. There was never any sign of anger or harshness in his character. Yet he possessed such powerful eyes that one could not look at his face and if one's gaze fell on his face, it would immediately lower itself. When one saw him one would remember Allah.

Birthplace and Residence

Qibla Alam's birthplace is a village named Checheyan Sharif.[3] The village is part of the Fathpur hamlet as this area was named after Sultan Fath Muhammad Khan Ghakkar *Rahmatullah Alayhi*. The Ghakkar tribe was given land grants in this region, during the reign of the famous Mughal emperor Awrangzaib Alamgir *Rahmatullah Alayhi* (1658-1707). From the earlier times, this family controlled the social, political and military landscape in this region. Therefore all the rulers tried to maintain good relationships with them by showing them honour and giving them land. This tribe controlled the route and borders to Afghanistan, Iran and Central Asia. Sultan Fath Muhammad Khan's brother Mira Khan *Rahmatullah Alayhima* founded the city of Mirpur in 1051 AH/1641CE.

Chechi is a sub-branch of the Gujjar tribe; this suggests that in the earlier period this tribe resided there. In historical terms it is not clear when this tribe settled there or why or when it migrated from that area. During the period 1819-1846 when Qibla Alam's ancestors lived there, this area was abandoned and there were no signs of a previous settlement except for a graveyard, which was the only reminder of the bygone era.

During this period the Sikhs ruled the area and according to Qibla Alam's family accounts, it appears that the Sikhs destroyed Mirpur city and indiscriminately killed the local Muslim population. Qibla Alam's family which resided in this area during the period was also the target of the Sikh tyranny. In order to protect their honour, the womenfolk of this noble family chose to jump into wells and end their lives and attain the rank of martyrs rather than be subjected to the Sikh brutality. From the descendents of Qadi Muhammad Masum only two people namely: Qadi Muhammad Khan Muhammad and Hafiz Khwaja Muhammad Akbar Ali *Rahmatullah Alayhim* survived. The latter settled, passed away and was buried in Checheyan village. On 19th April 1993, his blessed body was moved to Kaladeo, Jhelum. He was the grandfather of Qibla Alam *Rahmatullah Alayhi* and the first of his ancestors to settle in Checheyan.

---

[3] Next to Gorsian

Genealogy

Qibla Alam ℛₐₕₘₐₜᵤₗₗₐₕ ₐₗₐᵧₕᵢ is from Quresh lineage and a descendant of Sayyiduna Abu Bakr Siddiq ﷺ. His genealogy links him with the leader of the faithful, Sayyiduna Abu Bakr Siddiq ﷺ, through his eldest son Hadrat Abd al-Rahman ﷺ (d.53 AH) after 37 generations; the family tree is as follows:

1. Qadi Muhammad Sultan Alam ﷺ
2. Qadi Muhammad Rukn Alam ﷺ
3. Qadi Khwaja Muhammad Akbar Ali ﷺ
4. Qadi Ali Muhammad ﷺ
5. Qadi Ghulam Hasan ﷺ
6. Qadi Muhammad Naqshband ﷺ
7. Qadi Muhammad Masum ﷺ
8. Qadi Fath Allah ﷺ
9. Qadi Fard Allah ﷺ
10. Qadi Abd al-Basit ﷺ
11. Qadi Abd al-Jalil ﷺ
12. Qadi Shaykh Abd Allah ﷺ
13. Shaykh Muhammad ﷺ
14. Shaykh Abd al-Majid ﷺ
15. Qadi Muhammad Hakam ﷺ
16. Qadi Fadal Allah ﷺ
17. Qadi Qadan ﷺ
18. Qadi Hidayat Allah ﷺ
19. Qadi Imad al-Din ﷺ
20. Qadi Iftikhar al-Din ﷺ
21. Qadi Qiwam al-Din ﷺ
22. Qadi Husam al-Din ﷺ
23. Qadi Nizam al-Din ﷺ
24. Qadi Fakhr al-Din ﷺ
25. Qadi 'Ala al-Din ﷺ
26. Qadi Mu'in al-Din ﷺ
27. Qadi Kamal al-Din ﷺ
28. Shaykh Imam al-Din ﷺ
29. Shaykh Shams al-Din ﷺ

30. Shaykh Husam al-Din ﷺ
31. Shaykh Ahmad ﷺ
32. Shaykh Mahmud ﷺ
33. Shaykh Abu Bakr al-Thani ﷺ
34. Shaykh Ibrahim Abu al-Barakat ﷺ
35. Shaykh Ismail ﷺ (*ta'bi*)
36. Shaykh Abd Allah ﷺ (*ta'bi*)
37. Hadrat Abd al-Rahman ﷺ (*Sahabi*)
38. Sayyiduna Abu Bakr Siddiq ﷺ, (the foremost in Islam and the first *khalifa*)

Ancestor's Arrival in Iran

Shaykh Kamal al-Din Yemeni *Rahmatullah Alayhi* was the *amir* of Yemen. He left his rule and migrated to Madinah Sharif and taught Hadith in the Prophet's Mosque for many years. The great Suhrawardi Sufi master of the Indo-Pak subcontinent, Hadrat Shaykh Baha al-Din Zakariyya Multani *Rahmatullah Alayhi* (d.666 AH) was one of his students, who gained permission to transmit the famous books of Hadith known as the 'Six Authentic Collections'. Shaykh Baha al-Din Zakariyya had another distinction; during his five year stay in the blessed Hijaz every year he performed Hajj with his teacher Shaykh Kamal al-Din Yemeni *Rahmatullah Alayhima*. Later Shaykh Kamal al-Din Yemeni *Rahmatullah Alayhi* migrated to Sistan [4] and became the *qadi* (judge) of Jjnayr. For the subsequent five generations his descendants such as Shaykh Mu'in al-Din, Shaykh 'Ala al-Din, Shaykh Fakhr al-Din, Shaykh Nizam al-Din and Shaykh Husam al-Din *Rahmatullah Alayhim* occupied that position.

Ancestor's Arrival in the Indo-Pak subcontinent

The sixth descendant of Shaykh Kamal al-Din Yemeni *Rahmatullah Alayhi* was Qadi Qiwam al-Din *Rahmatullah Alayhi* who migrated to Delhi. At that time Delhi was ruled by the Tughluq dynasty (720-815 AH). In Delhi, Qadi Qiwam al-Din *Rahmatullah Alayhi* became a follower and deputy of the Sultan of the Masters, Shaykh Nizam al-Din Awliya *Rahmatullah Alayhi* (d.725 AH). The Sultan of Delhi appointed Qadi Qiwam al-Din *Rahmatullah Alayhi* as a judge of Rohtak.[5]

---

[4] Iran/Afghanistan
[5] Located between Hansi and Delhi

When the Muslim rule in India came to an end many families of Sayyids and Quresh moved to Rohtak. Qadi Qiwam al-Din *Rahmatullah Alayhi* married a lady from the Qureshi family in Rohtak from whom his numerous descendants trace their lineage. The prominent posts of judge, chief justice, inspector, scholar and orator stayed in this family from generation to generation. Even during the British occupation some members of this family occupied key posts. The British paid tribute to the services of this family in the Delhi Coronation in 1911. Qadi Qiwam al-Din *Rahmatullah Alayhi* was without a peer in both knowledge and piety and he was well known for his spirituality. In his proclamation dated Rabi' al-awwal 1117 AH/12th June 1705, Awrangzaib Alamgir *Rahmatullah Alayhi* granted him the title of *Zubda-tul Awliya*. One can surmise that despite the fact that three centuries had passed since Qadi Qiwam al-Din's demise, the great emperor still remembered him with such honour and respect.

Arrival in the State of Jammu and Kashmir

In order to seek knowledge one of the beloved sons of this family, Hadrat Qadi Fath Allah ibn Qadi Fard Allah *Rahmatullah Alayhima* travelled from Rohtak to the madrasa of Sayyid Mubarak Shah (1081AH/1670) *Rahmatullah Alayhi*.[6] During that period Sayyid Mubarak Shah *Rahmatullah Alayhi* who was well known for his knowledge and piety. He was the principal of the highly reputed madrasa, where a number of prominent scholars taught religious knowledge. The fame of this madrasa spread far and wide and students came to study here because of its excellent reputation. It is for this reason that Hadrat Qadi Fath Allah *Rahmatullah Alayhi* chose to study at this madrasa. A gifted teacher like Sayyid Mubarak Shah *Rahmatullah Alayhi* quickly saw the potential in his bright student and treated him with love and affection. Hadrat Qadi Fath Allah *Rahmatullah Alayhi* became a favourite student of his teacher and benefactor.

Not only was Sayyid Mubarak Shah *Rahmatullah Alayhi* a learned scholar but he was also well versed in spiritual matters. He was an authorised deputy of Hadrat Khwaja Muhammad Ya'qub and Hadrat Muhammad Hasan Rohtasi *Rahmatullah Alayhima* in the Shattariyya order. Apart from teaching, he was very fond of worship and asceticism. Despite having wealth he avoided the pleasures of the world and was very scrupulous in his conduct and often spent his time in seclusion.

---

[6] Alipur Sayyidain,Behra, situated about three kilometres north-west of Sargodha

During his studies, the desire to find a spiritual guide grew in the heart of Hadrat Qadi Fath Allah *Rahmatullah Alayhi,* without a doubt this was also due to the blessing of his teacher Sayyid Mubarak Shah *Rahmatullah Alayhi.* When the teacher saw the genuine desire in his gifted student, he began to inform him about the high spiritual rank his master Hadrat Muhammad Hasan Rohtasi *Rahmatullah Alayhi* occupied. This intensified the passion further and in order to reach the spiritual guide he was instructed by a Darwish to perform the forty day seclusion and within a few days he began to see the results. His sincere request was accepted by Allah and Hadrat Muhammad Hasan Rohtasi and another saint Hadrat Sharaf al-Din Muhammad *Rahmatullah Alayhima* came to visit the madrasa and thus the seeker and the sought met.

Hadrat Muhammad Hasan Rohtasi immediately saw the potential in Hadrat Qadi Fath Allah *Rahmatullah Alayhima* and instructed him to come to Rohtas with him. Despite the fact that he was about to complete his studies, he did not hesitate to obey his guide. Hadrat Muhammad Hasan Rohtasi *Rahmatullah Alayhi* was a complete master but had a strange personality; for example many prominent scholars and Sayyids came to become his followers but he did not accept them. Indeed, he would inform them that his association was akin to poison and advised them to stay away from him.

Hadrat Muhammad Hasan Rohtasi *Rahmatullah Alayhi* stated, "The Sufi path cannot be attained without giving up the world and required constant struggle, seclusion, asceticism. All of these things are difficult for the people of the world. The fortunate soul who sets off on this path becomes useless to the world. Thus one should only accept those sincere people who have the capacity to bear all the hardship and continue travelling on the path." Hadrat Qadi Fath Allah *Rahmatullah Alayhi* fulfilled all of these difficult pre-requisites of his guide. So Hadrat Muhammad Hasan Rohtasi *Rahmatullah Alayhi* put him through rigorous spiritual training which he successfully completed. Despite the painstaking discipline he never failed to serve his master and guide with all his heart. Therefore after many years of hardship he successfully completed the nine stages of the Shattariyya order and gained authorisation and *khilafat* from Hadrat Muhammad Hasan Rohtasi *Rahmatullah Alayhi* who then ordered him to go and settle in Mirpur, which was then ruled by the Ghakkars.

The Mirpur region was under the rule of Sultan Fath Muhammad Khan Ghakkar *Rahmatullah Alayhi* who had been granted[7] and the surrounding areas and was given the title of 'Sultan' from the central government in Delhi. This post remained in this family for four generations. Along with the high worldly position he was a caring, pious, practising person who supported learning. He was so impressed with the charismatic personality of Hadrat Qadi Fath Allah *Rahmatullah Alayhi* that he made him his son-in-law and it is from this wife that descendants trace their lineage.

First of all Hadrat Qadi Fath Allah built a mosque and a lodge on the land donated by Sultan Fath Muhammad Khan Ghakkar *Rahmatullah Alayhima*, this was the first mosque and spiritual centre in this city. The first house of the al-Bakri al-Siddiqi family was also built here. A spacious madrasa was built with the mosque complex where students from afar would come to study. There was sufficient accommodation for both students of knowledge and spirituality. The Delhi central government appointed Hadrat Qadi Fath Allah *Rahmatullah Alayhi* as the chief judge of the sate of Mirpur. For thirty years he performed his duties as a judge, teacher and a spiritual guide and passed away on 8th Sha'ban 1088 AH/1688. He was buried in the bestowed cemetery next to the mosque. Due to the building of the Mangla Dam his shrine was submerged and gradually eroded and therefore people were unable to pay their respects. For the benefit of the visitors his blessed body was moved and laid to rest in Masjid al-Firdous[8] and his shrine is now the centre of attraction. Qibla Alam is the seventh descendant of Hadrat Qadi Fath Allah *Rahmatullah Alayhima*.

Qibla Alam's Education

Qibla Alam *Rahmatullah Alayhi* grew up in a learned, religious and spiritual family. His home was an abode of religious and spiritual learning. His early education and upbringing took place in an environment that had love for the *din*, knowledge and spirituality, which made a lasting impression on his personality. There is a well established family tradition in which children are taught basic religious knowledge alongside practical knowledge of how to live one's life. Hence knowledge and actions complement one another. The aim of such an upbringing is that a person is not merely trained to be a preacher, debater, scholar or a religious political figure but someone who is perfect in following

---

[7] Dāngali
[8] Kotli, Azad Kashmir

the *Sunnah* of the Prophet ﷺ. Outward show is frowned upon in this family and instead the focus is on purifying one's inner self. The members of the family should be pious themselves and they should have the ability to guide others as well. The family members deem their *din* far more precious than anything else in the world and so a deep attachment to the *din* becomes their ultimate goal in life.

Worship and awareness of Allah is the purpose of human existence and if one dedicates one's whole life in the pursuit of external knowledge then this objective cannot be attained, indeed a major part of one's life should be spent in the pursuit of true knowledge. True knowledge is connected with the heart and spiritual attention and one cannot travel on this path without refinement, sincerity, struggle and self-discipline. It is for this reason that even today these principles are adhered to in the family of Qibla Alam *Rahmatullah Alayhi.*

Every effort is made to protect the members of the family from the ill effects of society. From the outset they are trained in both religious knowledge and proper upbringing and guided towards worship and self-discipline. As a result, an unconditional observance of religious obligations and with it non-obligatory practices are foremost in their mind and Allah willing this way of life shall continue.

It is important to stress that Qibla Alam's family is not against higher education or gaining degrees. Indeed due to his spiritual blessing dozens of people are studying in prominent institutions throughout the country. What is important however is that one should be well versed with one's religious obligations and practice so one is steadfast in faith and would not be adversely affected by external influences.

Qibla Alam *Rahmatullah Alayhi* received his initial education and training at home. Then he was enrolled at the madrasa.[9] This madrasa was chosen keeping in mind all the qualities that are valued in the family. The madrasa is now located in new Dadyal. During his education some miraculous events took place, due to which his esteemed teacher became very anxious and informed Qibla Alam's father. As a result Qibla Alam *Rahmatullah Alayhi* returned home with his father.

---

[9] Sahaleye Mandi, *Vichla Mohra*

13

Bay'a: Oath of Allegiance

When Qibla Alam was twelve years old, his father Khwaja Muhammad Rukn Alam *Rahmatullah Alayhima* took him to take the oath of allegiance from a great master at Bawali Sharif in Gujarat as he was a follower of this spiritual centre himself. The masters of Bawali Sharif were linked with the noble Naqshbandiyya Mujaddidiyya order. Khwaja Muhammad Rukn Alam's master, Khwaja Muhammad Khan Alam *Rahmatullah Alayhima* had passed away and he had two sons: Khwaja Muhammad Bakhsh (known as *Lendey Wallay Pir*, west area) and Khwaja Ghulam Muhyi al-Din *Rahmatullah Alayhima* (known as *Chardey Wallay Pir*, east area). The Bawali Sharif Khanqah was well liked by the local people and the contemporary scholars and Sufis trusted the masters of this lodge.

Khwaja Muhammad Rukn Alam had made the intention of visiting the shrine of his master Khwaja Muhammad Khan Alam *Rahmatullah Alayhima* and so on the journey he explained the etiquette of the visit to his son and instructed him to make a supplication at the shrine, in order that Allah would grant him guidance. As instructed Qibla Alam *Rahmatullah Alayhi* began to make his supplications and his father went into meditation. When his father raised his head from the meditation he saw his son praying and tears were flowing down his cheeks. "Baba Ji has completed my son's task," he remarked. In this trance like state Qibla Alam *Rahmatullah Alayhi* was neither aware of time nor place. This was the first time that he experienced a strange mystical incident. Then his noble father handed him over to Khwaja Muhammad Bakhsh who accepted Qibla Alam *Rahmatullah Alayhima* into the Naqshbandiyya Mujaddidiyya order. Qibla Alam displayed signs of sincerity and Khwaja Muhammad Bakhsh *Rahmatullah Alayhima* began to train him by starting with the *bismillah* on his spiritual heart. Qibla Alam *Rahmatullah Alayhi* made rapid spiritual success and began to pass through the stages of *fana* and *baqa* (the process of subduing the carnal soul) by his sincere and hard work.

Sometimes Qibla Alam *Rahmatullah Alayhi* was overwhelmed by his spiritual states which can only be understood by those who have had similar experiences. The following incident beautifully illustrates his mystical stages during his training. Qibla Alam's uncle Khwaja Fadal Ahmad *Rahmatullah Alayhi* relates that, "One night I was reading my daily *wird* (litany) in which I had to read *sura Ya-Sin* 70 times. During this time Muhammad Sultan Alam began to shout: "You are in me and I am in you, *tu meray vich mein teray vich*" and this affected my concentration. So I told him numerous times to say it quietly but to no avail. Finally I became upset and I shouted at him." The son of Khwaja Fadal Ahmad, Khwaja Muhammad Fadil *Rahmatullah Alayhima* continues the story, "That night my father suddenly woke up and began to ask for forgiveness. I enquired as to why he seemed so worried, he replied, "I made a mistake by shouting at my nephew. He shall occupy a high rank and thousands of people shall benefit from him." The next morning Qibla Alam *Rahmatullah Alayhi* was sat on the balcony near his bed when Khwaja Fadal Ahmad *Rahmatullah Alayhi* came and said, "I feel like touching your feet as I made a mistake." Qibla Alam *Rahmatullah Alayhi* remained silent.

For twelve years Qibla Alam *Rahmatullah Alayhi* served his master with exemplary standards. One day his master said, "If we go away on our travels then seek the company of Hafiz Muhammad Hayat, *agar assain wanday safar chaly gay teh tussi Hafiz Muhammad Hayat de sohbet ikhtiyar karna.*" He then gave him permission to go home. These words were like a bolt of lightning for Qibla Alam *Rahmatullah Alayhi* as he understood the demise of his master was imminent. He began to cry at the prospect of never seeing his master again. The master was deeply touched by the sentiments of his loyal follower. Following his master's instruction he went back home and within a few days as he had feared, his master passed away.

Completion of Spiritual Training

Qibla Alam *Rahmatullah Alayhi* had served his master in Bawali Sharif for twelve years. During this time he was the focus of attention. His caring master gave him special attention and trained him in the Naqshbandiyya Zubayriyya path. During these twelve years under the supervision of his master, Qibla Alam *Rahmatullah Alayhi* fulfilled the obligations of worship, self-discipline and struggle. He devoted his energies to obtain the path. However before he could complete his training and obtain authorisation his master passed away.

Following the demise of his master he acted upon his instructions and went to serve his master's deputy Khwaja Hafiz Muhammad Hayat[10] *Rahmatullah Alayhi* (d. 3rd Rabi' al-awwal 1325 AH/1916 CE) and to complete his training. Khwaja Hafiz Muhammad Hayat *Rahmatullah Alayhi* was very considerate towards him and always treated him with kindness. After serving him for 12 years he was granted permission and given *khilafat*.

---

[10] Dangrot Sharif, District Jhelum

The path of Khwaja Hafiz Muhammad Hayat *Rahmatullah Alayhi* was the Zubayriyya path. During this time a major development took place. Hadrat Pir Sayyid Muhammad Neyk Alam Shah *Rahmatullah Alayhi* (d. 22 *Rabi' al-awwal* 1319 AH/1899 CE)[11] was a qualified scholar and the *qutb* (pole) of the time and followed the Naqshbandiyya Mujaddidiyya order. He was the deputy of Hadrat Shaykh Hajji Muhammad *Rahmatullah Alayhi* of Bafa Sharif.[12] His method of training was the Sayfiyya way and that's how he used to train his followers. Once Khwaja Hafiz Muhammad Hayat met Pir Sayyid Muhammad Neyk Alam Shah *Rahmatullah Alayhima* who said to him, "Hafiz Sahib we want to give you a share of the blessing." He replied, "The benediction of Bawali Sharif is sufficient for me." Pir Sayyid Muhammad Neyk Alam *Rahmatullah Alayhi* reiterated, "You have a share with us, take it, keep your main contact there and visit us now and then." Following this Khwaja Hafiz Muhammad Hayat began to visit Hadrat Pir Sayyid Neyk Alam *Rahmatullah Alayhima* who became his master in the Sayfiyya method.

Regarding the Zubayriyya and Sayfiyya training there is an important narration by Qibla Alam's noble successor Hadrat Sahib *Rahmatullah Alayhima*. He states that, "Once in Gulhar, Kotli, Azad Kashmir, Hadrat Abu al-Hasan Zaid Faruqi Delhawi *Rahmatullah Alayhi* enquired from me, "Is there any difference between the Zubayriyya and Sayfiyya training?" I replied, "There must be" Hadrat Khwaja Abu Sa'id and Hadrat Khwaja Abd al-Rauf Ahmad Mujaddidi *Rahmatullah Alayhima* both of whom had *khilafat* in the Zubayriyya method, went and studied the Sayfiyya method under Hadrat Shah Ghulam Ali Delhawi *Rahmatullah Alayhi* and subsequently both taught the Sayfiyya method throughout their lives. Hadrat Sahib *Rahmatullah Alayhi* stated that this was his personal opinion and Allah knows best. Qibla Alam *Rahmatullah Alayhi* had been trained in both the Zubayriyya and Sayfiyya methods, in addition he had permission in other Sufi orders but he used to take the oath of allegiance in the Sayfiyya order and give instructions according to the Mujaddidiyya order.

Khilafat and Authorisation

Qibla Alam *Rahmatullah Alayhi* became a fully fledged spiritual guide at the age of forty. By this time he had completed the purification of the inner self and

---

[11] Gorah Sayyidain, District Mirpur
[12] Mansera, Hazara

was fully competent to train students. Allah granted him a great deal of blessings and as predicted by the saints earlier he guided thousands of people.

Sangi

Qibla Alam *Rahmatullah Alayhi* always referred to his followers as '*Sangis*' and this tradition continues in his family to the present day. 'Sangi' is a very meaningful term and in the local dialect it means: a) fellow traveller, b) companion and c) friend. Indeed the spiritual guide and the novice are 'fellow travellers' on the path, 'friends' in both public and private and 'companions' in both worldly and religious matters. No better word can be substituted in the local dialect for the term *murid* (disciple) other than 'Sangi'. Indeed there is a sweetness and attraction in the mere sound of the word.

First Sangi and First Authorised Deputy

According to reliable sources, the first person to take the oath of allegiance at the blessed hands of Qibla Alam *Rahmatullah Alayhi* was Sain Umar Din and the first authorised deputy was Miyan Shah Wali.[13]

The Spiritual Power at the Outset of His Guidance

When Qibla Alam *Rahmatullah Alayhi* began to guide people, such was his spiritual impact that if anyone touched any part of his blessed body, that person's body would start to remember Allah. Mawlana Abd al-Khaliq Chachi *Rahmatullah Alayhi* [14] was a learned scholar who had taught at many institutions throughout the subcontinent, and he came to Qibla Alam *Rahmatullah Alayhi* in order to purify his inner self. He narrates his own experience, "One day I was sat in the Checheyan Sharif mosque and Qibla Alam *Rahmatullah Alayhi* was stood next to the window reading some book when he called me over and said, "Move forward and have a look." As the book was in his hands I had to lean forward and a part of my body touched his and from that part of my body I could hear "Allah, Allah.""

---

[13] Both lived in Dadyal
[14] District Attock

Qibla Alam *Rahmatullah Alayhi* always dressed according to the *Sunnah*. He liked plain and simple clothes. His clothes were mostly made of cotton, woven on the hand weaving machine. He was very informal when it came to clothes and avoided any type of pretence. He only had one pair of clothes and at the time of his demise that is all he possessed. That pair has been preserved as a relic. His *kurta* (long shirt) was below his knees and his *dhoti* (sarong) was always above his ankles. He probably never wore a *shalwar* (loose trouser) although there is one account that once during winter he had a thin woollen *shalwar* made but there is no evidence to suggest that he ever wore it. He normally wore a five pointed cloth cap on his head. In summer he would wear a plain shawl and in winter he would use a black cashmere shawl. When he wore his shawl one could only see his face. He wore local pointed footwear and normally had just the one pair of shoes.

Once his authorised deputy Khwaja Muhammad Akbar Ali *Rahmatullah Alayhi* brought him a cashmere long shirt, he wore it for some time and it had stains of his perspiration. After his demise the shirt was hung up on a hook. Sometime later Qibla Mai Sahiba *Rahmatullah Alayha* handed it back to Khwaja Muhammad Akbar Ali *Rahmatullah Alayhi*. During the partition in 1947 when he migrated to Pakistan he was carrying the shirt on his head out of respect, considering it a precious gift and guarded it with his life. Presently this blessed shirt is a family heirloom and kept in Pakpattan Sharif. In order to protect it from dust, damp and insects it is kept inside a cover.

Not everyone is aware of how to tie a *dhoti;* according to the clear command of the Shari'ah it should rest above the ankles but some people out of sheer arrogance let it drag on the floor. Qibla Alam's authorised deputy and the author of the *Tohfa-e Sultaniyya*, Hajji Mawlana Baqa Muhammad (d.15th August 1976) *Rahmatullah Alayhi* relates his own incident. "After I had been a follower for some time I was advised by Qibla Alam *Rahmatullah Alayhi*, "Hajji Sahib lead the prayers." So according to the command I led the prayers for a few days. One day he summoned me and said, "Maulvi Sahib, I shall recite the Qur'an and you listen." I understood that this was a subtle way of correcting my faults. As my *dhoti* would drag on the floor I would have to pull it up again and again during the prayers. Qibla Alam *Rahmatullah Alayhi* said, "Maulvi Sahib, let me show you how to tie the *dhoti* correctly so that you shall be saved the inconvenience of having to pull it up again and again." Then he showed me how to pick the sides and tie a tight knot which would stay wherever you set it." Hajji Baqa Muhammad *Rahmatullah Alayhi* states that this became his lifelong practice.

Diet

Rasul Allah ﷺ said, "Allah has freed me from pretence." Qibla Alam's life was a manifestation of this tradition. He had few needs or desires and was free from all types of pretence. His way was so natural that one cannot imagine a simpler way of life. In food, as in other matters he followed the *Sunnah*. He never made great effort or formality with his food. Whatever was easily available would suffice. In those days tea was not common and he was not in the habit of eating breakfast. From *fajr* to sunrise he would be busy with the *Sangis* in *dhikr* and then would perform his prayers after sunrise. He would eat his lunch before mid-day and rest for the siesta before the *dhur* prayer. He would eat his evening meal between *maghrib* and *isha*. After *isha* he despised talking about *dunya* and instead preferred that the *Sangis* went to sleep early so they could rise for the *tahajjud* prayer. Staying awake late after *isha* might result in one missing the *tahajjud* prayer, observance of which is an essential part of the path.

He normally liked to eat plain chapatti and chutney and sometimes used curry as well. He always used to carry the ingredients of the chutney mix with him whether at home or on his travels. The mixture of the chutney was made from the following ingredients: pomegranate seeds, mint, Fenugreek (*methi*), *timbr* (herb similar to black pepper), salt and black pepper. In times of need he would add some water to the mixture and make chutney and eat his food with it. He did not like greasy food and if there was a buttered chapatti in the meal he would give it to another *Sangi*. He did not avoid sweet dishes, if they were presented he would eat them, otherwise he would never express a desire to eat them or make an effort to obtain them.

Qibla Alam's temperament was cold and for this purpose he used the Philosopher's mixture. He liked *kerla* and roasted black chick peas, in his view they were greatly beneficial to someone suffering from phlegm related illness. If food was unpleasant he would never complain. Sometimes he would eat on his own or but often he would eat with the *Sangis*. He would eat his food on the table spread and before starting to eat he would wash his hands and read *bismillah* in the beginning and *al-hamdulillah* at the end and also recite the

Sunnah du'a. His method of eating was in line with the *Sunnah* as he lifted his right ankle and rested on his left and ate with three fingers and whilst eating he would often repeat *al-hamdulillah.* This method of eating is still the practice amongst *Sangis* today. On numerous occasions Miyan Sattar Muhammad (deputy and senior *Sangi*)[15] ate in the same plate as Qibla Alam *Rahmatullah Alayhi.* After eating he would wipe his plate clean so it seemed as if it was washed. He normally liked to eat in clay made pots.

Qibla Alam *Rahmatullah Alayhi* would accept the invitation of sincere *Sangis* but with the condition that no great effort was made to prepare tasty dishes as it was his wish to eat whatever food was normally cooked for the family. During his travels he would stay in the mosque. If the host offered to bring the food into the mosque he would say, "That will be inconvenient for you, this humble servant will come himself." During one of his journeys in 1929 he accepted the invitation of Raja Karim Dad Khan known as Kimanh Khan,[16] Mawlana Ata' Allah Shah Bukhari was also invited.

Hospitality

Hospitality is an important feature of Islam. Indeed the Arabs are renowned throughout the world for their hospitality. Qibla Alam *Rahmatullah Alayhi* inherited the passion for hospitality from his ancestors. Even today one is surprised at the extent of people being fed through this hospitality. Everyday hundreds of people are fed at the family's table spread.

Qibla Alam's period was a time of poverty and hardship and there were none of the facilities we enjoy today. In addition he lived outside the city in a little remote village and the guests would walk there on foot. One could not predict when and how guests would arrive. The *Sangis* could arrive at any time of the day or night and had to be fed. There was no chef to take care of them.

In fact Qibla Mai Sahiba *Rahmatullah Alayha* had to carry out all these chores: grinding wheat, kneading flour, cooking chapattis in the clay oven and making curry. In winter she would heat water for the *Sangis* to make *wudu.* She would also provide bedding according to the weather. In addition she had to take care of her family's needs, truly Qibla Mai Sahiba *Rahmatullah Alayha* had remarkable

---

[15] Amb, Tehsil Dadyal
[16] Manor, Panjera, Kotli

determination. Despite all these commitments food was served on time and everyone was fed, the food would be the same for everybody except in the case of an ill person or someone with special dietary requirements. Everyone's needs were met. The food was always served from the right even if an important person was sitting on the opposite side.

Sometimes Qibla Alam *Rahmatullah Alayhi* would eat with the guests, at other times he would help wash their hands and serve them food. His sources were confined to the income from his land. He would attribute the land to his *Sangis*, and he would say, "Go and show them their land," as he considered this gift from Allah was for the purpose of serving his guests. If a guest came from afar, on his departure he would be given food for the journey back. This food would consist of one buttered chapatti, one plain chapatti, pickle or fried eggs or both. Boundaries were set on all four directions to say farewell to the guests. Qibla Alam *Rahmatullah Alayhi* would say farewell to the guest at those respective boundaries and pray for their safe return, sometimes due to wisdom he invited the guest back and requested that they stay for a further few days.

The guests were given permission upon their request. The guest from afar was considered a guest for the period of three days. After this period if someone wanted to stay longer then there was no restriction. Some *Sangis* would stay for months in order to purify their inner selves. Some of the poorer *Sangis* would be given money for their travel costs.

This passion for hospitality is evident in the last moments of Qibla Alam's beloved wife Qibla Mai Sahiba *Rahmatullah Alayha*. The eye witnesses to this incident are still alive. Hajji Punnu (*Sangi*) from Kotli was travelling back to the UK with his family and went to say a final farewell at Khanqah-e Sultaniyya, Jhelum. Qibla Mai Sahiba *Rahmatullah Alayha* was unwell and kept becoming unconscious. After she had met these visitors she fainted again. The whole family was worried. When she regained her consciousness at night, the first thing she enquired was, "Have you served tea and sweets to the guests?" Shortly afterwards she passed away. This passion for hospitality was due to the training of Qibla Alam *Rahmatullah Alayhi* which entered every cell of her being. Due to Qibla Alam's teachings everyone in his family, including the *Sangis* who lived there, were eager to serve the guests. There is another incident a few days prior to Qibla Mai Sahiba's demise. Some *Sangis* wanted to leave after they had paid a visit to enquire about Qibla Mai Sahiba's health. Qibla Mai Sahiba *Rahmatullah Alayha* said, "Have food before you go, the chapattis shall soon be brought from the oven." But the *Sangis* insisted on leaving so Qibla Mai Sahiba *Rahmatullah Alayha* instructed, "Wrap two chapattis each and pickle for them."

Lawful Livelihood

Qibla Alam *Rahmatullah Alayhi* gave great importance to lawful livelihood. He used to stress the need for lawful livelihood to his *Sangis* and took great care in this matter. All his life he refrained from eating doubtful food. Indeed, his needs were so basic that he survived on chapattis and chutney. For livelihood he had his land in which there was no room for oppression of any kind, illegal profit or denying someone's rights. He used to sow seeds, plough, grow wheat and feed himself and the *Sangis* from the produce of his land. Throughout his life he was never involved in any capacity with the government and never asked anyone for help. He was a very independent minded person and despite being a master of the path with numerous followers and many deputies, his method of guidance was far from the norm; he sat and resided in the mosque and used it to train the seekers of the path. When he travelled to train and instruct the *Sangis* he would stay in the mosque. He would guide them to the way to Allah and save them from falling into innovation and error.

All of his *Sangis* had some form of occupation: farming or other forms of employment. He would order them to do good deeds and refrain from evil deeds and kept a watchful eye on them. Most *Sangis* took on his characteristics and worked hard for their livings and were not a burden on people. His objective was to distribute love for Allah and the Prophet ﷺ to the people. Therefore he never encouraged people to make offerings to him, nonetheless he would accept gifts in order not to hurt the feelings of his *Sangis*. He was so detached from the world that when he passed away apart from some grain in the containers, there was not a single penny in the house. His whole life was based on the belief that Allah is enough for His servant and this noble tradition is his legacy.

Mode of Speech

Qibla Alam *Rahmatullah Alayhi* would mostly hold his gatherings in the mosque; evidently one cannot talk about worldly matters in the mosque. He would explain the deeper meaning of both religious matters and good moral conduct and the *Sangis* would listen attentively with their heads lowered. The *Sangis* would pay attention to his every word and tried their best to put it into practice. He would never be upset with people's questions however due to his presence and awe people would rarely ask questions. If he asked someone a question then that person would reply. His voice had power and majesty in it and he would talk in a clear tone. Every word could be clearly heard and understood by the listener.

During his speech his voice was neither loud nor muted and depending upon the topic he would raise or lower his tone. During the talk he would repeat the key points so that they could be remembered. His mother tongue was Mirpuri and he spoke in this dialect keeping in view the intellect and ability of the audience. If any *Sangi* made a mistake and he wanted to reprimand him then he would not criticise him directly but would indirectly mention what was desirable and what was not, which was very effective. Most of his talks focused on improving one's inner self and in order to re-enforce the point he would cite stories of the saints and encourage his *Sangis* to adopt the way of piety and purity and to subdue their egos. He never expressed anger over any unpleasant incident. Allah had granted him such forbearance that he always remained calm. From this one can imagine what a firm grip he had on his ego.

Once Qibla Alam *Rahmatullah Alayhi* was staying in a mosque, [17] and the nearby vast land, which had numerous trees, was owned by a Chaudary Ya'qub. When someone cut one of his trees he became angry and came to the mosque and hurled abuse at the *Sangis* thinking they had cut the tree. He said to Qibla Alam *Rahmatullah Alayhi*, "You have gathered all these robbers and thieves around yourself, and one of them has cut my *palai'* tree." Qibla Alam *Rahmatullah Alayhi* talked to him in a calm and polite manner and said: "*Sangiyya* (Friend) we teach them good things and stop them from doing bad deeds and do not misguide anyone." Then pointing in a certain direction, he said, "Look over there." Interestingly the Chaudary Sahib found his tree which had been cut into planks. So he realised this could not have been the work of the *Sangis*. As Allah had written guidance for him this incident led to his conversion.

Chaudary Ya'qub was now ashamed of the accusation he had made and was greatly impressed by the tolerance of Qibla Alam *Rahmatullah Alayhi*. He began to come to his gatherings and quietly listen but would never stay for the prayer. Neither Qibla Alam *Rahmatullah Alayhi* nor any *Sangi* scolded him for doing this. One day he realised his own mistake and told his wife to bring him some clean

---

[17] Gorah, Dadyal

clothes as he felt embarrassed every time they were praying and he had to come home as his clothes were not pure. From that day he began to offer his prayers. Afterwards he became a *Sangi* of Qibla Alam *Rahmatullah Alayhi* and strived hard and began his progress in the spiritual ranks. Due to Allah's Mercy he became a saint and thereafter was known as Sain Muhammad Ya'qub and this title has stayed with his descendants. Similarly there were other such incidents but Qibla Alam *Rahmatullah Alayhi* always remained calm and won people over due to his good manners.

Qibla Alam's speech was precise and free from unnecessary chatter. He spoke in a gentle and considerate manner. He would avoid praise or criticism, he neither exaggerated someone's qualities nor criticised anyone's weaknesses. If a *Sangi* tried to allude to someone's faults he would stop him and say, "One should worry about one's self. The only one who can criticise others is the one who is sinless himself." He would tell *Sangis* to beware of the tricks of the ego and think good of other people.

In times of joy he would smile and keep his gaze lowered. At times of sadness he kept his dignity and grace. Regarding himself he always forgave people and kept his emotions in check and would answer harshness with gentleness. But when it came to matters of the Shari'ah if someone ridiculed or made a derogatory remark about any matters of *din* he would not tolerate it. There were incidents of this nature but it is not appropriate to go into details at this point.

Observance of the Sunnah

The complete obedience to the way of Rasul Allah ﷺ is the soul of the faith and the life of spirituality. Qibla Alam's focus was always on the *Sunnah* and he observed its every detail. He encouraged the *Sangis* to follow the *Sunnah*. He was linked with the Naqshbandiyya Mujaddidiyya order which places a great deal of importance on observing the *Sunnah*. In this order it is considered doubtful to even loosely follow the permissible acts. In the view of the masters of the path it is just as important to avoid doubtful things as it is to avoid forbidden matters. And besides, Qibla Alam *Rahmatullah Alayhi* studied for 12 years at the centre of guidance in Bawali Sharif where the masters were extremely cautious; one day Khwaja Khan Alam *Rahmatullah Alayhi* became aware that one person who did not offer his prayers was amongst the people who cut the grain in the field. So he forbade that day's crop from being used in the *langar sharif* (communal food).

Qibla Alam's life was the epitome of love for the Prophet ﷺ and true love makes one follow the beloved. He dedicated his whole life to following the noble *Sunnah* and gained great comfort and joy from it. He would always drink water whilst sitting down in three sips and ate food in clay dishes. He would place the *wudu* water jug towards the direction of the *qibla*. His complete successor Hadrat Sahib narrates: "Sometimes after *isha* I would have the good fortune to place the jug near the headboard and he would instruct me, "Point its head towards the *qibla*. Similarly he would always place his shoes facing the *qibla*. He would sit on his knees and approved of this posture."

Piety

Qibla Alam *Rahmatullah Alayhi* was always in the state of awe of Allah and worried about his salvation as situations change day and night. Apart from the Prophets no one is safe from these changes, i.e. loss of faith. He tried to fulfil his obligations and in addition even the non-obligatory matters. To avoid what Allah and His Prophet ﷺ have forbidden is piety. The consequence of sins is always bad and besides that one faces the anger and wrath of Allah. To refrain from sin and save one's self from bad consequences and Allah's wrath is called piety.

For this reason Qibla Alam *Rahmatullah Alayhi* was very cautious about things, for example he would perform the desired acts and always chose to follow the difficult option rather than take concessions. He was very careful about purity and hence would take great care to remain in *wudu*. He would often be occupied in *dhikr*, contemplation and recitation of the Qur'an and stayed in the mosque. In order to fulfil the obligation of *wudu* he would always perform two units of prayer afterwards known as *tahiyya tul wudu*. In a similar manner his *Sangis* would remain in the state of purity and offer two units afterwards on a regular basis.

He was very careful about the source of his food and avoided doubtful provisions. He would never eat anything that was prepared in the Bazaar. He would encourage his *Sangis* to follow the path of piety. One simpleton *Sangi* who stayed with Qibla Alam *Rahmatullah Alayhi* was not aware that he had to shave under his armpits and pubic hair. Qibla Alam *Rahmatullah Alayhi* would make hints for him to clean his unwanted hair but the man never understood the signs. One day Qibla Alam *Rahmatullah Alayhi* was taking him to a private area to tell him to shave his hair and on the way he met Mawlana Muhammad Zaman *Rahmatullah Alayhi* who took this duty upon himself.

Sain Muhammad Husayn narrates that, "One day I brought some wood from the field as fuel for the clay oven. Qibla Mai Sahiba *Rahmatullah Alayhi* enquired as to where I got the wood from and when I informed her, she said, "There is other people's wood there as well, go and make sure you have brought what is ours and only then prepare the oven." Due to Qibla Alam's training this was the level of piety in his family. Unfortunately people do not consider such things important nowadays.

Humour

Qibla Alam's disposition was mild mannered and the *Sangis* would sit in his company with awe. But sometimes in order to break the silence he would enquire about their situation, family, children and daily affairs. During such occasions sometimes the *Sangis* would joke amongst themselves and as they were aware of his likes and dislikes these acts of humour stayed within the boundaries of Shari'ah. Often he would be amused by these antics and smile and this reaction was according to the *Sunnah* as well.

Poetry

Qibla Alam *Rahmatullah Alayhi* was neither a poet nor an author but he had good taste in literature and understood poetry well. He mainly liked religious poetry which truly reflected the spiritual path. There are some spiritual incidents related to poetry in his life. He had two *Sangis* neither of whom was a poet, one was literate and the other illiterate but both enjoyed poetry. The literate one was Sufi Faujdar Khan who was a customs officer, a sincere *Sangi* and deputy of Qibla Alam *Rahmatullah Alayhi*. He worked in the customs department in the Pūnch area. One day he met a poet who was a follower of the famous Sufi poet Baba Sahib Ji[18] *Rahmatullah Alayhi*. Sufi Faujdar Khan states, "I thought to myself that there was no poet amongst Qibla Alam's *Sangis*. That night I saw Qibla Alam *Rahmatullah Alayhi* in a dream who said, "*Sangiyya*, you think there are no poets amongst our *Sangis* look at the tablet of your heart." When I looked at my heart

---

[18] Larr Sharif

I saw that the tablet of my heart had opened and poems were written upon it in different languages. Then he enquired, "In which language would you like to recite poetry," so I replied, "In Panjabi." He said, "Then fine, recite." When I awoke everything I said was in rhyme and so I began to compile a collection. The topic of these poems was spiritual matters."

Sufi Faujdar Khan narrates that, "After the *urs sharif* as I was sat near Qibla Alam *Rahmatullah Alayhi*, he said, "We have heard that our *Sangi* has become a poet." So I asked a *Sangi* with a nice voice to read some poems from my collection in front of Qibla Alam *Rahmatullah Alayhi*. After listening to a few verses which were in his praise, he got up and left as he did not like to hear his own praises." He did not approve of dedicating one's whole life to poetry and was of the view that it was better to focus on the heart rather than spend time on metre and rhyme.

The illiterate *Sangi* was Baba Abd al-Ghafur commonly known as Baba Ghafuri. Hadrat Sahib relates that, "Once Qibla Alam *Rahmatullah Alayhi* was in a mosque in Kotli.[19] This mosque is situated next to the DC House in Kotli and is now called the Sultaniyya mosque. Hajji Mawlana Baqa Muhammad *Rahmatullah Alayhi* and some other *Sangis* were also present. Qibla Alam *Rahmatullah Alayhi* stated that, "Baba Ghafuri desires to be a poet, pray that he becomes one." Afterwards, the doors of poetry opened for him and he began to compose poems, although he could not even read the alphabet." If one reads his poetry one would not imagine that this person is illiterate. Once he met a visiting *pir* from the Panjab and composed the following poem about the incident.

La libas kar ras shaklanh,
Dawa ban key turan faqirian dey.

Wear the appropriate dress and correct your appearance,
Before you go around claiming to be a Faqir,

Rakan asp aswarian karan wallay,
Shokat shan dikhan amiriyian dey.

They keep race horses,
And show off as wealthy people.

---

[19] Deygala

Dunya jan missal murdar miyan
Jama' mal kardey dolat giriyian dey.

Sire, the world is like a carcass,
Yet they hoard wealth.

Ta,mim, ein begahir noktey,
Khali hal ghafur akhairin dey.

The letters *ta, mim* and *ein* (greed) are without dots,
Oh, Ghafur, they shall be without a rank on the last day.

And

Pir de nazar aksir hoindi,
Sang dilain nunh karey lal kiyun na?

The gaze of the master is an elixir,
Why should it not turn the stone hearted into gems?

Marey chamak koh tur de nur wali,
Qiymat pawey be-had kamal kiyun na?

When it strikes like light from Mount Sinai,
Why should it not become priceless?

Pakr karu qurbani de karey niyyat,
Howay nal takbir halal kiyun na?

If you grab it with the intention of sacrifice,
Why should it not become *halal* with Allah's name?

Ranjaey vich sama ghafur jawey,
Churey hir tammam ganjal kiyun na?

When Ghafur is absorbed in Ranjah (master)

Why should not Hir (disciple) leave all troubles behind?

Hadrat Sahib narrates that another *Sangi* Sain Muhammad Husayn recited this couplet as Qibla Alam *Rahmatullah Alayhi* was about to leave the area[20].

Kammi nah awey badshain nunh jey ik lal geya tanh?
Ayya malang sawali husayniah dada tang peya tanh.

What do the kings lose if they give away a gem?
The poor beggar Husayn has come in utter desperation.

Social Etiquette

Qibla Alam's social manners presented a beautiful example of Islamic social life. He would be the first to give *salam* and reply with, "*Wa-alaykum as-salam wa ramatullah wa-barakatu.*" He would give a full *salam* according to the *Sunnah* and did not consider it sufficient to merely wave his hand or nod his head in response. The Shari'ah has promised thirty virtues for such a response. He did not pay much attention to writing letters and would instead train his *Sangis* in person. Most *Sangis* would come themselves to be spiritually re-charged. During the last period of his life Mawlana Fadal Din Sahib[21] wrote a letter to him. This letter was found in his copy of *Dalail al-Khayrat* and is preserved. A few days after this letter had arrived he passed away. Some *Sangis* lived in Rangoon, Burma and they wrote a letter and on someone's request Qibla Alam *Rahmatullah Alayhi* expressed his willingness to write a reply but it never transpired, although he could have written the letter himself or have had it written from some learned *Sangi*.

Handshake

Qibla Alam *Rahmatullah Alayhi* used to shake hands with his *Sangis* and embrace those people who had come to meet him after a long time or lived far away. He did not permit anyone to kiss his feet and also did not approve of bowing during shaking hands. Some *Sangis* would out of love kiss his hands

---

[20] Rada, Sensa
[21] Chak No: 45, Sahiwal

29

after shaking them. As for himself he would kiss the feet of his masters with love and devotion.

Hijab

The rules regarding *hijab* for women are clearly stated in the Qur'an and the *Sunnah*. Qibla Alam's whole family strictly adhered to this command and great care was taken in this matter. Once a visiting lady, who was very pious and belonged to a noble family stayed in Checheyan Sharif for a period of time. One day as she was reciting the Holy Qur'an in an audible voice and a scholar who walking past the window stopped to hear her recitation as it was according to the rules of *tajwid* (rules of recitation). Qibla Alam *Rahmatullah Alayhi* did not approve of this and gave strict command to the woman to recite inside the room.

Qibla Alam's family is fortunate that none of its members take any type of intoxicants or waste their time in useless activities. And they do not indulge in wrongful activities in the guise of leisure. Their weddings are according to the Islamic etiquette and all Hindu customs such as the henna ceremony, dancing and music are prohibited.

Picture

There is no picture of Qibla Alam *Rahmatullah Alayhi* as there is no custom of making or keeping portraits in the family. In those days the government did not require such things as ID cards or passports, therefore no photo was taken. Bearing in mind how meticulous Qibla Alam *Rahmatullah Alayhi* was in adhering to the Shari'ah, one would not expect anything less from him.

Guard Dog for Protection of Land and Livestock

Qibla Alam *Rahmatullah Alayhi* had some land[22] in a remote village and Qibla Mai Fath Begum *Rahmatullah Alayha* (Hadrat Sahib's grandmother), lived there. Some *Sangis* stayed there to take care of the land and for this purpose a guard dog was kept for the land and the livestock, this is in line with the Shari'ah.

Social Interaction

---

[22] Duliya Jattain

Qibla Alam's social customs were unlike other scholars and Sufi masters as there was no special stage made for him and there was never a special place reserved for him. He would sit amongst the *Sangis* wherever there was space. He would often be dressed similar to the *Sangis* and he would not be seated above them and it was difficult for strangers to tell them apart.

However, Qibla Alam *Rahmatullah Alayhi* always treated people according to their status, for example he showed a great deal of respect for the elderly, weak, scholars and Sayyids and in his view love for the Prophet's family was a part of faith. He would not fail in his obligations as a host. He personally greeted, embraced and bid farewell to his guests. He would visit the sick and was keen to attend the funerals. He called even the youngest person by his full name and treated him with affection. He never minded carrying out his own chores, indeed whilst performing *wudu* he would not seek assistance from anyone. He would treat the *Sangis* as if they were a part of his own family and would always enquire about their private, family, social, religious and spiritual matters. It was for this reason that the *Sangis* sincerely obeyed him and considered service to his family a source of great benefit in both worlds.

Training Spiritual Students

Qibla Alam *Rahmatullah Alayhi* studied for twenty four years with the great masters in the Naqshbandiyya Mujaddidiyya order. He strived hard and completed his spiritual training and became a master of the discipline. He was acutely aware of the intricacies of the stages of the spiritual path. He was a skilled master of the Naqshbandiyya spiritual path and was renowned in this field. Hence many seekers of the path who for some reason had become stuck at a particular stage sought his help and gradually progressed to a higher level.

One such person came and stayed at Checheyan Sharif for this purpose. He did not tell anyone his name. He remained silent and had no dealings with anyone and always focused on his heart. He used take a lot of snuff. He presented his spiritual dilemma to Qibla Alam *Rahmatullah Alayhi* and was given help in the matter. Another person was a Qari Sahib[23] who needed help in spiritual matters, Qibla Alam *Rahmatullah Alayhi* appointed him as an *imam* and his problem was resolved. Another learned Sufi had some spiritual obstacles to overcome.

---

[23] Jand Sharif, District Gujarat; the *qur'a* of Jand Sharif were renowned for their recitation of the Qur'an.

He heard about Qibla Alam's ability to guide people in the matter. As he was searching for some great master to help him, he set out for Checheyan Sharif. When he arrived in Jhelum he mentioned his quest to some companions who in turn guided him to a *Sangi* of Qibla Alam *Rahmatullah Alayhi*. When he contacted the *Sangi* he was informed that Qibla Alam *Rahmatullah Alayhi* had passed away a few days earlier, he was very upset but what could be done? There are many other examples of this nature as people came from afar to seek his guidance and benefitted according to their capacity.

The Stages of Development

There was a particular method used by Qibla Alam *Rahmatullah Alayhi* by which students were taught the different stages of the spiritual path. During this development great care was needed and special attention was given to the students. Information was gathered about their progress and continuous guidance and counselling was required. Qibla Alam *Rahmatullah Alayhi* always used to start the spiritual training with the *latifa* (subtle centre) of the heart. This *latifa* is a bridge between the world of command and the world of creation. In the beginning he would teach the seeker *ism-e zat,* 'Allah', as God is unseen and cannot be comprehended by the senses and has no likeness or example, therefore this remembrance of 'Allah' acts as a purifying agent and is greatly beneficial for cleaning the heart. The continuous remembrance of 'Allah' gives strength to the heart and subsequently the ego is subdued and a person begins to gradually attain angelic characteristics.

On the next stage the remembrance of 'Allah' is done on different *lata'if* (subtle centres) which, including the ego and *sayyid al-adhkar* (the leader of the remembrance) amount to seven. 'Allah' should be repeated twenty five thousand times a day. This is followed by meditation on *nafi/asbat* (negation and affirmation), which is done by holding the breath and also by the tongue. In the spiritual development the role of the master is of paramount importance. The master experiences the mystical sensation at any moment and during these moments his gaze has extraordinary power and whoever comes into his gaze receives tremendous benefits. For example two senior deputies of Qibla Alam *Rahmatullah Alayhi*: both Miyan Fath Muhammad and Mawlana Baqa Muhammad *Rahmatullah Alayhima* were the products of such a glance. One glance from Qibla Alam *Rahmatullah Alayhi* changed their lives and brought them into the spiritual path. Both achieved high spiritual ranks as discussed later.

In the spiritual path the connection with the master is of great importance, this spiritual connection guarantees further progress. Effectively the master plants the seed of Allah's love in the heart of the seeker. By maintaining a close connection, the master's focus, the seeker's obedience to him and with hard work, this seed blooms into a healthy tree which bears fruit. One way of keeping this connection is to physically meet the master; the second way is to keep the master's image in one's mind. If the seeker is steadfast only then can the training of the master reap benefit. In the beginning the seeker has a lot of enthusiasm and shows keen interest in worship and reciting formulas but with time this passion fizzles out and it becomes difficult for him to even perform the necessary worship. Such a seeker never succeeds. Therefore the seeker needs to follow a moderate method. It is necessary for the seeker to follow the instructions of the master. This is best for him, as the master is fully aware of the capabilities of his student and hence guides him accordingly. It is for this reason that different seekers are given diverse formulas in accordance with their ability. Sometimes the results are not immediate but one must persevere.

Regarding the connection and association with the master, Qibla Alam *Rahmatullah Alayhi* states, "The association and company of the master is a great gift as through this even the less able seeker attains more passion for the spiritual path. Like a wet piece of wood catches fire alongside a dry one, in a similar manner the less able seeker can receive benefit from the advanced seeker.

Qibla Alam *Rahmatullah Alayhi* always instructed people who belonged to other Sufi orders to maintain their links and follow the instructions of their respective masters. However in order not to hurt their feelings he would offer them some form of guidance.

The first advice he used to give the seekers is to follow the path of *Ahl-e Sunnat wa-al-Jama'at* as its beliefs were in line with the Qur'an, the *Sunnah* and the views of the Companions. He used to warn them to stay away from charlatans who impress people with 'miraculous' powers. He would take into consideration the daily duties of the *Sangis* before giving them formulas to read. The advanced *Sangis* were an excellent example of their master. Anyone who met or dealt with them would testify to this statement. The master is like a philosopher's stone for the seekers, whoever he touches, turns to gold. He would state that, "Our job is to try to correct the condition of the *Sangi*; however guidance is in the hands of Allah, who is the real Architect."

Qibla Alam's whole life revolved around worship, self discipline and struggle. When he was studying with his masters he went through a great deal of hardship. When he became a master himself he increased his asceticism. His personal struggle and asceticism continued alongside his other responsibilities such as: guiding *Sangis*, serving Allah's creation and playing host to the visitors. There was never a time when his services were not needed. He was a source of joy and comfort for the needy. Indeed, his whole life was nothing but worship.

In the beginning he used to lead the prayers but in the latter part of his life this practice changed. However in times of necessity he would still lead the prayer. On one such occasion he led the *isha* prayers in the mosque[24] in which he recited verses from *sura Sajda*. His prayer was of moderate length and whether he was the *imam* or the follower he read the prayer with great care and was mindful lest the prayer should become burdensome for some people. Hence he would recite short chapters or some verses from long chapters; however he used to prolong the *fajr* prayer.

Qibla Alam *Rahmatullah Alayhi* began his prayers at *tahajjud* time. There is no evidence to suggest that he ever missed this prayer in his life. He used to offer eight units of prayer. In addition he would offer two units for *wudu* in which he would recite *sura Ikhlas* three times in each unit. In the early period of his life he used to recite *sura Ya-Sīn* in the first unit and *sura Muzammil* in the second, in this way he would complete each *sura* four times. But in later life this practice changed. He would recite *sura Ikhlas* eleven times in the first, nine times in the second, seven times in the third, five times in the fourth and three times each in the remaining units. Nowadays the *Sangis* pray according to this method. He had advised the *Sangis* that if they missed the *tahajjud* prayer they should make it up during the day.

After the *tahajjud* prayer he would recite the following *istaghfar*; *astagfirullahhiladhi la ilaha illah huwa alhayyul alqayyum* 111 times. After the two *Sunnah* of *fajr*, he would recite 11 times *durud sharif*, 100 times *subhan Allah wa bihamdihi subhan Allah al-azim wa bihamdihi* and *durud sharif* 11

---

[24] Amb, Dadyal

times. In addition he would recite 11 *durud sharif, sura Fatiha* 41 times and 11 times *durud sharif* by joining the last *mim* of *bismillah* with *sura Fatiha*.

Initiatly he would read *la ilaha ill lallah* 5000 times after *tahajjud* in his breath, and 10,000 on the tongue. Later he read it 500 times and 5000 on the tongue. Apart from this he read the name of 'Allah' 25,000 times daily on different *lata'if*.

Qibla Alam *Rahmatullah Alayhi* would regularly offer the non-obligatory four *Sunnah* before *asr* and *isha* in which he would recite the four *suras* starting with the *qul*. He would also read the *khatam sharif* of Hadrat Khwaja Muhammad Khan Alam *Rahmatullah Alayhi*; *sura Fatiha* once, *ayatul kursi* once, *sura Ikhlas* with *bismillah* 15 times and *durud hazara* 7 times and send the blessing upon his soul.

After *asr* he would read the *khatam sharif* of Imam-e Rabbani Mujaddid Alf Thani Hadrat Shaykh Ahmad Sirhindi *Rahmatullah Alayhi*: 100 times *durud sharif*, 500 times *la hawla wala quwata illah billah* and at every hundred adding *al-aliyul-azim* once, *durud sharif* 100 times and then send the merit to his blessed soul. After *maghrib* he would read the *khatam sharif* of Hadrat Shaykh Abd al-Qadir Jilani *Rahmatullah Alayhi*, 100 times *durud sharif*, 500 times *hasbunallahu wa ni'mal wakil* and every hundredth time *ni'mal mawla wa-ni'manasir*, once and then 100 times *durud sharif*. And send the merit to the soul of Hadrat Shaykh Abd al-Qadir Jilani *Rahmatullah Alayhi* and if he could not read on time he would make it up later.

The famous *khatam-e khawajgan* of the Naqshbandiyya order has always been part of the family practice. This *khatam* is normally read after the *fajr* or *asr* prayer as the situation permits in the company of the worshippers in the mosque. Qibla Alam *Rahmatullah Alayhi* used to read it on a regular basis and this practice continues in his family. In the beginning he used to recite the complete *Dalail al-Khayrat* on a daily basis. But later his practice was to read it completely on Mondays, Thursdays and Fridays. In later life he would only recite the daily portion. The copy of *Dalail al-Khayrat* that was in his use is preserved in Khanqah-e Sultaniyya.

He would recite the book of supplication entitled *Hizb al-Azam* every day. He would also read the names of the Companions who took part in the battles of Badr and Uhud but there is no evidence to suggest that he advised any

Sangi to read them. In addition he would read *durud mustaghas* and the spiritual genealogy.

He always read a chapter from the Holy Qur'an after every prayer. For example he would recite *sura Ya-Sīn* after *fajr*, *sura Nuh* after *dhur*, *sura Naba'* after *asr*, *sura Waq'iah* after *maghrib* and *sura Mulk* and *Sajda* (21st *para*) after *isha*. He would recite the Qur'an with the proper *tajwid*, and was careful not to let melody overtake the correct pronunciation. He preferred to read from the book rather than memory as he considered this worship of the eyes.

In the early period of his life he used to teach children and those people who were his students were well aware of the rules of recitation. According to Mawlana Muhammad Zaman the masters from Bawali Sharif said to Qibla Alam *Rahmatullah Alayhima* in a dream that, "There are many who teach this type of outer knowledge but you must focus on the inner knowledge." Following this instruction he gave up teaching and focused on spiritual training. Many seekers benefitted from him and purified their egos and achieved high ranks in spirituality. Some of them were able to guide others whilst few became intoxicated and roamed in the deserts; the prime example is of Muhammad Buta the wrestler who originally came from Jullundur to take part in a wrestling match in Jhelum.

There were many non-obligatory prayers which were part of his daily routine. He would read *salatul tasbih* after *maghrib* every day and used to advise the *Sangis* to read it as well.[25] Some *Sangis* like Hajji Muhammad Ashraf and Sain Muhammad Hasan *Zulfain Wallay* read *salatul tasbih* daily throughout their life. Most *Sangis* regularly read *salatul tasbih* on Friday. Khwaja Muhammad Bakhsh *Rahmatullah Alayhi Lendey Wallay Pir* of Bawali Sharif would read *salatul tasbih* after the sunrise and sunset prayers. Qibla Alam *Rahmatullah Alayhi* would read six units of *awwabin* prayer after *maghrib*; he would recite *sura Ikhlas* 3 times in each unit and this is also the regular practice of most *Sangis*. Between *maghrib* and *isha* Qibla Alam *Rahmatullah Alayhi* would recite the following supplication 41 times; *Ya ayyuhal Muzammil, zammilni, zammilni, zammilni bequdratil khafi wa adrikni qada'i hajati ya Ahmadu sal lallaho alayhi wa-salam.* (Oh, the one wrapped in the mantle (the Prophet ﷺ), cover me, cover me, cover me by the hidden power and come to my aide to fulfil my needs, Oh, Ahmad ﷺ). It was his practice to meditate in the mosque after *fajr* prayer; this

---

[25] Roli, Kotli and Potha Bungash, Dadyal

was collective meditation, the *Sangis* would join in. He always performed *ishraq* prayers after sunrise. He would perform 4 units of prayer and recite *sura Ikhlas* 3 times in each unit.

Some of Qibla Alam's practices were related to certain days or events. For example *du'a-e ashura* was a regular family practice and all the elders in the family recited this *du'a* and in the year they passed away they would forget to read this prayer. Hadrat Sahib relates that, "Once on the *ashura* day I enquired from Qibla Alam *Rahmatullah Alayhi* if he had read the *du'a*? He went into a deep thought and replied, "May Allah grant you a long life, we are old now and have seen life." After thirteen days on 23rd of Muharram he passed away. This *du'a* is written in the Farsi book of Hadrat Qadi Fath Allah Qadiri Shattari *Rahmatullah Alayhi* entitled the *Khaza'in Fathiyytul Asrar* the only known manuscript of which is preserved in Darbar Sharif.

On the mid-Sha'ban night *shab-e barat* (Night of Salvation) Qibla Alam *Rahmatullah Alayhi* would perform 100 *nafals* and advised the *Sangis* as well. Once Hajji Sakhi Walayat[26] *Rahmatullah Alayhi* was in Qibla Alam's presence and he encouraged him to do the same. However Hajji Sakhi Walayat *Rahmatullah Alayhi* was a very intelligent and logical person and would not accept anything without proof. He relates that, "I had not come across evidence for these *nafals* and so was reluctant, but it was necessary to obey the master, which I did, but the doubt still remained in my heart. Coincidently I was a guest at someone's house and as I was an avid reader I would carefully read any piece of paper. The room in which I was staying had a shelf and on it was a booklet. There was no cover on the booklet so it was not possible to know the author's name. However from the first page it discussed the matter of the *shab-e barat nafals* and he provided clear evidence that to perform the 100 units of prayer was worthy of merit. Not only was I convinced but I also marvelled at the spiritual power of my master."

Muraqabah (meditation) played an important part in the practice of Qibla Alam *Rahmatullah Alayhi*. *Muraqabah* literally means to lower your head or to protect, but in spiritual terms it means a special state. Meditation is to focus on the heart and await spiritual down-pouring from Allah via the masters of the path. The master's focus plays an important part in this process. Qibla Alam *Rahmatullah Alayhi* used to hold gatherings of meditation after *fajr* and after *maghrib*. He would sit facing the *Sangis* and they would sit facing the *qibla*. All the

---

[26] Mehnder

Sangis would cover their faces and focus on the heart. And Qibla Alam *Raḥmatullāh ʿAlayhi* would give appropriate attention to each *Sangi* in order to purify their hearts. Regarding meditation two incidents are mentioned:

Mawlana Hajji Baqa Muhammad initially met Qibla Alam *Raḥmatullāh ʿAlayhima* by chance. He was performing his duties in the Underhill area. He had heard about the spiritual greatness of Qibla Alam *Raḥmatullāh ʿAlayhi* from a *Sangi* and a desire grew in his heart to meet him but he made no effort to pursue this matter. However, divine matters take place at appointed times. Hajji Baqa Muhammad *Raḥmatullāh ʿAlayhi* relates, "Once I spent the night in[27] and in the morning I set off for my destination. It was extremely cold and I could not walk any more in that condition and began to look for a shelter. In the village[28] I noticed a mosque. So I sought shelter until the weather became warmer. The door of the mosque was opened and I was surprised to see a group of people sat with cloth over their faces and focusing on the heart. They were not aware of anything in the world. A similar clothed holy person was sat facing them. Nearby was a stove and that was what I needed. The mosque was totally silent and there was a sense of tranquillity in the place. Slowly the rays of the sun began to appear. First of all the leader of the group lifted the cloth from his face. His eyes were so powerful that I could not look at them and lowered my gaze and I felt numb. Gradually the other people lifted their cloths from their faces and they all performed 4 units of *ishraq*. Afterwards the leader; Qibla Alam *Raḥmatullāh ʿAlayhi* asked about my welfare and why I had come. At that moment an old lady shouted, "Take the *rotis* and milk inside." The *roti* was made of *bajra* (millet bread) maybe this was his breakfast. Noticing that I was a stranger he placed the food in front of me. This was the first time I enjoyed his hospitality. His first glance made an impression upon my heart. And when I learned that he was the master from Checheyan Sharif (whom I was seeking), my heart was drawn towards him.

Afterwards I came home but my love for him made me travel to meet him again.[29] I requested him to include me in the Mujaddidiyya order and he obliged. I was given my first lesson in *ism-e zat* ('Allah'). That night there was a gathering of *dhikr* and Qibla Alam *Raḥmatullāh ʿAlayhi* pointed towards me and instructed Miyan Fath Muhammad the 2nd *Raḥmatullāh ʿAlayhi*, "Focus on him as he is a

---

[27] Mohra Kinyal
[28] Amb
[29] Chinar

mullah." I was new to the path and my ego was at its peak and when I heard these words I became anxious. Then I was instructed to focus on the heart. During that time Miyan Fath Muhammad *Rahmatullah Alayhi* shouted, "Allah hu," and despite me being a heavy person I jumped to the ceiling and back. After this all my *mullah* characteristics left me and I became engrossed in the remembrance of Allah. Thereafter I would carry the luggage of Qibla Alam *Rahmatullah Alayhi* that contained his books and felt very tranquil."

The incident of Miyan Fath Muhammad the 1st *Rahmatullah Alayhi* is of a similar nature. He lived in Chinar and was going back home after buying a buffalo from the animal market. On his way home he stopped to rest near a mosque. It was time for the predestined event to take place. In that very mosque Qibla Alam *Rahmatullah Alayhi* was in meditation. When he finished, his first glance fell upon Miyan Fath Muhammad *Rahmatullah Alayhi*. This glance hit its mark and whatever was left was transmitted by the short conversation he had with Qibla Alam *Rahmatullah Alayhi*. He was transformed and decided to spend the rest of his life in the company of Qibla Alam *Rahmatullah Alayhi* in Checheyan Sharif. Later he called the rest of the family to join him there. He was one of the great deputies of Qibla Alam *Rahmatullah Alayhi*.[30]

Qibla Alam Rahmatullah Alayhi and Politics

The masters of Qibla Alam *Rahmatullah Alayhi* were great personalities of the time. These masters were endowed with both knowledge and spirituality and dedicated their lives to the spiritual training of the individuals and left other areas to people who were more suited for those duties. These masters would sit in the mosque, lead prayers, hold gatherings of *dhikr,* give spiritual attention to the followers and spent every moment in the remembrance of Allah. Hence they neither had the opportunity to attend religious gatherings nor give public sermons. It is for this reason that these masters stayed away from politics. Their priorities were elsewhere as the saying goes, "We do not seek power but we seek to reform those in power," whereas the aims of politics are totally different. There is no middle ground between the two. However as these masters genuinely loved and cared for the Muslim nation they made supplications at early dawn for its welfare.

---

[30] He had a large following in the Mendher, some of his followers can still be found in the occupied Kashmir

Qibla Alam *Rahmatullah Alayhi* was trained by such masters and hence held their worldview. He dedicated his life to following the way of his masters and therefore used the mosques as the centre of his activities. He never took part in any political movement or attended any such gatherings. The Pakistan independence movement had not even begun at that stage. He never kept any contacts with either those in power or the leading individuals in society. His greatest provision was trust and total reliance upon Allah and this is what he shared with the *Sangis*. Hence his followers were totally dependent upon Allah. However, anyone who visited the Checheyan Sharif regardless of his position was treated with dignity and respect and no effort would be spared in his service. He gained pleasure from being a host and considered it an honour to personally serve the guests. He would personally say farewell to the guests. Apart from the spiritual training that he provided for the people it is an exaggeration to associate him with any political affiliations. However, there is some evidence that his deputy Khwaja Muhammad Akbar Ali *Rahmatullah Alayhi,* participated in the Pakistan independence movement.

Litanies for the Seekers

Qibla Alam *Rahmatullah Alayhi* gave *bay'a* in the Naqshbandiyya Mujaddidiyya order. He had permission to give *bay'a* in other orders as well, but he chose to train people in the Mujaddidiyya path. He would start with the name of 'Allah' on the heart, then move to the spirit, secret, hidden and most hidden. He would train the follower about these *lata'if* and take them through each stage personally. At the beginning one would be instructed to say 'Allah' with the tongue pressed against the back of the throat. Due to this the follower's heart would be purified and pollution of the world would be removed; helping open the door for further progress. After the *lata'if* of the realm of command the *lata'if* of the realm of creation, ego and the leader of the remembrance, the name of 'Allah' would be practised on the above. During this process the name 'Allah' is considered as the substitute for God Almighty and focusing on the *latifa* one sees this name as a source of divine outpourings. In total the name of 'Allah' is set at 25,000. After every 100 the following sentence should be repeated once, *tunh hain maqsood mera attay riza teri, ah, khuda, ishq attay mohabat meray dil nunh merbani kar."* (My purpose is You and Your pleasure, O, God please grant me Your love and passion in my heart).

40

After the name of 'Allah', Qibla Alam *Rahmatullah Alayhi* would train the follower to repeat the affirmation and negation formula. This would be done by both the tongue and the breath, he would explain: "Bring the *la* from the navel to the forehead." Bring the *Ilaha* from below the right shoulder and strike *illallahu* on both your breasts. For some followers he would recommend 500 and for others 5000. After this a person would be instructed to focus on the heart after every prayer for the length of two units of *nafila* prayer or as long it takes one to drink three sips of water with three breaths.

After the *ism-e zat* and *nafi/asbat* the *Sangi* would be taught the various meditations ranging from the meditation of *ahadiyyat* (Oneness) to the circle to *la ta'ayyun* (non-determination) and some would be taught and trained up to the meditation of *masharib* (spiritual links). With this intention: "*Meinu faiz awandey heh uss zat pak theian jeyri musum heh nal sifatain kamalian deh aur pak heh sariyian eybain theian, bi wasta piran-e kiram dey, upper dil meray deh.* (I am receiving spiritual blessings in my heart from that Pure Being (Allah) who is perfect in His attributes and free from all faults by the channel of the great masters, may Allah have mercy upon them).

After the *dhikr* Qibla Alam *Rahmatullah Alayhi* would instruct the *Sangis* to read the *khatam*: after *asr* the *khatam* of Hadrat Mujaddid Alf Thani, after *maghrib* the *khatam* of Hadrat Shaykh Abd al-Qadir Jilani *Rahmatullah Alayhima* and some would be instructed to read the *Khatam-e Khawajgan,* and this *khatam* was read regularly in the Darbar Sharif as well.

As far as written *waza'if* are concerned *Dalail al-Khayrat* would take precedence over other things. This book is a collection of salutations on the Prophet 🕌 and with eight daily sections. Most *Sangis* are given a daily portion to read, some are told to recite the whole book, whilst others are instructed to read the full book on Fridays and just the daily section on other days. The *Sangis* were also told to read *durud hazari* and *durud mustaghas* as well. Some were advised to read the *Hizb al-Azam* and *Qasida Burda* (Poem of the Mantle). Others were told to recite *durud tunajjina* 313 times. It is due to the blessing of this particular *durud* that a kidnapped lady from Lahore was found in the Ambala encampment, the details of which shall be mentioned later.

As for *nafals* he advised the *Sangis* to read two units after *wudu,* two units upon entering the mosque, four units after sunrise, and six units after *maghrib* and *salatul tasbih.* Qibla Alam *Rahmatullah Alayhi* would personally instruct people how to read *salatul tasbih*, for example he taught this prayer to Sufi Ghulam Haydar after the *maghrib* prayer.[31]

Qibla Alam *Rahmatullah Alayhi* would stress the importance of reciting the Holy Qur'an. Every *Sangi* was required to recite different portions of the Holy Qur'an. Some *Sangis* would finish the whole Qur'an in seven days, others two and a half *para* per day and most *Sangis* would recite one and a quarter *para* daily. In the month of Ramadan this portion would be increased and most of the *Sangis* would recite the complete Qur'an at least four times. The *Sangis* were advised to recite *sura Ya-Sin* and *sura Muzammil* in the morning and *sura Mulk* and *sura Waqi'ah* after *isha.*

The *Sangis* were instructed to read the *tasbihat-e Fatimi* (*subhan Allah* 33 times, *alhamdulillah* 33 times and *allahu Akbar* 34 times) and *durud khidri* 11 times after every prayer. In addition the *Sangis* were advised to read *istaghfar* 100 times, *durud sharif* 111 times and 100 times *subhanallahi wa-bihamdihi subhanallahil-azim wa bihamhamdihi astaghfirullah wa atubuilaihi* with *durud sharif* 11 times in the beginning and at the end. In addition, *sura Fatiha* 41 times by joining the *mim*, with *durud sharif* 11 times in the beginning and at the end. One can speculate what types of outer and inner results would emerge from such training.

It is vital to explore an exceptional aspect of Qibla Alam's training. Often it is assumed that when a person does not feel any joy in the remembrance of Allah one should suspend the *dhikr* until the previous state resumes. Indeed some people act upon this. In spiritual terms this condition is called *qabdh* (contraction) and the opposite state is named *bast* (expansion).

Qibla Alam *Rahmatullah Alayhi* stressed the need to continue the *dhikr* regardless of whether one is in a state of contraction or expansion, as it is not possible for the spiritual states to always continue. Therefore if one continues *dhikr* during this delicate period the heart is purified. Qibla Alam *Rahmatullah Alayhi* would cite the example of the metal till which due to constant use becomes clear like a mirror. Another example he would give was that it is common practice amongst farmers that when one puts the wheat inside the big drum and beats it, the wheat falls out of the drum but with constant slower beating one eventually

---

[31] Hill Sanyaranh, District Jhelum

sifts rice or wheat from the straw. If one loses heart in the beginning and stops trying, then one is bound to fail.

Once a follower asked his master whether it was possible to focus on spiritual matters whilst one was occupied with other things? According to Qibla Alam *Rahmatullah Alayhi* such a thing was possible and he cited the example of the women who carry two or three water pots on their heads and at the same time converse with each other. Sometimes they move their heads but the water pots stay where they are. The reason for this is that despite their conversations their focus is on the water pots. The Holy Qur'an supports such a view as it states that, *"By men whom neither traffic nor merchandise can divert from the Remembrance of Allah."*

In Service of the Masters Rahmatullah Alayhim

Qibla Alam served his master Khwaja Muhammad Bakhsh *Rahmatullah Alayhima* (*Lendey Wallay*) from Bawali Sharif for twelve years and learned the Zubayriyya path from him. Some details of the service he carried out during the twelve years are preserved. During one meeting Hadrat Mai Sahiba *Rahmatullah Alayha* (Bawali Sharif) informed Hadrat Sahib that during his stay in Bawali Sharif, Qibla Alam *Rahmatullah Alayhi* carried out his duties in an exemplary manner. Apart from matters of routine and emergency, the tasks that he performed were: to assist his master in *wudu*, massaging him, in the summer sometimes cooling him with the hand fan all night, bringing fresh water from the station well, heating the clay oven and assisting with cultivation. Whilst regularly performing his spiritual devotion, he would first offer his *tahajjud* prayer then wake his master up. Hadrat Mai Sahiba *Rahmatullah Alayha* stated that he had so much respect for his master that he never put his feet on his bed (this bed is preserved in Bawali Sharif). Hadrat Mai Sahiba *Rahmatullah Alayha* continues, "Although he seemed a simple person, nature had given him a tremendous amount of ability and steadfastness in order to achieve high spiritual stations."

In his lifetime Khwaja Muhammad Bakhsh had advised Qibla Alam to continue his training with Khwaja Hafiz Muhammad Hayat *Rahmatullah Alayhim*. He passed away, shortly after. According to the instructions of his master Qibla Alam went to study with his master's follower and authorised deputy and served Khwaja Hafiz Muhammad Hayat *Rahmatullah Alayhima* for many years and was finally authorised by him. During this time he served his master with his heart and soul. He served food at his master's lodge and only ate after everyone else had been fed. It is well known that he would survive on the leftovers of his *Sangis*, he would not break a fresh *roti* in case some new guests arrived and it could be used for them.

This area[32] was a desolate and rocky plain. It was an impossible mission to turn this area into a land that would cultivate crops. However with his will of iron, Qibla Alam *Rahmatullah Alayhi* did just that, even his master's son acknowledged this fact. Due to his sacrifice, service and humility he gained the trust of his master and would act on his behalf in his absence. He attained such a rank due to his sincerity, devotion and humility. This close relationship between the master and disciple is mentioned by Khwaja Hafiz Muhammad Ali who states that his father, Khwaja Hafiz Muhammad Hayat *Rahmatullah Alayhima* said to him, "Muhammad Ali, as you are my son, in the same way Sultan Alam is my son."

Once, Khwaja Hafiz Muhammad Hayat sent his youngest son Hafiz Ali Ahmad to Checheyan Sharif to see Qibla Alam *Rahmatullah Alayhim* regarding some matter. By now Qibla Alam *Rahmatullah Alayhi* was a spiritual guide. Hafiz Ali Ahmad was instructed to return the same day but Qibla Alam *Rahmatullah Alayhima* requested him to stay the night, so he apologised that he did not have permission. Qibla Alam *Rahmatullah Alayhi* said, "We shall obtain permission." He then closed his eyes and focused on the heart. "Permission has been granted," he said. Hafiz Ali Ahmad *Rahmatullah Alayhi* narrates that, "The next day when I returned home my noble father did not enquire about my delay, I informed him what had transpired, he simply smiled and remained silent."

Khwaja Hafiz Muhammad Hayat's statement, "If you put my son in a woman's cloak and put him to sleep you will not know whether it's a man or a woman," *meray puttar nunh aurat neh bukl vich sula deo teh patta neh chaley gah ke aurat heh yeh mard*, testifies to the chaste nature of Qibla Alam *Rahmatullah Alayhi*. Due to his master Khwaja Hafiz Muhammad Hayat, Qibla Alam was able to meet and serve the pole of the time Hadrat Pir Sayyid Muhammad Neyk Alam *Rahmatullah Alayhim*. One day in the presence of his master, Qibla Alam *Rahmatullah Alayhi* was plastering the chamber of Hadrat Pir Sayyid Muhammad Neyk Alam *Rahmatullah Alayhi* who was very impressed by Qibla Alam's utmost devotion in carrying out the task and so he went inside and brought out a register of

---

[32] Dangrot Sharif was situated near the river banks of Jhelum

Meditations and offered to grant him permission but Qibla Alam *Rahmatullah Alayhi* humbly requested that such an honour should be bestowed upon his master and he would receive it from him and this is what transpired as he obtained the Sayfiyya path in this manner.

Another incident that expresses Qibla Alam's love and devotion for his master is related by Hadrat Sahib. Once Qibla Alam *Rahmatullah Alayhi* had to travel upon the request of *Sangis*[33] and his son and successor Hadrat Sahib was with him. Qibla Alam's masters' grave was on the same trail. The noble wife of Khwaja Hafiz Muhammad Hayat was still alive and Qibla Alam *Rahmatullah Alayhim* sent some money and clothes with his son to present the gifts to her, whilst he waited outside. Hadrat Sahib narrates that, "When I entered the house I saw her spinning some wool and as soon as she saw me she enquired *"Ajji kuthe neih,* Where is your father?"* I replied that he was stood outside. She said, *"Unh keh beganay hoi gay ho,* Has he become a stranger now?"* When Qibla Alam *Rahmatullah Alayhi* heard her voice, all the past memories came to his mind, he came running without his shoes and placed his cap on her feet and began to cry out loud and tears began to flow from her eyes as well. She asked him to stay the night but he replied, "I have promised the *Sangis* and they are waiting," so she did not persist.

Once Khwaja Hafiz Muhammad Hayat sent his son, Khwaja Hafiz Muhammad Ali to obtain mustard oil from Qibla Alam *Rahmatullah Alayhim* who immediately emptied the container in which the seeds were kept and carried the sack full of seeds and had the oil pressed[34] and then carried the mustard oil with his master's son to the river Jhelum. Often Qibla Alam *Rahmatullah Alayhi* would send grain from the harvest for his master's *langar*.

One *Sangi* from Bawali Sharif called Miyan Muhammad *Rahmatullah Alayhi* who used to herd the goats there, got upset over some matter and moved to Checheyan Sharif. As long as he remained in Checheyan Sharif, Qibla Alam *Rahmatullah Alayhi* never turned his back towards him and he advised the *Sangis* to show the proper respect and take good care of Miyan Muhammad *Rahmatullah Alayhi* as he was linked to Bawali Sharif.

---

[33] Hill Sanyaranh
[34] Tangdeo

Qibla Alam *Rahmatullah Alayhi* made only a few short journeys in his lifetime. He was mostly busy with his own devotions and training of the *Sangis* and had little time for travel. There was a constant traffic of *Sangis*, who wanted as much time as possible to benefit from him. Many of the *Sangis* belonged to the Underhill area, so there was constant traffic between the Underhill area and Checheyan Sharif. Some wise person commented that, "The constant flow of the *Sangis* reminded one of the armed forces' movements during the World War." There is some truth in this as group after group would come and go from Checheyan Sharif on a daily basis.

Qibla Alam *Rahmatullah Alayhi* mostly travelled towards the Underhill area.[35] His travels were not for the sake of travelling, nor for pleasure or any worldly benefit. All of these journeys were solely for teaching or training purposes. His centre would be the mosque, where many *Sangis* from the surrounding areas would gather. He would hold gatherings of meditation and *dhikr* in order to purify the rust from their hearts. And in a light manner some points of spirituality would be mentioned. Some seekers would enter these gathering and request the oath of allegiance. During these few days he would assess the situation of the *Sangis* and encourage them to persevere and highlight their shortcomings and direct them to improve their condition and would lead them by his example. His practices were the same whether he was travelling or at home, there would not be the slightest difference. The *Sangis* who accompanied him would be instructed to focus on their hearts and useless talk would strictly be forbidden during these journeys. Whenever it was time for prayer, the rows would be formed and he would lead the prayers.

Once, Qibla Alam *Rahmatullah Alayhi* intended to visit Bawali Sharif and he began his journey from the Kokkhar village (situated near Khanqah-e Sultaniyya). The train was to depart early in the morning so he set off on his journey by horse before dawn. The *Sangis* began to talk amongst themselves but he reprimanded them, "These are priceless and blessed moments, spend them in the remembrance of Allah." As they approached the Court turning in Jhelum it was time for *fajr*, so he immediately stopped his horse, straightened the rows

---

[35] Beyli Batar to Gorah mosque and he would stay at the Tajpur mosque or Potha Bungash, Amb, Sarthala or the Samlotha mosque

and led the prayer. Indeed every moment of his life was a source of guidance for the *Sangis*.

Apart from the Underhill area, the Kotli province can be considered as his second area of training. He travelled to this region on three or four occasions and stayed at various locations [36] These journeys were also with the intention of comforting and guiding the *Sangis*.

Qibla Alam *Rahmatullāh Ǎlayhi* travelled to pay his respects to various shrines of his masters.[37] His journeys were mostly on foot or on a horse. However he travelled to Bawali Sharif on a train.[38] During the journey he brought with him the chutney mixture and other basic needs. He took utmost care not to inconvenience any *Sangi* on his travels.

During these travels some incidents took place that indicate Qibla Alam's great foresight, we shall only mention two such events. Once he was travelling on a horse.[39] On the way he suddenly stopped at a place near Kotli.[40] At that time this place was a forest and uninhabited. He said to the *Sangis*, "See if you can find any graves here." The *Sangis* looked in the thorn bushes but did not find any signs of graves. Then he said, "Look over there." When the *Sangis* searched that particular area they found some old graves. After examining one of the very old graves Qibla Alam *Rahmatullāh Ǎlayhi* commented that this person's spiritual connection was superior to a great saint. This suggests that the buried saint was a contemporary of the famous saint. Qibla Alam *Rahmatullāh Ǎlayhi* made no further comment on the matter. Based on this incident about sixty years later Qibla Alam's son Hadrat Sahib *Rahmatullāh Ǎlayhi* built a shrine over the five graves and built a mosque adjacent to them and also living quarters for the *imam* and his family. This beautiful place has now become a sight of pilgrimage.

During the journey mentioned above, when Qibla Alam *Rahmatullāh Ǎlayhi* finally arrived at the village,[41] he visited the grave of a sincere *Sangi*. Whilst he was there people mentioned that the dead *Sangi*'s brother was in a wretched state. When Qibla Alam *Rahmatullāh Ǎlayhi* personally met him and saw his state of

---

[36] Nakka Kurti, Latu'i, Roli, Khad, Manor, Kulla, Rajur and Saroha
[37] Bawali Sharif, Dangrot Sharif and Gorah Sayyidain
[38] Jhelum to Karyala then to Dina
[39] Kartot Khad via Nakka Kurti
[40] Jameyri Tahthi
[41] Kartot Khad

poverty, he felt compassion for him and advised him to plant a banana farm. When the *Sangis* heard this they smiled, as this area was arid land and there was a shortage of water, but they had complete faith in their master. So the poor *Sangi* took Qibla Alam's advice and amazingly the bananas grew in abundance. As a result the *Sangi* became wealthy. These bananas used to be sold in large quantities[42]. In 1947 this farm was used by the army and freedom fighters as a fort against the enemy forces.

Another sign of Qibla Alam's blessing is that wherever he stopped or rested during his journeys, beautiful mosques have been built on those sites. The teaching of Holy Qur'an takes place in these mosques and many *huffaz* are trained there. Hadrat Abu al-Hasan Zaid Faruqi Delhawi *Rahmatullah Alayhi* visited Gulhar Sharif, Kotli on several occasions. He was very impressed with the structure and maintenance of these mosques.

Hadrat Abu al-Hasan Zaid Faruqi Delhawi *Rahmatullah Alayhi* met an old *Sangi* called Baba Sattar Muhammad,[43] who had a rosary with thick beads in his hands. These types of rosaries were used by the *Sangis* in Qibla Alam's time. These rosaries were made by Sufi Ghulam Muhyi al-Din,[44] who did not follow any school of jurisprudence, but due to his profession he met and became a sincere *Sangi* of Qibla Alam *Rahmatullah Alayhima*. Later he travelled to Sirhind Sharif with Hadrat Sahib. So when Hadrat Zaid *Rahmatullah Alayhi* saw this big rosary in Baba Muhammad Sattar's hands, he was very happy and conversed with him for a while. Then he turned to Sahibzada Muhammad Maruf Sahib ibn Qadi Muhammad Latif *Rahmatullah Alayhi*, and said, "This old man is worthy of respect as he is connected with your grandfather." Then Hadrat Zaid *Rahmatullah Alayhi* enquired from Baba Sattar Muhammad, "Did Qibla Alam *Rahmatullah Alayhi* ever visit this area, and if so, how did he travel?" He replied "Qibla Alam *Rahmatullah Alayhi* used to come here on foot." Hadrat Zaid *Rahmatullah Alayhi* stated, "How much hardship he went through for the sake of the *din,* those people had such great resolve and determination. He planted this garden and now it is producing fruit."

---

[42] Pagorah Mohra Road
[43] Rajur
[44] Dadhala, District Jhelum

Qibla Alam *Rahmatullah Alayhi* married three times. Qibla Alam's first marriage was to his cousin named Muhammad Bi; her father's name was Qadi Nur Alam *Rahmatullah Alayhi*. This marriage was not successful as the couple's personalities did not match. Qibla Alam's house was an abode of guidance which meant that it was not possible to guess when and how many guests would arrive. Some *Sangis* came to seek spiritual training and their stay would extend over many days. All their needs had to be met by the family. In those days life was harsh and the modern facilities did not exist. Everything required a great effort, grinding the wheat, kneading flour, preparing food and providing bedding according to the weather. In addition the domestic chores had to be carried out. The noble lady was not interested in serving people and often expressed her displeasure on these occasions. By contrast, hospitality played a pivotal role in Qibla Alam's life. There was no way to reconcile these differences and thus separation became inevitable. The noble lady was given her dowry, the receipt of which is dated[45] and is preserved with Qibla Alam's other documents.

Qibla Alam's second marriage was to Hadrat Begum Ji *Rahmatullah Alayhima*. Her education and upbringing took place at Checheyan Sharif, where she learned the Holy Qur'an from Baba Faqir Muhammad *Potha Wallay* *Rahmatullah Alayhi*. She recited the Holy Qur'an with the proper *tajwid*. She did not live long, she fell ill and her illness became complicated and resulted in her untimely death. She had given birth to a baby daughter called Amina Bibi who died in her infancy.

It is related that on her deathbed she asked for Qibla Alam *Rahmatullah Alayhi* and said: "I have never asked you for any material thing, neither comfort, wealth nor jewellery. Whatever you gave I happily accepted. I always gave preference to your wishes. Now I make a final request, please pray for my salvation. I always served the *Sangis* in order to please you." And she added, "Faqir Muhammad from Potha is my teacher, he taught me the Holy Qur'an, and he has left his kith and kin and has devoted his life to you. He has a harsh temper, but please take care of him." At that time her mother *Rahmatullah Alayha* was also present, she had been given permission by Qibla Alam *Rahmatullah Alayhi* to guide women.

---

[45] Poh 1976, Bikrami (Hindi Calendar)

Qibla Alam's third marriage was to Hadrat Sajjaddah Begum also known as Qibla Mai Sahiba (the Elder) who was the elder sister of Hadrat Begum Ji *Rahmatullah Alayhima.* The virtues of Hadrat Qibla Mai Sahiba *Rahmatullah Alayha* are often mentioned and there are many eye witness accounts of her spiritual powers. Even though she was illiterate, she had been granted a great deal of hidden knowledge and wisdom by Allah. Everyone testifies to her beautiful manners and her exceptional service to people. She was a source of comfort for both the *Sangis* and strangers.

One of the outstanding features of Hadrat Qibla Mai Sahiba's life is that after the demise of Qibla Alam *Rahmatullah Alayhi* in 1934, she did not let the spiritual movement be suspended. She not only managed the spiritual movement but was also a source of inspiration for the *Sangis* during that difficult time. For three centuries this noble family had been a source of guidance and with the demise of Qibla Alam *Rahmatullah Alayhi* it was feared that this would come to an end, as his son was only thirteen years old at the time. It seemed no one could fill the void left by Qibla Alam's death but Hadrat Qibla Mai Sahiba *Rahmatullah Alayhima* took all these responsibilities upon herself and as hundreds of thousands of people have testified for the next fifty years, she led this spiritual movement. Not only did she continue Qibla Alam's mission, she also laid such strong foundations that the superiority of the Shari'ah and mysticism in the form of sincerity was inseparable from the Islamic law (they were imbedded in all her children and the *Sangis*). With tact and wisdom she guided the *Sangis* and her children so that they did not miss the presence of Qibla Alam *Rahmatullah Alayhi.* She organised the movement in such a way that the teaching of the Holy Qur'an became the nucleus of all activities and the mystical element prospered as well. Allah accepted her sincere intentions and all her noble efforts bore fruit. Her way was the path of charisma and love. She passed away on 10th January 1985; her funeral prayer was led by Mawlana Hafiz Muhammad Fadal Sahib[46] *Rahmatullah Alayhi* and she was buried in Khanqah-e Sultaniyya in Jhelum. The present work is dedicated to her memory. Hadrat Qibla Mai Sahiba's favourite poem:

Ism apne de shoq ilahi hardam devhin meinnu,
Waqt nazah deh shoqanh ander yad karanh mein tehnu.

Grant me a longing for Your blessed name in every breath,
So that I may remember You with longing at the time of death.

---

[46] Dangari Sharif (Dangrot Sharif)

Allah, Allah kardiyanh jivanh vich Allah marjavanh,
Jahnh, jahnh ruh jushey vich howhey tera ism pakavanh.

Chanting Allah, Allah, may I live and die,
Remembering Your name as long as I am alive.

Bahj tere kujj nazar na aveh jitval nazar uttahavanh,
Utthdianh, benhdianh, turdianh, phirdianh tera zikr pakavanh.

Wherever I look, may I see nothing but You,
And in every movement remember You.

Qalb munawwar kardeh mera barkat ism ilahi,
Jitval dekhainh tu hi dissenh ghair na disseh ka'ie.

Enlighten my heart with the blessing of Your name,
Wherever I look may I see no one else but You.

Allah, Allah kardiyanh rabba, meri jan kadahainh,
Murshid, mah, pyo razi rehveinh fazal kare rab sainh.

Take my life in as I remember You,
May my Guide and parents be pleased and You too.

Children

All of Qibla Alam's children were borne by Qibla Mai Sahiba *Rahmatullah Alayhima,* Allah granted them one son and four daughters. Their names are as follows:

1) Hadrat Khwaja Muhammad Sadiq, born on Saturday 25th December 1921/22nd Rabi'a al-akhar 1340 AH/10 Poh 1978 Bikrami. He is the present master and the epitome of his noble ancestors. A voluminous book is needed to discuss his services and contributions to the *din*. The

present work was not published when on 31st December 2008/2nd Muharram 1430 AH, he passed away at around 11.15 pm and his blessed soul reached the Divine Presence. *"Truly we are from Allah and to Him is our return."* His funeral prayer was led by his eldest son, Hadrat Shaykh Hafiz Muhammad Abd al-Wahid 'Hajji Pir Sahib' after the *dhur* prayer on 1st January 2009 at the Khanqah-e Fathiyya, Kotli. The noble Shaykh was buried next to his great ancestor Hadrat Qadi Fath Allah Shattari *Rahmatullah Alayhima*

2) Hadrat Maqbul Begum, she was married to Mawlana Muhammad Zaman *Rahmatullah Alayhima* (d.27th March 1976), who was a deputy of Qibla Alam *Rahmatullah Alayhi*. His shrine is in[47] next to the mosque.

3) Hadrat Manzur Begum, she was married to Hadrat Qadi Muhammad Latif Sahib who was a cousin of Qibla Alam and was the son of their deputy, Hadrat Qadi Muhammad Alam (d.7th Muharram 1352 AH/1934) *Rahmatullah Alayhim*.

4) Hadrat Rahmat Begum *Rahmatullah Alayha* she was married to Hadrat Miyan Fadal Ilahi[48] (d.3rd November 1992) who was a deputy and the son of the deputy Hadrat Miyan Fath Muhammad *Rahmatullah Alayhima*. He was the cousin of Hadrat Qibla Mai Sahiba *Rahmatullah Alayha*. Hadrat Rahmat Begum *Rahmatullah Alayha* passed away on 21st Dhul-hijjah 1424/13th February 2004 and all of the above are buried in Khanqah-e Sultaniyya, Jhelum.

5) Hadrat Fatima Begum *Rahmatullah Alayha* she was married to Qibla Alam's youngest uncle Qadi Chirag Alam's son, Qadi Muhammad Afdal *Rahmatullah Alayhima*. She died in young age and only had one daughter who is married to Sahibzada Muhammad Maruf ibn Qadi Muhammad Latif ibn Qadi Muhammad Alam *Rahmatullah Alayhim*

Demise

Qibla Alam *Rahmatullah Alayhi* passed away on Tuesday 9th May 1934/23rd Muharram 1352 AH, at *dhur* time. He was buried the next day, Wednesday 10th May 1934/24th Muharram 1352 AH in Checheyan Sharif. His illness was for a

---

[47] Mehta Losar
[48] He had a following, mostly in the Mendher, Pūnch area.

few days, resulting in a high fever. During those days a wooden plank was placed on his bed and suffering from the high fever, he would perform his prayers on it. On the day of his death he was offering his *dhur* prayers on the plank when his body swayed to one side. He was then carried to his bed and a few moments later he passed away. The loyal *Sangi* who assisted him in the *wudu* of his final prayer was called Baba Faqir Muhammad Pahariyya. Hadrat Sahib narrates that a few moments before his death, Qibla Alam *Rahmatullah Alayhi* enquired, "Have the *Sangis* eaten?" Fifty years later, Hadrat Qibla Mai Sahiba *Rahmatullah Alayha* made a similar enquiry before her death.

Fragrance

A strange incident occurred during the last days of Qibla Alam's life. His room would be engulfed in a powerful fragrance. There is no evidence of whether he ever used any type of perfume in his life. His avoidance of perfume was due to his extreme level of piety. Once some *Sangis* from Mandalay in Burma sent him some perfume as a present, but he did not use it. A pious lady called Sharfain Bi[49] who stayed in Checheyan Sharif to complete her training in the Mujaddidiyya order and was respected by the family for her nobility, tried her best to persuade Qibla Alam *Rahmatullah Alayhi* to use that perfume but he politely refused. He stated, "If one desires fragrance, then it is best to put some jasmine flowers into mustard oil and use it after a few days."

Faqir Muhammad Pahariyya

Faqir Muhammad came from the mountainous area and that is why he was called Pahariyya. He was a very sincere and loyal *Sangi* and dedicated his life to service in Checheyan Sharif. When Qibla Alam *Rahmatullah Alayhi* was on his deathbed, Faqir Muhammad was very keen to gain advice concerning his son and successor. Hadrat Sahib narrates that, "Baba Faqir Muhammad would continually present me in front of Qibla Alam *Rahmatullah Alayhi* in the hope that he would give some instructions." In response to his sincere request Qibla Alam *Rahmatullah Alayhi* said, "I leave you in Allah's care, everything shall be fine." Then he made supplications and advised the *Sangis*, "Be steadfast upon your prayers and preoccupy yourself in Allah's remembrance." From this incident one can imagine how much love and affection Baba Faqir Muhammad had for the

---

[49] Hill Sanyaranh

family. It also indicates Qibla Alam's deep concern for the welfare of the *Sangis* and his emphasis on prayer and the remembrance of Allah.

1934 the Year of Demise

1934 was the year of sorrow for the family of Qibla Alam *Rahmatullah Alayhi*. In addition Qibla Alam's cousin and dear friend Qadi Muhammad Alam *Rahmatullah Alayhima* passed away on 7th Muharram 1352 AH/1934. Both were very close and despite the fact that they were cousins Qadi Muhammad Alam never overstepped his limit with his master Qibla Alam *Rahmatullah Alayhima*. He died after a short illness and two weeks later Qibla Alam *Rahmatullah Alayhi* also joined his Lord. The physical separation of these two holy people was a great loss for the family.

Bathing and Burial

Such was his detachment from the world and his integrity, self reliance and generosity that when Qibla Alam *Rahmatullah Alayhi* passed away there was no money in the house. He was not in favour of hoarding wealth. Whatever income he had was spent upon the *Sangis* and the guests. The grain from the wheat crop had as yet not been separated. The family was trained by Qibla Alam *Rahmatullah Alayhi* and thus they did not forsake their Lord and turn to the people for help. Those who place their trust in the Lord, never despair of His mercy. On that very day money order arrived from the sincere *Sangi*, Sufi Faujdar Khan.[50] The money was sufficient to take care of the needs of the humble servant of Allah. The burial ceremony was simple and Qibla Alam *Rahmatullah Alayhi* was buried in a white cotton cloth.

Coffin

Qibla Alam's body was placed in a wooden coffin and buried. The coffin has a history of its own. Once Qibla Alam *Rahmatullah Alayhi* went to a village,[51] the wooden highchair on which he sat was made of wood and in the local dialect it was called '*Tun*' (Cedar). This wood is naturally protected from woodworm and silk worm. Out of interest Qibla Alam *Rahmatullah Alayhi* made enquiries about this particular wood. The *Sangis* considered the enquiry a sign of his pleasure and therefore went to the nearby village[52] and bought a tree and

---

[50] Stationed at Pūnch
[51] Kulla, Palandari
[52] Uday Chak

prepared a coffin from that wood. This was then carried by a group of *Sangis* who chanted the name 'Allah' with devotion and carried it on their heads all the long way to Checheyan Sharif. This coffin was prepared many years before Qibla Alam's demise.

Funeral

Qibla Alam's son in law and deputy Mawlana Muhammad Zaman *Rahmatullah Alayhima* bathed him, Baba Faqir Muhammad *Potha Wallay* and Sain Muhammad Hasan *Zulfain Wallay* assisted him in this task. The funeral prayer was led by the teacher of the teachers, Hadrat Mawlana Muhammad Abd Allah *Rahmatullah Alayhi* from Ladar; he was a pious and learned person and was authorised from Bawali Sharif. At the funeral Hadrat Khwaja Muhammad Fadal *Rahmatullah Alayhi* [grandson son of Khwaja Hafiz Muhammad Hayat *Rahmatullah Alayhi*] represented the lodge of Qibla Alam's master. Seeing the face of Qibla Alam *Rahmatullah Alayhi* for the last time, he commented, "I have never seen a more luminous and fresh face except for another one of his *Sangis* called Miyan Husayn Ali[53], whose face was similar after his death." Some relics from Bawali Sharif were buried with Qibla Alam *Rahmatullah Alayhi.*

Final Resting Place

Qibla Alam *Rahmatullah Alayhi* was laid to rest in the same chamber, which was the abode of light and where he had spent his life in worship and self-discipline. His grave was made of mud.

Tomb

Qibla Alam's chamber was made of mud and when it rained it would leak. This was a source of great inconvenience to the visitors. Finally with the consultation of the *Sangis* it was decided to contact the well known builder Muhammad Ibrahim,[54] who had built many mosques and shrines. He was a practising Muslim and would often spend his time reciting the Holy Qur'an. His piety can be assessed by the following incident: when he was working on the tomb in Checheyan Sharif, Khwaja Hafiz Muhammad Ali *Rahmatullah Alayhi* came and prayed behind Muhammad Ibrahim and was pleased with his recitation. Qibla Alam's tomb was built to provide comfort for the visitors. However, due to the

---

[53] Kas Harranh
[54] Akhnur

Mangla Dam this tomb is now submerged. In 1967, his body was transferred to Khanqah-e Sultaniyya, Jhelum. It is said that a *Sangi* has a photo of the shrine but as yet it has not been found. The work on the shrine was supervised by Hajji Baqa Muhammad *Rahmatullah Alayhi*, and no funds were raised for this purpose; in fact some family land was sold to cover its cost.

Urs Mubarak

Urs is a well known term. When gatherings are held in honour of saints in order to send merit to their souls such an annual event is called *urs*. On such an occasion devotees gather and they are informed about the teachings of the saint buried there. The main purpose of such a spiritual gathering is to awaken the desire in the devotee's heart to perform pious deeds and to follow in the footsteps of the saint. But unfortunately these days some innovations have been introduced into these sacred gatherings which bear no relation to the real spirit of such gatherings.

In the beginning Qibla Alam's *urs* was held according to the lunar calendar on 23rd Muharram. As the lunar date rotated in different seasons, once due to heavy rains the situation became unbearable. Afterwards the *Sangis* decided to hold the event according to the solar calendar. Now this blessed event takes place every year on 9th May at the Khanqah-e Sultaniyya, Jhelum. It is often called the big *khatam* or yearly *khatam* and the collective supplication, but most people refer to it as *urs mubarak*. This is a simple gathering. Every year the *Sangis* gather and this is the catalyst behind the congregation. This is a unique gathering as no attempt is made by the Khanqah-e Sultaniyya to publicise this event, either by posters, letters or any other form of communication. The scholars and preachers are not inconvenienced. It is as if the *Sangis* have written this date in their hearts and minds. Regardless of where the *Sangis* are in the world and barring any genuine reason or legal complications they try to attend the gathering of their own accord. A few days prior to the event, a large amount of people gather at the Khanqah-e Sultaniyya. The gathering offers the opportunity to the Khanqah-e Sultaniyya to play host to the *Sangis*. Many young volunteers, the family of Qibla Alam *Rahmatullah Alayhi* and the *Sangis* do their utmost to serve the guests. Every effort is made to take care of each individual in the gathering of thousands of people. Those people who have attended the *urs mubarak* know well how much effort is made to take care of the *Sangis'* needs.

The second special feature of this *khatam sharif* is that thousands of *Sangis* perform their devotions: daily *wird*, prayer in congregation, *nafila* prayers such as *ishraq, awwabin, tahajjud, wird* from books and other non-obligatory prayers. They make supplications to be steadfast in the future. In addition they spend a considerable time reciting the Holy Qur'an near the shrines. Despite the gathering of thousands, people are busy performing their devotions in peace and tranquillity with *wudu*. The third main feature of this *khatam* is that the admission of women and children is strictly prohibited. Both women and children are not allowed to enter the Khanqah-e Sultaniyya two weeks prior and two weeks after the gathering, so the environment of the place is not jeopardised. The fourth feature of this *khatam* is that during the *urs* ceremony no stalls or shops are allowed under the area controlled by Khanqah-e Sultaniyya. The *Sangis* are advised not to venture outside the building except for emergencies and to be satisfied with the hospitality that is offered and refrain from indulging in the pleasures of the ego. The fifth feature is that everything takes place on time. Thousands of people are served tea twice a day. The time set for food is strictly adhered to. Islamic etiquette is foremost during these occasions. After the *fajr* prayer tea and rusks are served as people are still sitting in their rows. Lunch is served before *dhur* prayer and the evening meal is served after *maghrib* prayer. The table spread is laid out and all the guests are served quickly. One never hears any noise or witnesses any lack of organisation and everyone gets fed.

The sixth feature is everyone is served the same food except for the sick or those with special dietary requirements. The *khatam* takes place at the shrine of Qibla Alam *Rahmatullah Alayhi* and starts every year on 9th May at 9 am; the full duration of the ceremony is one hour and thirty minutes. Half an hour before the ceremony begins, the chapters of the Holy Qur'an are distributed amongst the *Sangis*. Just before 10 a.m. the proper ceremony starts with the recitation of the Holy Qur'an. Afterwards a brief analysis of Qibla Alam's teachings is read out. The *Sangis* are asked to reflect on how many of the teachings that were read out the previous year have been practised. Then they are reminded of the fact that this gathering is held in order to guide and instruct them and it is hoped that they pay heed to this advice. Those *Sangis* who do not follow these teachings, are advised not to use this occasion as an excuse for a pleasure trip. They should not waste their time or money as the Khanqah-e Sultaniyya has no desire to fill numbers. Indeed it needs those *Sangis* who are sincerely willing to follow the commands of Allah and his Messenger ﷺ.

The seventh feature of this *khatam* is that the *Sangis* are instructed to spend money in their own neighbourhood mosque or madrasa rather than make offerings here. And to bear in mind that they shall not receive any preferential treatment due to offerings as anyone who comes here is an honoured guest and is worthy of equal respect. To come with pure and sincere intentions is the best offering of all.

After a brief talk the *khatam-e khawajgan* and then devotional poems by Hadrat Pir Sayyid Muhammad Neyk Alam Shah *Rahmatullah Alayhi* are read. Hadrat Qibla Mai Sahiba's favourite poem which reflects the instinctive love for Allah is also recited for blessings. Afterwards the customary *khatam* is read and the merit is sent to the occupant of the shrine, Qibla Alam and his ancestors *Rahmatullah Alayhim*. Finally all the *Sangis* are requested to correct their rows as food is served straightaway. Once the *Sangis* have eaten they have permission to leave, however if anyone wishes to stay they are most welcome.

Unique Features of Qibla Alam *Rahmatullah Alayhi*

Qibla Alam *Rahmatullah Alayhi* was a complete master and whoever sat in his company, took his share of the blessings. The special features of his life as narrated by the *Sangis* are mentioned as they are not without benefit. He held the beliefs of *Ahl-e Sunnat wa- al-Jama'at* and followed the school of Imam-e Azam Abu Hanifa *Rahmatullah Alayhi*. He was very learned and studied religious books throughout his life. Although he spent his life with the great scholars, such was his caution that whenever he was asked about a matter of *fiqh*, if he had investigated that particular issue he would relate it, otherwise he would advise the questioner to ask a Sunni scholar.

The homes of the pious people are the places of hope for those in despair. The needy, oppressed and distressed come to seek guidance and remove their burdens in such places. Indeed many types of people came to Qibla Alam *Rahmatullah Alayhi* to seek help. He would try to comfort them and no one went away empty handed. He would advise the visitors to place their trust in Allah and consider Him as the real Source and it was not beyond His mercy to resolve their problems. Dozens of people would seek his help on a daily basis. He would grant amulets to some and to others he would advise some *wird* to read. For example, he would advise someone to read *ya-salamu* 125,000 times and to another to read *sura Fatiha* 41 times after the *fajr Sunnah*. Some people would complain about being possessed by Jinns and they would be given seven amulets for four lunar months. With Allah's mercy the previous complaint would go. His method was unlike other practitioners as he would not blow on them but relied upon Allah and used his spiritual focus. His every act and deed was based upon the Shari'ah. If someone acted contrary to the Shari'ah he would express his displeasure. One *Sangi* was interested in alchemy and he was very pious and loyal to Qibla Alam *Rahmatullah Alayhi*. However Qibla Alam *Rahmatullah Alayhi* did not approve of this and reprimanded him on many occasions. He used to say, "The real alchemy is to control your ego. One should work on that so one can progress in spiritual ranks."

Qibla Alam *Rahmatullah Alayhi* would always be occupied in *dhikr*, contemplation, worship and self-discipline. He would teach the students with wisdom. It is due to his constant worship that if anyone stayed with him for a few days, even though they were not *Sangis,* they would feel change within themselves. Two people were once sat in the company of a Shaykh, who encouraged them to take the customary *bay'a*. They replied, "We have sat in the company of Qibla Alam *Rahmatullah Alayhi* and although we did not formally take *bay'a* with him yet we felt a change within ourselves and we consider that as an oath of allegiance." If a person spent a few days in his company he would regularly pray five times a day. It was the blessing of his association that even people who were followers of other masters would benefit from him, some of whom later became masters themselves.[55] Apart from those listed above there were many others who benefitted in a similar manner.

Qibla Alam *Rahmatullah Alayhi* had a compassionate nature and he was extremely generous and would never embarrass the person by talking about his previous oath of allegiance. He would always encourage such people and inform them that their previous oath of allegiance was sufficient, and advised them to remember Allah. In his view sincerity was the only criterion which was needed for a potential master. Things like caste and a high worldly position had no bearing in this matter. Whoever was sincere attained spirituality and the following case of Sain Ranjah is a prime example. Sain Ranjah belonged to the *musalli* 'low' caste. He used to herd animals of the local people in the Kokkhar area. He had no kith or kin and no connection with those in authority to speak of. A wealthy farmer named Baba Ghulam Husayn was a devotee of Qibla Alam

---

[55] Miyan Fath Muhammad (Chinar), Maulvi Abd al-Aziz (Jhelum), Hajji Baqa Muhammad (Kurti) Qadi Karam Din (Tekhyala), Miyan Karim Bakhsh (Pakhrani,Banah), Miyan Fadal Ilahi, (Kulla), Maulvi Ghulam Nabi (Bār), and Khwaja Muhammad Akbar Ali (Pir Karriyanh, Pakpattan Sharif)

Rahmatullah Alayhi and was also related to Qibla Alam's mother. When Qibla Alam *Rahmatullah Alayhi* used to visit Bawali Sharif he would stay at his house and Sain Ranjah would serve him.

Once when Qibla Alam *Rahmatullah Alayhi* set off early in the morning with his cousin and deputy Qadi Muhammad Alam *Rahmatullah Alayhi*, Sain Ranjah walked with them to say farewell, good fortune was about to smile upon him. Qibla Alam *Rahmatullah Alayhi* enquired from his cousin, "Have you taught Sain Ranjah 'Allah', 'Allah'?" He replied in the negative, so he said, "Teach him." Hence Sain Ranjah was given the oath of allegiance, *wird* and some remedy for cure. (Later he used this remedy to good effect and cured many people). He was also instructed to teach the Holy Qur'an to children. Within a short time, Ranjah the *musalli* became the mystic Sain Ranjah and people began to flock to him for benefit. Nowadays he has a shrine and an annual ceremony takes place there. It is very rare that someone from such a status has achieved honour and respect within the local community. Sain Muhammad Ashraf would joke, "This is the greatness of our master that he turned a low caste into a saint." In this context Hadrat Sahib narrates an interesting incident. "Once I was riding a horse and passing through Qamroti, when suddenly a person began to shout my name and ran towards me. By his appearance he seemed crazy but when he came near me he enquired, "Are you not the son of he who turned the illiterates into saints?""

The term 'ignorant Sufis' refers to those people who have merely inherited the title from their ancestors but have not completed spiritual training under a guide and only teach their followers from books. Regarding such people Shaykh Yahya Maudh Razi *Rahmatullah Alayhi* warns, "Avoid the company of three types of people: the heedless scholar, the charlatan mystic and an ignorant Sufi."

Qibla Alam *Rahmatullah Alayhi* used to sit on his knees, there was no special seat reserved for him, he would sit wherever there was room. He did not follow norms in dress and appearance. If he entered a gathering and the *Sangis* tried to stand up out of respect for him, he would tell them not to do that. He would not permit anyone to sit or stand up for his sake. He would tell the *Sangis*, "If you get up it hurts me." If a new or full-sized person came to visit him and he noticed that it was uncomfortable for him to sit in the kneeling posture he would say to him, "Sit as you are comfortable, we are used to this posture from our childhood." He would be very happy in the company of the *Sangis* as these people were simple and sincere. He did not seek the company of the wealthy or community leaders. As he was independent minded, he neither liked to praise nor did he want to be praised, even if it was from a dear old *Sangi*. For example, once when Sufi Faujdar Khan *Rahmatullah Alayhi* read some couplets in his honour in one gathering, he showed his displeasure by walking out.

He would give the oath of allegiance for reforming and training purposes only. Hence he never kept a record of his devotees, from which one could estimate the number of his followers. His focus was the purification of the *Sangis* and he was not concerned with increasing numbers. He did not seek fame, recognition by the masses or any material benefit, hence the absence of such a record. He never gave a written authorisation and did not encourage anyone to assume the mantle of a master. Whoever he considered fit, he gave him permission to teach 'Allah, Allah'. None of his deputies had a written authorisation from him. However in the *wird* book of Hajji Baqa Muhammad *Rahmatullah Alayhi*, Qibla Alam's signature is found, which has been preserved. He did not like to walk in a procession with the *Sangis*. At the most he would have one or two *Sangis* with him on his travels. If by chance there were more than two *Sangis* he would advise them to, "Walk ahead, do *dhikr* of 'Allah' and avoid useless conversation." He would give amulets for different purposes. Mostly his amulet consisted of the word 'Allah'. For particular situations he gave different amulets, but he never accepted any money in exchange for these amulets.

According to the masters, miracles and unveilings are minor matters and he would avoid the display of such things. If a *Sangi* mentioned his own experience of a miraculous incident, he would simply respond, "This happened due to the blessings of the masters, all of this is their grant." If any miracle was attributed to him he would become upset and state, "All of this is the exaggeration of the *Sangis*, otherwise this humble being is not capable of any goodness or perfection."

One of his special features was that on 12th *Rabi'a al-awwal* he would celebrate the birth of the Prophet ﷺ with the utmost of devotion. Nowadays the term *Eid Milad al-Nabi* ﷺ is used for this occasion but in Qibla Alam's time this term was not in use. Often on these occasions he sat with the *Sangis* and related authentic narrations from the *salaf as-salihin* (the pious generations) from the *sira* (Biography of the Prophet ﷺ) or read the *Dalail al-Khayrat* in full. The *Sangis* read *durud sharif* 125,000 times inside the mosque. Whatever food was available would be presented and supplications made and then it was served to the *Sangis,* after which they had permission to leave. They were advised to honour the blessed day by constantly remembering Allah. This practice continues in the family and on the blessed day 125,000 times *durud sharif* is read in the mosques under the supervision of Darbar Sharif and food and sweets are distributed amongst the *Sangis.*

A Few Sayings

Some sayings of Qibla Alam *Rahmatullah Alayhi* as narrated by the *Sangis* are related for the benefit of guidance.

1) Some fake *pirs* assume the mantle of guidance with the intentions of gaining worldly benefit. They establish contacts with the wealthy people and use them as the ladder to reach their goal. This method is against the pure spirit of Sufism. The real purpose of Sufism is to make the ego the servant of the Shari'ah. Sufism is the process by which the soul is purified. Bringing the ego under control is a step towards *fana fillah* (to lose one's self in the will of Allah).

2) Hadrat Sahib narrates that Qibla Alam *Rahmatullah Alayhi* used to state, "If a Shaykh is on his way to meet a *Sangi* and on the way he thinks of some worldly benefit that might come out of this visit, he must turn back immediately."

3) It is often assumed that one should not consult the *pir* for worldly matters but Qibla Alam *Rahmatullah Alayhi* disagreed, "Actions depend on intentions, this world is a place of means. Every matter is tied to a mean. Even worldly matters should be presented to one's Shaykh as it is possible that a worldly matter might lead to religion and the search for Allah." In evidence Hadrat Sahib narrates the story of Mai Jivini.[56] For some reason she left home and came to visit Qibla Alam *Rahmatullah Alayhi.* She came to seek a cure for her domestic problems but she was so impressed with the spiritual environment that her life was transformed. Subsequently she had no other desire than to seek Allah. When her son came searching for her to Checheyan Sharif, Qibla Alam *Rahmatullah Alayhi* explained to him the duties of a son and the rights of parents. He was ashamed of his previous behaviour and fell at the feet of his mother and took her home. Mai Jivini stayed steadfast upon her *wird* of reciting 'Allah' 25,000 times and regularly visited Checheyan Sharif. In her old age her eye sight failed her but

---

[56] Borah Jungle, Dina

she still came to visit with her grandson. This story indicates that sometimes a worldly matter can lead to a spiritual transformation.

4) All the Sufi paths teach their devotees some words to make intention. Hadrat Sahib narrates that Qibla Alam *Rahmatullah Alayhi* used to teach these words to make intention, "I am focusing towards the heart, which is focused on Allah, and from Allah the divine down pouring is coming to my heart, and my heart is mentioning Allah with longing and desire."

5) Some people think that if one covers one's head during *dhikr* this is showing off, whilst others disagree. Qibla Alam *Rahmatullah Alayhi* was of the view that if one performed an action on a regular basis in both private and public and then performed such an act in front of others it could not be considered showing off.

6) Qibla Alam *Rahmatullah Alayhi* placed great importance upon the saying, "*Kam ghuftan, kam khurdan, kam khuftan,* Talk, eat and sleep less. He used to tell the *Sangis* to heed this advice and personally acted upon it all his life.

6) Regarding the holy month of Ramadan, Qibla Alam *Rahmatullah Alayhi* advised that apart from that which is necessary all other travel should be avoided in this month. He continued, "If the month of Ramadan is spent by regularly praying, fasting, reciting the Holy Qur'an and reading the *wird* then Allah willing the whole year shall pass in peace and harmony."

7) Once Hadrat Sahib said to Mufti Muhammad Amin Sahib from Faisalabad that, "Qibla Alam *Rahmatullah Alayhi* states that to recite 'Allah' yourself and teaching others to repeat it is the real knowledge and training. The word 'Allah' is all encompassing and all elements of the Shari'ah such as probations and commands are contained in it. Hence this one word 'Allah' represents the whole Shari'ah.

8) Qibla Alam *Rahmatullah Alayhi* was very cautious about expressing his opinion of other people. It was extremely rare that he expressed his views about a contemporary. However it is known that he expressed his views about two contemporary masters; Pir Sayyid Jama'at Ali Shah Thani Alipuri and Ji Sahib

Abd Allah[57] *Rahmatullah Alayhima,* he made a similar comment about them both, "They follow the way of the old masters."

9) Qibla Alam *Rahmatullah Alayhi* always remembered the pious people with love and affection and if a pious person was mentioned in his presence, he would comment, "He is a pious servant of Allah Almighty."

10) Hadrat Sahib narrates that Mawlana Muhammad Zaman informed him that once he met Qibla Alam *Rahmatullah Alayhima* who enquired, "Where have you been?" He replied, "I went to visit your brother Qadi Muhammad Alam." Qibla Alam *Rahmatullah Alayhi* said, "Anyone who comes here should stay within the boundaries of the mosque, there is no reason to wander outside."

11) Qibla Alam *Rahmatullah Alayhi* placed great emphasis on lawful earnings. He stated, "Lawful earning, truthful speech, five prayers with Jama'at and *tahajjud* prayer are essential for spiritual development."

12) Qibla Alam *Rahmatullah Alayhi* used to strongly advise against sitting alone with a strange woman. Sain Muhammad Hasan *Zulfain Wallay* stated that Qibla Alam *Rahmatullah Alayhi* said, "There is magic in the forehead of strange women." And he also said, "There is danger for the student of the spiritual path from both women and youth."

13) Qibla Alam *Rahmatullah Alayhi* said, "The Darwish must not be greedy, he should not refuse and he should not hoard wealth. He should not desire anything from anyone, he should not refuse gifts that are offered without asking and not hoard what he has. His whole life was based on this principle and the *Sangis* were the living example of this.

14) He would often state, "*Hath kar wal dil yar wal,* the hands in work, the heart with the Lord."

15) Baba Ni'mat Ali[58] stated that Qibla Alam *Rahmatullah Alayhi* told him, "When you reach one hundred whilst reading 'Allah', then recite this *du'a:*

> *Maqsud-e man tu'i riza tu'i ya khuda,*
> *Irfan-e khwasheh ata kun dil-e mara.*

---

[57] Larr Wangat Pargana, Srinagar
[58] Khanyara, Dadyal

> Oh, Lord, You are my desire and Your pleasure my aim,
> Grant my heart Your love.

He also stated he had a hand written copy of this *du'a* from Qibla Alam *Rahmatullah Alayhi.*

Tried and Tested Remedies

The spiritual masters are physicians of the illnesses of the heart, but it seems they are also experts in dealing with the physical ailments as well. They have devised some remedies for physical illnesses and Qibla Alam *Rahmatullah Alayhi* sometimes used to suggest a remedy to the *Sangis*. Some tried and tested methods are listed below.

1) In winter the people who perform prayers often find that their feet or heels are cracked and sometimes it is very painful. For this ailment he recommends some mustard oil mixed with water rubbed on the affected area and *Insha Allah* the problem shall be resolved.

2) Cows or Buffalo that do not become pregnant should be fed a pound of millet bread with salt cooked as a chapatti for seven days, *Insha Allah* the aim shall be achieved. According to the *Sangis* after the third or fourth chapatti the desired result would occur.

3) If one had toothache, he would recommend two units after *maghrib* as a gift for Hadrat Awais al-Qarni ﷺ. *Sura Ikhlas* should be read three times in each unit and this prayer should be offered throughout life. One follower of Pir Sayyid Jama'at Ali Shah Alipuri called Fadal Ahmad[59] sometimes used to visit Qibla Alam *Rahmatullah Alayhima.* Once he made an offering of *churmah* (sweet *roti*) and brought some to Checheyan Sharif. That day he had a severe toothache. Qibla Alam *Rahmatullah Alayhi* instructed him to practise the above method and he states, "Forty years have passed since that incident and I never suffered from toothache again."

4) For the protection of teeth he used to recommend pure mustard oil mixed with table salt and wiped over the teeth. This method is very affective. Hadrat

---

[59] Bahjohti

Sahib states that a *Sangi* called Nur Muhammad claims that most dentists recommend this method.

5) Qibla Alam's authorised deputy Mawlana Baqa Muhammad *Rahmatullah Alayhima* used to suffer from migraines and sometimes the pain was unbearable. Qibla Alam *Rahmatullah Alayhi* advised him to soak seven almonds in water at night and to peel them first thing in the morning and to chew them properly. He added that one must not eat anything with these almonds. This is a great remedy for the brain.

6) The great masters continue to give blessings after death. Regarding this an incident involving Fath Muhammad Sahib[60] is related. He was a good natured person who often used to visit Qibla Alam *Rahmatullah Alayhi* at night. He possibly spent all his life as a bachelor. He narrates a story after the demise of Qibla Alam *Rahmatullah Alayhi*. "I had an abscess on my finger which is called '*mohri*' in the local dialect. The heat and pain was unbearable. This situation went on for many days. One day as I was leaning against the bed with my shoulder held up high, I suddenly felt drowsy. I saw Qibla Alam *Rahmatullah Alayhi* in the dream and he enquired about my problem and then suggested a remedy. He advised me, "No matter what people say do not use any medicine. Just warm some butter and pour it over the abscess. Allah shall make it better." When I woke up it was nearly time for *fajr*, so I thought that I would start the treatment after the prayer. When I came back from the prayer I saw someone sitting on a bed in the courtyard and I thought he must be a traveller from the Underhill area, as these people used to attend court dates in the morning and came into people's houses for water or *lassi*. When he saw me, he enquired, "What is the problem?" I told him about the abscess. He told me the exact remedy that Qibla Alam *Rahmatullah Alayhi* had recommended a short while ago and he used the same words. I was amazed and went inside to get the butter. When I came back, that person had left. To this day I have not been able to unravel this mystery."

---

[60] Gorsian

Ji Sahib[61] ℛahmatullah ℭlayhi

His blessed name was Abd Allah but he was known as 'Sahib Ji'.[62] After completing his spiritual training, he was advised by his master to move to Kashmir.[63] Although he was illiterate his Sufi poetry is very profound. His poetry is well known amongst the local people. He was a complete master of his time. He spoke in the Gujjari dialect. He expressed his view of Qibla Alam ℛahmatullah ℭlayhi in these words, *"Mirpur kohl ik janvaro mano mouch chanjge nazar ayeyo, I really like that man near Mirpur."*

Mawlana Nabi Bakhsh Halawa'i ℛahmatullah ℭlayhi

He was a great scholar and a Sufi. He wrote a memorable poetic commentary in the Panjabi language entitled *Tafsir-e Nabawi*. He was a firm Sunni scholar and a Darwish. His shrine is located in Lahore.[64] During one meeting in Lahore he commented to Hadrat Sahib, "He (Qibla Alam ℛahmatullah ℭlayhi) was a model of the pious generations."

Baba Alf Din ℛahmatullah ℭlayhi

He was known as Bahji and lived in the Kotli suburbs[65]. He was a mystic and a complete master. Many miracles are attributed to him by the local people. During his meeting with the father of Qari Muhammad Bashir, Sain Bahadur Ali[66], he enquired, *"Ap kit millian, thari ba'it kit heh?* Who are you linked with and where is your oath of allegiance?" When Sain Bahadur explained he was a *Sangi* of Qibla Alam ℛahmatullah ℭlayhi, he remarked, *"Qadi Sahib mouch faqir heh,* Qadi Sahib is a great mystic."

Sain Nur Majdhub ℛahmatullah ℭlayhi

---

[61] Larr Sharif
[62] Born Balakot, Sarhad, Pakistan
[63] Wangat Pargana
[64] Kotwali Gate Mosque
[65] Riya Gazan
[66] Khad Gujjaranh

He was always in the state of intoxication and his miracles were well known.[67] Once he met Qibla Alam and Miyan Fath Muhammad *Rahmatullah Alayhima* and said, "*Balle, balle, eh zamin howe, eh hal howe, is ki zamin vich bowh teh kun samaley,* (Wonderful, wonderful, if the soil is such and the till is such and the seed is planted who can count the crops)." This prophecy became true as Miyan Fath Muhammad *Rahmatullah Alayhi* was granted permission and authorisation and he spread spirituality in the Pūnch region. Once Sain Nur *Rahmatullah Alayhi* said about Qibla Alam *Rahmatullah Alayhi,* "He is a black cobra, the one bitten by him does not survive and no spell can work on him."

Sain Eido Majdhub *Rahmatullah Alayhi*

He used to answer questions in his intoxicated way which no one could understand.[68] Once he met Mawlana Muhammad Zaman *Rahmatullah Alayhi* and Hadrat Sahib was also present. When someone enquired about Mawlana Muhammad Zaman, Sain Eido *Rahmatullah Alayhima* said, "Sultan Khan was a big king and he is his slave."

---

[67] Near Dangrot Sharif
[68] Chathro, Dadyal

Chapter Two

Qibla Alam *Raḥmatullāh ʿAlayhi* and His *Sangis* as Narrated by Hadrat Sahib

Introduction

The most reliable source on Qibla Alam's personality, characteristics, spiritual status, method of training, and biographical data of his deputies and *Sangis* is the individual, his noble successor and custodian Hadrat Sahib Khwaja Muhammad Sadiq. Not only did he gather information about Qibla Alam *Raḥmatullāh ʿAlayhi* personally from the family members but he also collated from the *Sangis,* which he then related in his gatherings. In this way he passed on the spiritual teachings of the Naqshbandiyya Mujaddidiyya order and the legacy of the Khanqah-e Fathiyya for the future generations, so that the *Sangis* would gain guidance from such teachings. Allah granted the noble Hadrat Sahib an acute memory and an eye for detail, an analytical mind, desire and passion to preserve the family traditions, a remarkable zeal to transform people and a great ability to articulate his thoughts.

These recollections of Hadrat Sahib were gathered from 4th April 1989 to 25th November 1996 and were subsequently presented to him to amend and correct which he did. Thus these recollections have been authenticated. As the main topics of these recollections is Qibla Alam *Raḥmatullāh ʿAlayhi* and his *Sangis,* this information is included in the *Tazkira-e Sultaniyya.* Due to these memoirs a great deal of the family's spiritual history has been preserved. These narrations are presented in a chronological order.

1) Tuesday 4th April 1989

Hadrat Sahib related that the graves of his grandfather Khwaja Muhammad Rukn Alam and his great grandfather Khwaja Muhammad Akbar Ali *Raḥmatullāh ʿAlayhima* were side by side in Checheyan Sharif and there was just enough space to sit between the graves. Qibla Alam *Raḥmatullāh ʿAlayhi* used to sit there after *dhur* prayer and read his *wird*. Nearby was an acacia tree (*kikker*), there was an empty spot in the trunk and if the weather allowed he would place his book of *waza'if* there. It is important to point out that due to the Mangla Lake this area was submerged. Twenty six years later in 1993 the graves of

Khwaja Muhammad Rukn Alam and Khwaja Muhammad Akbar Ali *Rahmatullah Alayhima* were transferred to the Khanqah-e Sultaniyya, Jhelum, where they are buried to the right and left of Qibla Alam's grave. The graves in Checheyan Sharif were made and plastered in mud; this was also the tradition in Qibla Alam's life.

Hadrat Sahib narrates from Sufi Faujdar Khan that once Qibla Alam *Rahmatullah Alayhima* told him to sit near the graves and focus on their spirits and when he had meditated as instructed, Qibla Alam *Rahmatullah Alayhi* enquired, "Did you experience anything?" He replied that he saw a holy person with a white beard praying that, "O Allah grant good health to Miyan Fath Muhammad *Rahmatullah Alayhi* and remove his illness." Incidentally Miyan Fath Muhammad *Rahmatullah Alayhi* was in Pūnch[69] and had been taken ill.

Hadrat Sahib narrates that the chief of the Pūnch area, Khwaja Muhammad Abd Allah Ju *Rahmatullah Alayhi* was a Darwish-like person and a devotee of mystics. He greatly honoured the pious people. He used to host Miyan Fath Muhammad *Rahmatullah Alayhi* and his *Sangis* for many days and was happy to serve them. He was a practising Muslim and read his prayers, kept fasts and regularly read his *wird*. In order to express his devotion he paid a visit to Qibla Alam *Rahmatullah Alayhi*.

Hadrat Sahib narrates that it is related that Sain Muhammad Ya'qub *Rahmatullah Alayhi* had the ability to unveil the graves. Miyan Mardan Ali Naushahi[70] confirmed this in one of his poems;

> *Sain ya'qub amb wallah banda khas hazuri,*
> *Allah sahib rahmat kiti hoya kashf qaburi.*

> Sain Ya'qub from Amb is a special person,
> With Allah's grace he can unveil graves.

However, Qibla Alam *Rahmatullah Alayhi* did not approve of such an approach and so he forbade Sain Muhammad Ya'qub *Rahmatullah Alayhi* to use this method. Consequently he gave up this practice.

---

[69] Mehnder
[70] Pind Pinyam

Hadrat Sahib narrates that it is related that two old *Sangis*: Baba Faqir Muhammad Pahariyya and Baba Faqir Muhammad Pothiyya *Rahmatullah Alayhima* were at the forefront of *Langar* duties at Checheyan Sharif. Hadrat Sahib states that, "I grew up in the lap of Baba Faqir Muhammad Pahariyya and it was he who assisted Qibla Alam *Rahmatullah Alayhima* in his last ablution. When Qibla Alam *Rahmatullah Alayhi* was on his death bed Baba Faqir Muhammad Pahariyya presented me to him on several occasions and sought advice. Qibla Alam *Rahmatullah Alayhi* replied, "I leave you in Allah's care, everything shall be fine." He also advised the *Sangis* to be steadfast upon prayer and the remembrance of Allah."

Hadrat Sahib narrates that he was informed that when Hadrat Abu al-Hasan Zaid Faruqi Delhawi *Rahmatullah Alayhi* first visited Khanqah-e Sultaniyya in Jhelum, he pointed towards Qibla Alam's shrine and said to Sahibzada Muhammad Maruf, "Maruf Miyan, I will not say anything else about him, but this entire blossom is due to his blessing."

Hadrat Sahib narrates that, "Qibla Alam's way was based on, 'talk little', 'eat little' and 'sleep little'. He would advise the *Sangis* to practise this, which he acted upon himself, and trained me accordingly. He advised, "The secret of good health is to eat simple food and to eat a few morsels less than your desire."

2) *Wednesday 5th April 1989*

Hadrat Sahib narrated that Maulvi Fadal Ahmad[71] *Rahmatullah Alayhi* was a strong handsome person. When he entered the spiritual path, he completed his training under Khwaja Muhammad Akbar Ali *Rahmatullah Alayhi* and was authorised by him.[72]

3) *Thursday 6th April 1989*

Continuing with Maulvi Fadal Ahmad *Rahmatullah Alayhi* Hadrat Sahib narrates, that it was his practice that whenever he visited Checheyan Sharif and was about to say farewell he would stand near the shrine of Qibla Alam *Rahmatullah Alayhi* and read some poems of Allama Iqbal *Rahmatullah Alayhi* and then address him, "*Balihain koh balihian lajjain* (from the good ones we expect goodness)."

---

[71] Kuhtora

[72] His area of influence was Bahawalpur, Munchanpur and the surrounding areas. The minister of Chanba, Abd al-Samad was his follower. His shrine is in Hawali Lakha in the Okara District

Hadrat Sahib continued that Maulvi Sahib *Rahmatullah Alayhi* was a devout follower of his master. He was so dedicated to his master that he did not turn to any other *pir* or Khanqah and did not like the *Sangis* to do such things. Once Mawlana Muhammad Zaman, the authorised deputy of Qibla Alam *Rahmatullah Alayhima* went to visit Maulvi Fadal Ahmad[73] *Rahmatullah Alayhi* with another *pir,* who was also authorised and belonged to another Khanqah. Maulvi Fadal Ahmad *Rahmatullah Alayhi* was upset with this gesture and reminded him that it would have been better if he had come on his own rather than with that particular *pir.* Even if the trip was for the purpose of raising funds he would have been of more help. He stated "Our belief is that only Allah gives, and if after careful consideration we have taken a guide, what is the purpose of looking here and there." Hadrat Sahib recollects that he once met the above mentioned Pir Sahib who complained about the indifferent treatment he received from Maulvi Fadal Ahmad *Rahmatullah Alayhi.*

Hadrat Sahib continued, Hafiz Muhammad Ibrahim and Maulvi Fadal Ahmad *Rahmatullah Alayhima* were married in the Pūnch province.[74] It was due to these marriages that both became attached to Khwaja Muhammad Akbar Ali *Rahmatullah Alayhi,* consequently both became followers and later were granted authorisation. It was this Maulvi Fadal Ahmad to whom Qibla Alam *Rahmatullah Alayhima* said, "Take your *pir* to the Panjab." Upon hearing this, his master, Khwaja Muhammad Akbar Ali *Rahmatullah Alayhi* expressed his anxiety that there were great Sufis and scholars in the Panjab and they laughed at our local dialect. Qibla Alam *Rahmatullah Alayhi* replied, "Your task is not to chase people but to teach 'Allah', 'Allah' to those who come to seek it from you."

4) Saturday 8ᵗʰ April 1989

Raja Rang Baz Khan[75] was a follower of Pir Sayyid Jama'at Ali Shah Alipuri *Rahmatullah Alayhi* but mostly kept in touch with Hadrat Sahib. According to Hadrat Sahib, Raja Sahib used to visit Qibla Alam's shrine in Checheyan Sharif twice a day. After the body was transferred to Jhelum he used to go there. Once after visiting the shrine, he confided that, "Even my only son Mahmud Ahmad is not aware of what I am about to tell you and I want it to remain a secret during my life." He continued that, "One day I prayed at the blessed shrine, "O,

---

[73] Kuhtora
[74] Mehnder
[75] Ladar

72

Allah, for the sake of Qibla Alam *Rahmatullah Alayhi* grant me the ability to read a complete Qur'an everyday during Ramadan." With Allah's blessing I have been doing this for many years. I finish the whole Qur'an in three sittings and this continues through the six fasts of Shawwal as well, all of this is the blessing and focus of Qibla Alam *Rahmatullah Alayhi*."

5) Monday 10ᵗʰ April 1989

Hadrat Sahib narrates that Sain Muhammad Ismail[76] was the follower of Khwaja Ghulam Muhyi al-Din *Chardey Wallay Pir* *Rahmatullah Alayhi* of Bawali Sharif. His favourite phrase was, "*Dastgir jiya koi nahin,* There is none like the Helper (master)." He was a friend of Bakhshi Moti Ram[77] and when Moti Ram became minister of the Pūnch province, he went to visit him. During his visit he met the ruler of Pūnch, Khwaja Abd Allah Ju. Later Sain Sahib came to meet Qibla Alam *Rahmatullah Alayhi*.

Sain Sahib used to make loud *dhikr* and his voice was very feminine. Once he was in the company of Qibla Alam *Rahmatullah Alayhi* in the mosque,[78] when Baba Lal Din asked him to make *dhikr* of the first *kalima*, Sain Sahib said, "No, the snakes will come." Baba Lal Din said, "You perform *dhikr*, no snakes will come." So Sain Sahib began the *dhikr* when suddenly a snake appeared near the door. Sain Sahib said, "Look, *dastgir jiya koi nahin* the snake has appeared." All *Sangis* were amazed to see the snake and Baba Lal Din killed it.

As Nakka Kurti has been mentioned above it is necessary to give some background about this important place. Qibla Alam's first visit to the Kotli (AJK) region was in Nakka Kurti, he stayed in a house as there was no mosque there at the time. It was in that house that he led his first prayer in the Kotli region. Later a mosque was built on the same spot. Hadrat Sahib then built a new mosque there which was simple but very impressive in terms of architecture. This mosque comprised of a room and a courtyard. Later a university campus was built next to the mosque that offered courses in MBA, M.com and I.T. With increasing demands a bigger mosque was built on the site which encompassed the old mosque, however clear markings were made to indicate where the old mosque was situated.

---

[76] Potha Bungash
[77] Peel Siyakh
[78] Nakka Kurti

(Mujaddidi Sahib writes; Whilst inspecting today's post Hadrat Sahib remarked), "He has the rare manuscript, which has been protected by the Hidden hand. From this manuscript we have gained a great deal of information which had remained a mystery and subsequently some of our anxiety has subsided."

Later he briefly mentioned the history of this manuscript. Hajji Mawlana Baqa Muhammad, the authorised deputy of Qibla Alam *Rahmatullah Alayhima,* wrote this book of his own accord and there was no expressed desire directly or indirectly from Qibla Alam *Rahmatullah Alayhi* in this matter. This book consists of spiritual matters and in addition mentions some stories, states and experiences of his master. Seventy to eighty years ago this manuscript was taken to publishers in Lahore called, 'Allah Wallay', they liked it and promised to publish it. The aim was to announce its publication on the occasion of Qibla Alam's *urs* ceremony. The *urs* ceremony was near and it was not published in time and the manuscript remained with the publishers. For the next twenty to twenty five years there was no progress in this matter. After considerable difficulty the manuscript was brought back from the publishers.

The famous business man Hajji Sakhi Walayat[79] *Rahmatullah Alayhi* who was the follower of the author expressed his desire to have it published in the Pūnch press but he was unsuccessful in this attempt. For the next twenty five years this manuscript remained on the book shelf in the mosque.[80]

Once Hadrat Sahib happened to visit Mehnder and stayed at Hajji Sakhi's mosque. In the mosque cabinet there were files of the monthly magazine, '*Maulvi*' that was published in Delhi. As he was browsing through these files, he found the manuscript. Maybe nature had postponed its publication until the appropriate person came along. With Hajji Sahib's permission he brought the manuscript with him. Many years passed and the partition took place and now Mehnder is in occupied Kashmir.[81]

After all these hurdles finally today, 10th April 1989, the original manuscript and its draft typed copy arrived in the post, so that it could be proof read (prior to publication). Hadrat Sahib read some passages from the book,

---

[79] Mehnder
[80] Mehnder
[81] In 1947 Hajji Sakhi Walayat migrated to Kotli, died and was buried in Dhamal.

74

which shed light on many matters which were shrouded in mystery. For example despite all efforts in the past it was not possible to establish when Qibla Alam *Rahmatullah Alayhi* actually first visited the Kotli region. However, through this book it was confirmed that Qibla Alam *Rahmatullah Alayhi* first arrived here in 1920/1977 Bikrami. Indeed, one year before Hadrat Sahib's birth. This visit was in regard to a purchase of some land in this area. His stay was in Nakka Kurti and he prayed at the only *Ahl-e Sunnah wa- al-Jama'at* mosque in Kotli.[82] From the above account one can assess the importance of the Nakka Kurti mosque. (This important book was finally published in 1993 entitled '*Tohfa-e Sultaniyya*')

6) Tuesday 11th April 1989

Today Hajji Abd al-Rashid Bengali arrived and when Hadrat Sahib saw him he said, "*Aa gay ho*." He then explained the story behind this quote; he narrated a story from the *Sangi* himself. There were two *Sangis* called Muhammad Hasan in the Underhill area, one was known as 'Suda'i' and the other as 'Zulfain Wallay'. This story is about Muhammad Hasan Suda'i *Rahmatullah Alayhi*; who had relatives in Kotli.[83] He was a follower of Qibla Alam *Rahmatullah Alayhi*, who had trained him in the Zubayriyya path. In this path a person would experience states of spiritual ecstasy. So when Muhammad Hasan *Rahmatullah Alayhi* experienced this type of ecstasy, he would often feel drowsy or restless. His *dhikr* of the heart opened up. His family had all sorts of doubts and some thought he had lost his mind, whilst others thought he was possessed by a Jinn. As a result they tried to confine him indoors and placed a person on guard duty. He would be tied to his bed at night. They thought this mystic was a mad man and tried various ways to control him, all of which failed.

During this time an *amil* (exorcist) was brought to cure him. He brought his bag and sat on the opposite bed and he had hardly taken off one of his shoes, when suddenly Muhammad Hasan Suda'i *Rahmatullah Alayhi* sat up on his bed and as he was a tall and stocky young man, he looked fiercely at the exorcist and said, "*Aa gay ho*, you have arrived." The exorcist was so frightened that he ran off with just the one shoe. Standing far away he asked people to bring his bag and shoe to him as he was afraid to go near Muhammad Hasan *Rahmatullah Alayhi*.

---

[82] Baliyah
[83] Rajur

He said he was unable to perform the exorcism as the matter was above him; he was so shocked that he did not stay for food.

When Muhammad Hasan *Rahmatullah Alayhi* could no longer tolerate this pain he asked for help via the masters[84] of Qibla Alam *Rahmatullah Alayhi* to take back what he had given him, because it was beyond his endurance. One morning he felt as if there was something dripping from his heart like a few drops of the morning meadows and he felt at ease. Later on despite every effort he could never achieve that feeling and could not bring the image of Qibla Alam *Rahmatullah Alayhi* into his mind.

In the same gathering Hadrat Sahib narrated some stories of a simpleton *Sangi* called Sain Ilm Din *Rahmatullah Alayhi*. One can always find such simple personalities at the lodges of the masters. Although Sain Ilm Din *Rahmatullah Alayhi* was a simple person, he was a sincere and dedicated follower. He had great love for Qibla Alam *Rahmatullah Alayhi* and always tried to be with him, Qibla Alam *Rahmatullah Alayhi* was very compassionate towards him.

As a result of his simple nature, Sain Ilm Din *Rahmatullah Alayhi* did not behave in a formal manner and this was his distinction. He never did anything without permission and in his view Qibla Alam's wishes took precedent above other things. His common phrase was *"Allah be prawa'iy*, Allah is independent."

Once Qibla Alam *Rahmatullah Alayhi* was staying in the mosque[85] with some *Sangis,* and Sain Ilm Din was asleep and Muhammad Hasan Suda'i *Rahmatullah Alayhima* opened his eyes and put a pinch of snuff in them. Sain Ilm Din woke screaming in agony and Muhammad Hasan *Rahmatullah Alayhi* ran off. Sain Ilm Din went and complained to Qibla Alam *Rahmatullah Alayhima* *"Tussain sarey suda'i pal rakhey hain,* You have nurtured all these disloyal people." Qibla Alam *Rahmatullah Alayhi* expressed his sympathy and instructed him to wash his eyes to get rid of the pain.

Sain Ilm Din *Rahmatullah Alayhi* used to request Hadrat Sahib's maternal grandmother to make a *prataha* (buttered chapatti) but one day she was unable to fulfil his request. So he went to Qibla Alam *Rahmatullah Alayhi* and said, *"Bai*

---

[84] Bawali Sharif, Dangrot Sharif and Gorah Sayyidain
[85] Samloth

horainh ke khuda nein bakhshana, Allah will not forgive dear mother." He continued, "She slaps the face according to its status." She had informed him that there was no butter so she would make him one tomorrow, to which he responded, "If there is no butter today, then make the *prataha* with water."

Once Qibla Alam *Rahmatullah Alayhi* stayed in the Amb mosque with some *Sangis* and Sain Ilm Din asked Baba Faqir Muhammad Pothiyya *Rahmatullah Alayhima* to cut his hair. In mischief Baba Faqir Muhammad shaved Sain Ilm Din's moustache as well and when he realised he went running to Qibla Alam *Rahmatullah Alayhi* to complain about the incident. In the meantime Baba Faqir Muhammad *Rahmatullah Alayhi* hid from sight in case he got into trouble. After listening to Sain Ilm Din's complaint Qibla Alam *Rahmatullah Alayhi* said, "You sat quietly when your moustache was being shaved, what good is it to make commotion now." There are many incidents which indicate his simplicity but these are the ones which are of common interest.

Then Hadrat Sahib explained how Sain Ilm Din *Rahmatullah Alayhi* died. He was stung on the leg by a bee, which resulted in an infection and he had to be admitted into the hospital in Mirpur. Qibla Alam *Rahmatullah Alayhi* went to visit him in the hospital with a few of the *Sangis*. Sain Ilm Din *Rahmatullah Alayhi* loved *mishri* (sugar candy) so it was purchased on the way to the hospital. As soon as Qibla Alam *Rahmatullah Alayhi* entered through the gate, Sain Ilm Din *Rahmatullah Alayhi* saw him from his room and stood up out of respect. Qibla Alam *Rahmatullah Alayhi* instructed him to lie on the bed and then he mentioned the whole incident about how he got stung by the bee. Afterwards Qibla Alam *Rahmatullah Alayhi* gently stroked his head, chest and shoulders, and after a short stay returned. It was this minor incident which led to Sain Ilm Din's death.

Hadrat Sahib narrated that Mawlana Muhammad Zaman related that once a *Sangi* came to Qibla Alam *Rahmatullah Alayhima* and complained that his house was full of insects. He had tried every method to get rid of them but to no avail. He was so fed up that he was thinking of moving house. Qibla Alam *Rahmatullah Alayhi* advised him to grab one insect and start walking whilst reading *sura Ya-Sin* and not to converse with anyone on the way and when the *sura* was completed to throw away the insect. He did as he was advised and never had that problem again.

7) Saturday 15ᵗʰ April 1989

Hadrat Sahib stated that, "On the persistent request of Mullah Muhammad Ramadan *Rahmatullah Alayhi* I went to his village.[86] Mullah Muhammad Ramadan stated that on many occasions he invited Qibla Alam *Rahmatullah Alayhima* to visit Gurdaspur. However, on one occasion, a strange thing occurred as Qibla Alam *Rahmatullah Alayhi* enquired, "Which is the way to Gurdaspur?" I replied, "Via Wazirabad to Narowal." He enquired, "What they call Wazirabad, is it a city or a village?" And he repeated this question; I understood that he was in some mystical state so I remained silent."

Hadrat Sahib stated that, "Khwaja Muhammad Akbar Ali *Rahmatullah Alayhi* used to celebrate Qibla Alam's *urs* ceremony in his village.[87] Due to the partition in 1947 and the battle to liberate Kashmir he had to migrate.[88] The *Sangis* decided to continue the practice of holding an *urs* ceremony in Qibla Alam's honour. So it was decided that the ceremony would be held in Chandowal. In this context the *Sangis* invited me to attend. I went to Chandowal with the following three *Sangis*: Master Sain Khan Sahib, Hajji Bustan Sahib and Hajji Faid Alam Sahib.

The ceremony took place in a local school. When we arrived we did not recognize anyone. An old man, Master Abd al-Ghani from Kakaza'i, B.A and *Munshi Fadil* was discussing some matters. He was a well educated and well mannered person who also had knowledge of the *din*. He was probably a follower of Pir Jama'at Ali Shah Sahib *Rahmatullah Alayhi* although he had also taken some lessons in spirituality from Khwaja Muhammad Akbar Ali *Rahmatullah Alayhi*. It was said about him that he was an exceptionally disciplined person and had set aside a particular time for every activity. When we got there he was talking about the concept of *bay'a*. He stated that, "The saint is a means to reach Allah and the role of the saint is to guide one to the nearness of Allah. But if the person himself is not near Allah how can he guide others? Nowadays mostly it is these kinds of people who are giving *bay'a*."

Master Abd al-Ghani said, "People say if you eat a lot then you become healthy, but I say that if you eat less it is better for your health." He would not even drink tea unless it had been blessed. Through Khwaja Muhammad Akbar

---

[86] Dera Baba Nanak
[87] Kotli Kala Ban, Rajouri
[88] He stayed in Chandowal and Narowal for some time

Ali *Rahmatullah Alayhi* he used to visit Darbar Sharif until his death, his wife would also come with him."

Hadrat Sahib mentioned Hajji Sayd Muhammad,[89] who read the *wird* of the path regularly. He was a conscientious person and a loyal follower of his master. Once he was travelling from Mirpur city to Checheyan Sharif and on the way he met Dr Gul Bahar[90], who enquired, "Sufi Sahib where are you going?" He replied, "Checheyan Sharif." Dr Gul Bahar asked, "Why do you go there? What do you gain from there?" Hajji Sayd Muhammad was uneducated and a simple villager, but the answer he gave is worthy of note. He said, "I am an uneducated person, I do not have the capacity so that I can achieve anything. However everyone benefits according to his ability. All I know is that I was very far from religious commands such as prayers and fasting. I do not know about my ancestors but I know what I was like. Due to these pious people we pray regularly and by Allah's grace also perform *ishraq*, *awwabin* and *tahajjud* every day. When one comes here (Checheyan Sharif) the desire for the world is subdued. One's mind is on matters of purity and impurity. This is all due to the association with these pious people." Upon hearing this Dr Gul Bahar remained silent.

When Hajji Sayd Muhammad was on his death bed, he was of sound mind and when someone remarked that his illness was perhaps due to the effect of the poison, he responded, "If poison can have an effect on Hadrat Siddiq-e Akbar ﷺ, who is Sayda?" Later he expressed his regret that despite the fact that by the grace of Allah and the blessing of his master most of his children prayed and fasted regularly, unfortunately one of his sons did not. He would state, "People say that my son has achieved high status and respect in the community but I would rather see him pray five times in the mosque and that would give me greater pleasure."

Hadrat Sahib also mentioned Mawlana Ghulam Nabi who had great love and affection for Qibla Alam *Rahmatullah Alayhima* He used to tell the *Sangis*, "Although my body is in my village,[91] my soul is always wandering in the streets of Qibla Alam *Rahmatullah Alayhi*." When he used to say farewell to Qibla

---

[89] Khattar Saylainh, Kotli
[90] Fathpur
[91] Chak No:18

Alam *Rahmatullah Alayhi* he used to break down and cry bitterly. When he stayed at Checheyan Sharif, Qibla Alam *Rahmatullah Alayhi* would appoint him as the *imam*.

Hadrat Sahib stated that he was still a young boy when Qibla Alam *Rahmatullah Alayhi* passed away therefore he was unable to witness the earlier period of his life. It is a well established fact that Qibla Alam *Rahmatullah Alayhi* used to lead the prayers in the early period of his life. However due to certain circumstances he did not lead prayers in the latter part of his life.

Hadrat Sahib stated that, "My first and foremost teacher was Qibla Alam *Rahmatullah Alayhi*. In contrast to customary fashion he taught me the alphabet and began to teach me the Holy Qur'an. He made me memorise *sura Ya-Sīn*. According to Qibla Mai Sahiba *Rahmatullah Alayhi* I memorised up to the fourth *para*. Qibla Alam *Rahmatullah Alayhi* was busy during the day so I would read my lesson to him at night. It was during this period that I accompanied Qibla Alam *Rahmatullah Alayhi* to Kulla.[92] Allah knows best what reason lay behind this but I became seriously ill. The illness lasted for forty days so the physicians recommended that I give up memorising the Holy Qur'an."

Hadrat Sahib continued, "On many occasions Qibla Alam *Rahmatullah Alayhi* would let me sleep with him. At midnight he would wake up and sit on his knees and would often read couplets like these from the poetry of Hadrat Pir Sayyid Muhammad Neyk Alam Shah *Rahmatullah Alayhi*:"

> *Jeraha lewehe pechan sajan nunh jani nunh ke karsi?*
> *Puttar, dehaian, daulat, dunya fani nunh ke karsi?.*

He who recognises his Beloved, what use is life to him?
What need are children wealth and the transitory world to him?

> *Kar ke jahlla dewehe alam do jag de sultani?*
> *Jahlla us da do jag de sultani nunh ke karsi?*

Alam, He grants the kingdom of the two worlds, after you become mad,
One burnt in His love, what need for him the kingdom of two worlds?

---

[92] Near Panjera, Kotli

Afterwards Qibla Alam *Rahmatullah Alayhi* would offer his *tahajjud* and other prayers.

Hadrat Sahib states that Mawlana Ghulam Nabi *Rahmatullah Alayhi* was a firm Hanafi and he would strictly follow the rulings of this school. He would perform matters of purity with great care.

8) Sunday 16th April 1989

In today's session Hadrat Sahib mentioned Baba Wazir Muhammad Khan[93] *Rahmatullah Alayhi* who was a very outspoken and pious person. Once the discussion turned to *kashf* (unveiling) and he stated that, "One should hide these matters as a woman hides her menstruation." He would state that, "The outstanding feature of the Naqshbandiyya is that they do not waste a single breath without the remembrance of Allah."

Baba Wazir Muhammad Khan's love and affection for his master was such that his master loved horse riding and so he treated this activity like worship. He would buy a filly and personally cut the grass and feed it himself. At *asr* time he would soak the chickpeas and feed the filly at night. When the filly was ready to be saddled he would send it to his master. He often visited Qibla Alam *Rahmatullah Alayhi* and there was a lot of love and affection between the two. Hadrat Sahib states that he went to visit Baba Wazir Muhammad Khan *Rahmatullah Alayhi*. At that time he was very old and he would often remain in meditation.

Then in the same context Hadrat Sahib mentioned the two brothers Jammu and Gammu, who were notorious thieves.[94] Once a thief from Bar heard the fame of these brothers and came to visit them. He told them he was a famous thief himself and had come to pay them respect. He requested they show him some of their special skills. One of the brothers was sitting on a stool, he spun the stool in such a way that he landed on the roof. In old age they both repented at the hands of Baba Wazir Muhammad Khan *Rahmatullah Alayhi* and became his followers. He advised them to return the goods they had stolen and seek forgiveness from the people, as these matters were the right of people and one would be questioned regarding them. They apologised that they could not return

---

[93] Chibalpur, he was a follower and deputy of the Rupar Sharif Khanqah
[94] Buha Dangri

the goods as they no longer had them and they could not openly confess to their crimes as this entailed punishment from the authorities. They would state, "We are hoping for Allah's mercy." Hadrat Sahib narrates that, "Once I went into their area to buy a horse. One of the brothers had died and the other had finished his prayers and was busy in *dhikr*."

An incident that reflects the outspoken nature of Baba Wazir Muhammad Khan *Rahmatullah Alayhi* is related: The local chief Chaudary Gul Muhammad[95] and his father were the followers of Rupar Sharif. Once he invited the sons of his master to his house, Baba Wazir Muhammad Khan *Rahmatullah Alayhi* was also invited. During the meal the sons of the master asked Baba Wazir Muhammad Khan *Rahmatullah Alayhi*, "What is the reason that despite all our efforts we do not achieve the spiritual states of our ancestors?" Baba Wazir Muhammad Khan *Rahmatullah Alayhi* boldly stated, "Because they did not eat the food from the chief's table."

Hadrat Sahib states that Qibla Alam *Rahmatullah Alayhi* did not like lengthy titles. His personality was firmly grounded on reality and he hated show and exaggeration and did not like to be praised.

9) Tuesday 18th April 1989

Hadrat Sahib narrates that brother Muhammad Zaman related that, "Once I was massaging Qibla Alam *Rahmatullah Alayhima*, he was lying down with his eyes closed and it seemed as if he was asleep. I was thinking about a person from the Rajput clan, whether he was a Sunni or a Shi'a? As sometimes he used to pray in our mosque and at other times he attended Shi'a gatherings. Qibla Alam *Rahmatullah Alayhi* became aware of my thoughts and immediately opened his eyes and said, "Without a doubt he is a strict Shi'a."

Mawlana Muhammad Zaman also related these two stories of Qibla Alam *Rahmatullah Alayhima*. The first story is about Chaudary Nadir[96] who wanted to marry a widow. The matter had developed to such an extent that he would often visit her. Once he was visiting Qibla Alam *Rahmatullah Alayhi* and intended to visit her after the *asr* prayer. But before he could gain permission, Qibla Alam *Rahmatullah Alayhi* covered his head with a cloth and began his meditation, so Chaudary Nadir

---

[95] Gul Pirah
[96] Thanpal

82

was very agitated. Suddenly Qibla Alam *Rahmatullah Alayhi* lifted the cloth from his face and said to him, "You will not finish your bad habits. Do not just look at my dark skin; I have been through every hair on your body." After this Qibla Alam *Rahmatullah Alayhi* focused on Chaudary Nadir's heart and he fainted and remained unconscious until night fall. Chaudary Nadir relates, "When I regained my conscious all thoughts of that woman were erased from my heart and despite her invitations I never met her again. If it was not for Qibla Alam's focus I might have landed myself in sin and destroyed my hereafter."

The second story concerns, Khushi Muhammad[97] who was the first *Sangi* in this area and was the cause of Mawlana Muhammad Zaman taking *bay'a* from Qibla Alam *Rahmatullah Alayhima* and becoming his deputy. Once Khushi Muhammad came to meet Qibla Alam *Rahmatullah Alayhi* in Checheyan Sharif but he had gone to the mountainous area. So Khushi Muhammad set off to meet him. On the way when he was in a particular area and as it was near nightfall he decided to spend the night in a house. Inside the house was a wicked woman who wanted to seduce Khushi Muhammad and commit sin. Khushi Muhammad relates that, "I was tempted by the woman and was willing to commit the sin but at that very moment my heart was filled with fear as I thought about Qibla Alam *Rahmatullah Alayhi*. In this state of anxiety I came out of the house and did not go back lest I commit a sin. By the grace Allah Almighty and due to the blessing of the great master I was saved from sin."

10) Wednesday 19th April 1989

Hadrat Sahib related a few stories about his noble grandfather, Khwaja Muhammad Rukn Alam *Rahmatullah Alayhi*. He stated that if a person was bitten by a snake, Khwaja Muhammad Rukn Alam *Rahmatullah Alayhi* would blow or give water to the person who brought this message and by the grace of Allah Almighty the affected person would be cured. He did not give the customary *ta'wiz* and would instead tell a person to lift a piece of wood or rock from one place to another. In later life he entered the state of mystical intoxication and his actions and states were beyond comprehension. During this period he was particularly fond of black bulls and spotted cows. If he saw such an animal he would bring it home and feed it and then take it back to its owner. And when he used to leave home and someone asked where he was going he would reply that he was, "Going on official duty."

---

[97] Metha, Dina

Khwaja Muhammad Rukn Alam only had one son Qibla Alam *Rahmatullah Alayhima* whose mother had died when he was an infant. Khwaja Muhammad Rukn Alam *Rahmatullah Alayhi* did not remarry. Due to his mystical state he would leave his only son on his own and wander off.

Some of the miracles of Khwaja Muhammad Rukn Alam *Rahmatullah Alayhi* were amazing. Once he was going on 'official duty'. The corn crop was not ripe, so he informed his son that he was going on 'official duty'. And it would be difficult for a young boy to take care of the crops, so he decided to sort it out before his departure. He dug a big ditch in the ground and cut the unripe corn and laid it down. He then watered the unripe corn and covered it with thorn bushes and left for his 'official duty'. When he returned all the people had gathered their harvest. He instructed his son to tell the local women to come the next day to his field and peel the corn. The villagers who knew the situation sniggered at the prospect of peeling the unripe corn. They said to one another, "Corn, what corn, how can corn grow like this?" The next day he went to his field with his son and the people were amazed to discover that the corn was in perfect condition and considerably more than the previous year's crops.

Regarding the term 'official duty' some people were of the opinion that Khwaja Muhammad Rukn Alam *Rahmatullah Alayhi* was from the category of saints known as the 'People of Service'.

Once Khwaja Muhammad Rukn Alam *Rahmatullah Alayhi* went away on 'official duty' and his son was left on his own. His son became ill with a fever and was looked after by his uncle and other relatives. When Khwaja Muhammad Rukn Alam returned from his journey his elder brother Qadi Fadil Ahmad *Rahmatullah Alayhima* reprimanded him for neglecting his only son in the state of illness. Khwaja Muhammad Rukn Alam *Rahmatullah Alayhi* remained silent and touched his son to assess his fever and finally said, "It is not as bad as he claims." When his son heard these words he began to cry, as he was expecting some words of comfort and affection from his father. He then took his son to the mosque and made him eat some leaves from the tree inside the mosque and then he went into meditation. His son went home and was soaked in perspiration and with that he recovered from his illness.

In the arid areas it is extremely difficult to reap the harvest as it requires a lot of water. Whenever Khwaja Muhammad Rukn Alam *Rahmatullah Alayhi* needed rain for this purpose he would take his water jug and prayer mat and go to the roof of the house. Even on a clear day the dark clouds would cover the sky and it would rain and in this way the work would get done. The local villagers used to wait for his harvest so they could be saved a great deal of effort and benefit from the rain.

Once Khwaja Muhammad Rukn Alam *Rahmatullah Alayhi* was staying at the mosque.[98] Mai Umari a pious lady lived near the mosque; she would bring water to the mosques and carried out other duties as well. Once Mai Umari was about to reap her harvest when dark clouds covered the sky. She became very anxious as there seemed to be no solution to the problem. Coincidently Khwaja Muhammad Rukn Alam *Rahmatullah Alayhi* was walking past, so Mai Umari asked him to pray. He had gone past her but he turned back and took off his shoes and faced the sky. According to one version he stood quietly and in another version he wrote something in the air with his finger, the dark clouds lifted and he put on his shoes and carried on walking.

11) Monday 24th April 1989

In today's session Hadrat Sahib mentioned a story about Hadrat Mujaddid Alf Thani *Rahmatullah Alayhi*. It is related that when he was given the final bath after his demise, his hands kept returning to below the navel, as in the posture of prayer. Hadrat Sahib narrates from two *Sangis*: Chaudary Nadir Ali[99] and Baba Lal Din[100] that when Qibla Alam *Rahmatullah Alayhi* was bathed after his demise a similar incident took place.

12) Saturday 29th April 1989

In this session Hadrat Sahib mostly talked about Sufi Faujdar Khan *Rahmatullah Alayhi*. He was stationed in the Pūnch Customs Office where Khwaja Muhammad Abd Allah Ju *Rahmatullah Alayhi* was the Superintendent. Khwaja Sahib *Rahmatullah Alayhi* was a good natured person and devotee of pious people. Once Sufi Faujdar Khan expressed his desire to visit Qibla Alam and Khwaja Sahib gave him some paper, caps and some money as an offering for Qibla Alam *Rahmatullah Alayhim*. According to Sufi Faujdar Khan *Rahmatullah Alayhi* the journey was on foot and he had his books of *waza'if* with him. When he reached,[101] a thought came to his

---

[98] Jabr
[99] Thanpal
[100] Khad Gujjaranh
[101] Palak

heart that the terms *fana* and *baqa* were often mentioned in the Sufi literature. "Is it possible that someone could possess these states nowadays?" These thoughts occupied his mind all the way to Checheyan Sharif.

It was hot weather and the mosque was made of mud and only had one door. When he opened the door he saw a bed with a sheet spread on it but there was no one on the bed. The mosque was small so it was not possible that someone could hide there. He placed his luggage on the floor and went to perform ablution. When he came back to the mosque he heard the sound of 'Allah', 'Allah' and saw Qibla Alam *Rahmatullah Alayhi* stretched out on the bed. Sufi Faujdar Khan *Rahmatullah Alayhi* states, "Later he embraced me and sat on the floor and asked about my welfare, and remarked, "You just set off whether it's an appropriate time or not." Sufi Faujdar Khan then presented the gifts from Khwaja Muhammad Abd Allah Ju *Rahmatullah Alayhima* to him but he did not touch them. He went outside and told him to rest. Later on a *Sangi* took the gifts inside. The call to prayer was said and after the prayer Sufi Faujdar Khan mentioned the matter of *fana* and *baqa* and how he did not see Qibla Alam on his bed to Miyan Fath Muhammad *Rahmatullah Alayhima* who said, "This is a type of *fana* and *baqa*."

In this context Sufi Faujdar Khan *Rahmatullah Alayhi* mentioned another personal experience. He narrated that it was the occasion of the annual *urs* ceremony in Checheyan Sharif and the teacher of teachers Hadrat Mawlana Muhammad Abd Allah *Rahmatullah Alayhi* from Ladar who was a saint himself was giving a talk. During the talk he mentioned the terms *fana* and *baqa*. Qibla Alam *Rahmatullah Alayhi* was sat in the back rows. A *Sangi* called Mukhtar was massaging his neck and shoulders, Qibla Alam *Rahmatullah Alayhi* indicated with his finger for him to stop. Qibla Alam *Rahmatullah Alayhi* then disappeared and was later seen at the time of the final supplication. Sufi Faujdar Khan *Rahmatullah Alayhi* was confused by what he saw. So he discussed the matter of *fana* and *baqa* with a *Sangi*, who replied, "This was the answer to your query, indeed the saints who experience *fana* and *baqa* still exist."

13) Monday 1ˢᵗ May 1989

Hadrat Sahib narrated that, "Once I went to the shrine of Hadrat Pir Sayyid Muhammad Neyk Alam Shah *Rahmatullah Alayhi* with the old loyal *Sangi* Baba

Faqir Muhammad[102]. On the way back as we reached the area[103] I asked him if Qibla Alam *Rahmatullah Alayhi* had given him some *waza'if* to read, he replied in the affirmative. He stated that Qibla Alam *Rahmatullah Alayhi* had instructed him to read the *khatam* of Hadrat Mujaddid and Hadrat Shaykh Abd al-Qadir Jilani *Rahmatullah Alayhima*, *sura Ya-Sīn* and *sura Mulk*. "But I sensed a hint of disappointment in his tone. So I said to him, Baba take this *wazifa* (litany) which thanks to Pir Sahib (Hadrat Pir Sayyid Muhammad Neyk Alam Shah *Rahmatullah Alayhi*) I have been granted today. But Baba Faqir Muhammad *Rahmatullah Alayhi* quickly stepped forward and stopped me saying, "Absolutely not, all thanks are due to my master, if he is happy then all others are happy and if he is upset then no one shall come to your aide." Sain Muhammad Ashraf *Rahmatullah Alayhi*, the personal servant used to state, "The strong beliefs of the illiterate people are a good example for the educated."

Hadrat Sahib narrates that once Qibla Alam's guide and benefactor Khwaja Muhammad Hayat *Rahmatullah Alayhima* came to the nearby village.[104] Qibla Alam instructed Baba Faqir Muhammad Pothiyya to prepare food for Khwaja Muhammad Hayat *Rahmatullah Alayhim*. As Qibla Alam *Rahmatullah Alayhi* had served his master for many years and played host to him on numerous occasions, he knew his master's taste. Once Qibla Alam *Rahmatullah Alayhi* stated, "If we were in a hurry we would have taken the skin off the chicken so it would cook quickly." So he instructed Baba Faqir Muhammad to prepare scrambled eggs and chapattis for Khwaja Muhammad Hayat *Rahmatullah Alayhima* and to start cooking as soon as he left Gorsian, as the master did not intend to stay overnight.

14) Saturday 20th May 1989

Hadrat Sahib narrated that Maulvi Muhammad Din Barauchi *Rahmatullah Alayhi* from Bombay went to perform Hajj in the blessed Hijaz. By a coincidence he met Sayyid Qai'm Ali Shah *Rahmatullah Alayhi* from Pūnch in Madinah Munawwara. Sayyid Qai'm Ali Shah's life was according to the Shari'ah. Maulvi Muhammad Din *Rahmatullah Alayhi* liked his life style and disposition and so he enquired about his spiritual connection. In response Shah Sahib informed him that he was a follower of Hadrat Pir Sayyid Muhammad Neyk Alam Shah *Rahmatullah Alayhima*,[105] who was still alive, Maulvi Muhammad Din *Rahmatullah Alayhima*

---

[102] Potha
[103] Nala Khad
[104] Gorsain
[105] Gorah Sayyidain, Mirpur, Jammu and Kashmir

87

came to visit him but by the time he arrived in Mirpur, Hadrat Pir Sahib *Rahmatullah Alayhi* had passed away. Whilst he was in this area he met Maulvi Abd al-Latif[106] who was a trustworthy and loyal follower of Hadrat Pir Sayyid Muhammad Neyk Alam Shah *Rahmatullah Alayhima*. Apart from his vast knowledge he was also advanced in spiritual ranks. Indeed, he had led the funeral prayer of his master and looked after the guests after his master's demise for forty days. Maulvi Muhammad Din was very impressed with Maulvi Abd al-Latif *Rahmatullah Alayhima* and came to the conclusion that, "This whole saintly family is full of spirituality." He asked to be included in the noble chain of transmission. Although Maulvi Abd al-Latif *Rahmatullah Alayhi* did not normally give the customary oath of allegiance, seeing Maulvi Muhammad Din's passion he accepted him into the spiritual path. The love and passion Maulvi Muhammad Din had for the masters and the path led him to Bafa Sharif where the master of Pir Sayyid Muhammad Neyk Alam Shah, Hadrat Hajji Muhammad *Rahmatullah Alayhim* was buried.

According to Hadrat Sahib, Maulvi Muhammad Din *Rahmatullah Alayhi* was plump and offered his prayers with great devotion. He originally had the small copy of the *Dalail al-Khayrat* printed that is used by the *Sangis*. He was very devout in reciting the *Dalail al-Khayrat* himself as well as other *waza'if.*

In the same context Hadrat Sahib stated that Qibla Alam *Rahmatullah Alayhi* used to read the *Dalail al-Khayrat* with great enthusiasm. He would advise the *Sangis* to begin the book on Friday and to focus on the *lata'if* and read it with the image of the Prophet ﷺ in mind. He stated that if one read it with such devotion one would feel the presence of the Prophet ﷺ. Qibla Alam *Rahmatullah Alayhi* would say, "We are old now and so is our spirituality but when we were both young then whenever we read the *Dalail al-Khayrat* with the utmost devotion we felt the presence of the Prophet ﷺ."

15) Tuesday 23rd May 1989

Hadrat Sahib said that Qadi Nadir Ali[107] *Rahmatullah Alayhi* was originally a follower of some other Pir Sahib, however for some reason that connection had been severed. He used to stay at home in the Underhill area. As there were many *Sangis* in this area, Qibla Alam *Rahmatullah Alayhi* often visited it. The people

---

[106] Gul Pirah (Abd Illah Pur, Mirpur)
[107] Potha Bungash

would often mention Qadi Nadir Ali to Qibla Alam *Rahmatullah Alayhima* but he would not comment on the matter. Qadi Nadir Ali *Rahmatullah Alayhi* was a proud person, due to his knowledge. Indeed, he had a vast amount of knowledge and did not accept anyone as a saint if he did not possess knowledge. After the break up from his master, he did not contact any other master. If he ever met Qibla Alam *Rahmatullah Alayhi* it was by a coincidence.

Although following the break up with his master, Qadi Nadir Ali *Rahmatullah Alayhi* lost his passion but he never gave up seeking spirituality. If a person is a sincere seeker then the Divine Hand comes to the rescue. Qadi Nadir Ali, the very person who never considered it worthwhile to meet Qibla Alam *Rahmatullah Alayhima*, arrived unexpectedly at Checheyan Sharif one day. The *Sangis* were surprised to see him and informed Qibla Alam *Rahmatullah Alayhi* about his arrival, but he remained silent. Instead of entering the mosque Qadi Nadir Ali *Rahmatullah Alayhi* went outside to examine the prayer niche. He then took out a piece paper and checked its contents with the mosque's surroundings. Later he suddenly entered the mosque and addressed Qibla Alam *Rahmatullah Alayhi*, "Last night I had a dream in which I was shown a map of this location and my heart wanted to come here and when I woke up I drew the map on a piece of paper. That is why I checked the surroundings to verify the location in the dream, and when everything matched I knew I had come to the right place. That is why I have now come to meet you."

During the discussion Qibla Alam *Rahmatullah Alayhi* said to him, "As you are linked with the Chishtiyya order and read many *waza'if*, it would be better if you put a chain and lock on the mosque door and after *fajr*, when the other worshipers have gone, then lock the chain from inside the mosque and sit quietly. Do not read anything during this period. Only bear in mind that you have pinned your hopes in Allah Almighty and wait at His gate, continue this until it's time for sunrise prayers. Repeat this practice between *asr* and *maghrib* as well."

Qadi Nadir Ali acted upon the advice of Qibla Alam *Rahmatullah Alayhima* and put a chain and lock on the mosque door. Although the mosque has now been renovated, the chain and the lock has been preserved. Due to this practice Qadi Nadir Ali's condition began to improve rapidly. *Dhikr* reached every hair in his body. He expressed his regret that he had met a perfect guide late in life. According to one narration he passed away within six months and according to the other report he died a year later. In any case he had achieved his goal. According to one report he composed some eulogies in honour of Qibla Alam *Rahmatullah Alayhi*, but had them destroyed as anything that would give pleasure to the ego had to be avoided.

16) Wednesday 24th May 1989

Hadrat Sahib narrated that Maulvi Abd al-Latif[108] belonged to the Ahl-i Hadith as did most of the villagers. Some *Sangis* narrate that Maulvi Abd al-Latif did not believe in the concept of *tasawwar-e shaykh*, (to focus on the master). Qibla Alam *Rahmatullah Alayhi* was visiting a nearby village.[109] Out of Islamic brotherhood and courtesy Maulvi Abd al-Latif came to meet Qibla Alam *Rahmatullah Alayhi*. Upon his arrival Qibla Alam *Rahmatullah Alayhi* handed an open book to a *Sangi* for Maulvi Abd al-Latif to read that discussed the concept of *taswwar-e shaykh*. After reading the relevant section of the book Maulvi Abd al-Latif said, "We do not reject, we accept."

According to the *Sangis*, Maulvi Abd al-Latif was so impressed by Qibla Alam's observance of the Shari'ah that he obtained the *dhikr* of 'Allah' from him and practised it all his life. Some *Sangis* were of the opinion that Maulvi Abd al-Latif had actually become a follower of Qibla Alam *Rahmatullah Alayhi*. After this incident whenever Maulvi Abd al-Latif went to Mirpur he would visit Qibla Alam *Rahmatullah Alayhi* in Checheyan Sharif. The fanatics amongst the Ahl-i Hadith would criticise him for visiting Qibla Alam *Rahmatullah Alayhi* and felt that in old age he had gone astray.

17) Monday 5th June 1989

In today's session Hadrat Sahib showed a photocopy of Qibla Alam's signatures: one was signed in *nastaliq* writing and read 'Qadi Muhammad Sultan' and the other 'Muhammad Sultan Alam'. Hadrat Sahib narrated that Qibla Alam *Rahmatullah Alayhi* recited poems in a melodious voice and would offer his unique commentary upon the couplets. "Miyan Muhammad Ibrahim had studied a Farsi book with Qibla Alam *Rahmatullah Alayhima* as did some other people but I cannot remember their names. Regrettably some important events of that period

---

[108] *Imam* of mosque in Potha Sher, Dadyal

[109] Mohrah Gujjaranh situated opposite Potha Sher

were lost due to neglect on my part. Now I regret the fact but I cannot rectify the situation."

Hadrat Sahib continued, "Once Qibla Alam *Rahmatullah Alayhi* taught the following couplet from the *Pandnamah* (Shaykh Farid al-Din Attar *Rahmatullah Alayhi*):

Suy'e o khasme teer andakhteh,
Pussha ay karash kifayat sakhteh.

The enemy who threw an arrow at him,
A mosquito finished him.

Qibla Alam *Rahmatullah Alayhi* provided a beautiful commentary on the above couplet. My sister who was very young at the time was stood nearby and she memorised this couplet and recited it the next day in the same melodious tone and Qibla Alam *Rahmatullah Alayhi* was very pleased with her.

Miyan Muhammad Ibrahim[110] *Rahmatullah Alayhi* (mentioned earlier) used to fetch water from the well at Checheyan Sharif. In those days the water was brought from the well. The local women also used to fetch water from the well. So Qibla Alam instructed Miyan Muhammad Ibrahim *Rahmatullah Alayhima* not to go to the well in the presence of women and to wait to one side until they had finished. He always acted upon this advice. He also used to give *adhan* and had shoulder length hair. He would often stay with Qibla Alam *Rahmatullah Alayhi*. When Qibla Alam went to the village[111], Miyan Muhammad Ibrahim *Rahmatullah Alayhima* was with him. A person came to meet Qibla Alam *Rahmatullah Alayhi* and perhaps his name was 'Jang'. He mentioned his problem that his children (boys) had died in their infancy. Qibla Alam *Rahmatullah Alayhi* said, "Bring a quarter pound of Khurasani fennel seed and a few ounces of black pepper." He then instructed Miyan Muhammad Ibrahim *Rahmatullah Alayhi* to recite following with the intention that Allah grants 'Jang' healthy children: *sura Was-shams* 41 times at midday on Monday. Due to Allah's blessing 'Jang' had twins, Yusuf and Musa. Hadrat Sahib states, "I have met them both." Later Qibla Alam would comment that the

---

[110] Para'i Anban, Kotli
[111] Potha Sher

breath of Miyan Muhammad Ibrahim *Raḥmatullāh ʿAlayhima* is very effective as Allah grants twins. "One of the brothers is still alive."

Hadrat Sahib mentioned that Raja Rahmat Khan[112] was a follower of Khwaja Ghulam Muhyi al-Din *Chardey Wallay Pir* and would spend some time in the company of Qibla Alam *Raḥmatullāh ʿAlayhima*. He was steadfast in his *waza'if* but his Rajput attitude would sometimes surface as he was very particular about his food. Qibla Alam *Raḥmatullāh ʿAlayhi* did not like this aspect of his character as it was against Sufi ethics. Qibla Alam *Raḥmatullāh ʿAlayhi* would state, "As yet Delhi is very far, *hanuz delhi dur ast.*" Meaning the humility which is required in the Sufi path is absent. "As yet you have not become accustomed to its spirit."

Hadrat Sahib then mentioned a pious person named Akbar Ali Khan,[113] he was slim and tall and had a grey beard. "He visited Qibla Alam *Raḥmatullāh ʿAlayhi* and I have seen him. Maulvi Ghulam Nabi from Bār narrates that once Akbar Ali Khan was about to leave Checheyan Sharif and Qibla Alam *Raḥmatullāh ʿAlayhima* had come to the boundary to say farewell to him, Akbar Ali Khan said, "I have visited many famous masters and shrines but alas have not achieved my goal. The heart is dead as before." Qibla Alam *Raḥmatullāh ʿAlayhi* said to him, "There is a pond where water is stored for irrigation purposes and the water has stopped reaching the field. If the direction of the water can be changed then maybe your problem might be resolved." (This is a cryptic saying that indicates that Akbar Ali Khan had some spiritual obstacle which had thus far prevented him from benefiting from the holy people and Qibla Alam *Raḥmatullāh ʿAlayhi* gave him a task so that the obstacle could be removed)

When he heard this Akbar Ali Khan postponed his departure and got a pickaxe and a spade and started digging. The task took fifteen days and during this time Qibla Alam instructed him to read the *khatam* of Hadrat Mujaddid *Raḥmatullāh ʿAlayhima* with every prayer. When the digging was completed Qibla Alam *Raḥmatullāh ʿAlayhi* enquired, "Did you read the *khatam*?" He replied, "My tongue is lazy, I had plenty of time at *fajr* and *isha* and read it regularly at these times but during the day I did not get the opportunity." Qibla Alam *Raḥmatullāh ʿAlayhi* said, "Today complete the *khatam sharif.*" Then Qibla Alam *Raḥmatullāh ʿAlayhi* turned his spiritual attention towards him and Akbar Ali Khan was overwhelmed. Seeing

---

[112] Gādari
[113] Domeli

his state some people commented that Qibla Alam *Rahmatullah Alayhi* gave so much spiritual power to Akbar Ali Khan that, "*faizunh nal tunni churaiyya,* he was overflowing with blessings."

Hadrat Sahib narrated that Akru Khan and Farmana Khan[114] and were followers of Mawlana Hajji Baqa Muhammad *Rahmatullah Alayhi*. They belonged to the Dulli tribe and used to bring merchandise from Gujjar Khan on their mules. In those days the situation was such that whomever Qibla Alam *Rahmatullah Alayhi* glanced upon would be filled with spirituality and this is what happened to Akru Khan and Farmana Khan.

Another *Sangi* was Neyk Muhammad[115] who met Qibla Alam via Sufi Faujdar Khan *Rahmatullah Alayhima*. He was a strong, tall young man with broad shoulders. He became so attached to Checheyan Sharif that he spent the remainder of his life there and died there as well. Qibla Alam *Rahmatullah Alayhi* had some land[116] and Neyk Muhammad was made in charge of it. At one time there were twenty one cows (big and small) grazing on this land. Qibla Alam *Rahmatullah Alayhi* used to state, "Three things are essential for a person, wood, grass and water." All three of these divine gifts were present in this area.[117]

18) Tuesday 6th June 1989

Hadrat Sahib told a story about Qibla Alam's childhood. Once a simple village girl went missing, in those days people really cared about one another. Honour, profit and loss were shared, so all the villagers set out to find the girl. Teams were made of young people and Qibla Alam *Rahmatullah Alayhi* and some people were given the task of searching for her in the Potohar area. When Qibla Alam *Rahmatullah Alayhi* reached the village,[118] the sun was about to set. There was a house situated near the canal where an old lady lived. So Qibla Alam *Rahmatullah Alayhi* went forward and enquired about the lost girl but the old lady was deaf and did not understand a word he said. She thought he was asking if he could stay the night in her house. So the old lady said, "If you want to spend the night there is plenty of space. A person does not take the house or the land with him. Who

---

[114] Mankot
[115] Muzaffarabad
[116] Duliya Jattain
[117] Duliya Jattain
[118] Dhok Mohri located between Potha Bungash and Khadimabad

knows what Allah has destined and what shall happen. You shall have a bed, food, water jug and a prayer mat." Qibla Alam *Rahmatullah Alayhi* tried his best to get some information about the girl from her but to no avail. So Qibla Alam *Rahmatullah Alayhi* and his team continued their search.

When the team came to the area[119] they saw a funeral which was accompanied by a large crowd, so they asked the people in the crowd if they had seen the simple girl. They assumed that these young boys were beggars and replied, "Why are you making excuses? If you want some charity grain, then join the queue of beggars and you shall be given your share." This story beautifully illustrates the social situation of the time.

Once upon the request of Baba Lal Din,[120] Qibla Alam *Rahmatullah Alayhi* went to his home. When he arrived it was night time. There were many *Sangis* with Qibla Alam *Rahmatullah Alayhi*. The wife of Baba Lal Din called Pattu had cleaned the house and prepared food according to her estimate. But when she saw the large group accompanying Qibla Alam *Rahmatullah Alayhi* she became anxious that the food might not be enough. Qibla Alam *Rahmatullah Alayhi* sensed her anxiety and gave his shawl to his deputy Mawlana Hajji Baqa Muhammad *Rahmatullah Alayhi* and instructed him, "Cover the basket of chapattis with this and then serve the *Sangis*. The *Sangis* have come to recite 'Allah', 'Allah' and food is of secondary concern." Baba Lal Din wanted to slaughter a goat but Qibla Alam *Rahmatullah Alayhima* stopped him and told him whatever was present would suffice. There was abundant unrefined sugar and the *Sangis* ate to their fill. Even the family ate the same food. The *Sangis* state there were still some chapattis left in the basket.

Baba Lal Din *Rahmatullah Alayhi* was a poor person. He only had a small piece of land near his house. He had no work or business but his love for Qibla Alam *Rahmatullah Alayhi* was such that he would stop every traveller going past his house and renew his faith by listening to stories about Qibla Alam *Rahmatullah Alayhi*. Once a shepherd stole a big wooden rosary from Checheyan Sharif, this rosary belonged to Khwaja Muhammad Rukn Alam *Rahmatullah Alayhi*. On the way he felt some pain and he thought it was because he had stolen the rosary. He became frightened and gave the rosary to Baba Lal Din *Rahmatullah Alayhi* so he could return it

---

[119] Miyan-e Ban
[120] Khad Gujjaranh

to its rightful place. When Baba Lal Din returned the rosary, Qibla Alam *Rahmatullah Alayhima* gave it back to him as a gift.

Once a Jogi came to Baba Lal Din's house and saw the big rosary hanging there and was eager to obtain it. So he said to Baba Lal Din *Rahmatullah Alayhi*, "I shall ask you for something but do not refuse." Baba Lal Din *Rahmatullah Alayhi* said, "Do not ask me something that is beyond my means." So the Jogi asked for the rosary but Baba Lal Din *Rahmatullah Alayhi* refused. Then the Jogi offered to buy it from him but Baba Lal Din *Rahmatullah Alayhi* said, "Even if you were to offer me a Rupee for each bead I would not sell." So the Jogi began to make threats, "What if the rosary comes to me." Baba Lal Din *Rahmatullah Alayhi* said, "If you can move the rosary, you can have it for free otherwise I shall beat you up." Baba Lal Din's wife Pattu persuaded the Jogi to leave.

Once Baba Lal Din *Rahmatullah Alayhi* was about to set off to Checheyan Sharif when a crow cried out. This was considered a bad omen in the local culture and his wife tried to stop him from travelling but Baba Lal Din *Rahmatullah Alayhi* said, "That crow is a devil and so are you if you stop me from visiting my master." Then he set off on his journey and safely arrived in Checheyan Sharif.

19) Thursday 15th June 1989

Hadrat Sahib narrated from Sufi Faujdar Khan that, "Once I was carrying the *waza'if* books of Qibla Alam *Rahmatullah Alayhima* and as we were passing through the area,[121] he said to me, "*Sangiyya*, today you are with me as Hadrat Abu Bakr Siddiq ؓ was with the Prophet ﷺ."

Later events proved that this prophecy was true as whenever Sufi Faujdar Khan had a problem he would receive spiritual help from Qibla Alam *Rahmatullah Alayhima*, even when there were no worldly means the image of the master would come to Sufi Faujdar Khan's aide.

20) Saturday 17th June 1989

Hadrat Sahib mentioned that the builder Muhammad Alam was linked to Chura Sharif. He had a fine voice and had learned some parts of the Holy

---

[121] Nala Khad

Qur'an from Khwaja Hafiz Muhammad Hayat *Raḥmatullāh Ꜥlayhi.* "We used to call him uncle." He used to work during the day and visit Qibla Alam *Raḥmatullāh Ꜥlayhi* at night as instructed. Sometimes Qibla Alam *Raḥmatullāh Ꜥlayhi* would ask him to lead the prayers. He was the *imam* in his village mosque.[122] This village was situated east of Checheyan Sharif. The inhabitants of this village mostly comprised of Bains Rajputs. He used to teach children in the mosque as well. Hafiz L'al Din (the blind) read some chapters of the Holy Qur'an from him and later was transferred.[123] Muhammad Alam gained some *waza'if* of the spiritual path from Qibla Alam *Raḥmatullāh Ꜥlayhi.*

Once Pir Sayyid Jama'at Ali Shah Alipuri came to Mirpur, and was invited by the teacher of teachers Mawlana Muhammad Abd Allah *Raḥmatullāh Ꜥlayhima* from Ladar, Muhammad Alam the builder was also invited. During the session the eldest son of Mawlana Abd Allah, Sahibzada Maulvi Abd al-Aziz mentioned to Pir Sayyid Jama'at Ali Shah *Raḥmatullāh Ꜥlayhima* that Muhammad Alam was also a follower of Chura Sharif. He replied, "I have never met him there." Muhammad Alam stated that he had never been to Chura Sharif. So Pir Sayyid Jama'at Ali Shah *Raḥmatullāh Ꜥlayhi* said, "Sire, if a couple is married and the husband lives in Karachi and the wife lives in Mirpur then how can they have children?"

Moving back to Sufi Faujdar Khan's account, he received special spiritual attention from Qibla Alam *Raḥmatullāh Ꜥlayhi.* Sufi Faujdar Khan *Raḥmatullāh Ꜥlayhi* worked in Customs and was stationed at the check post. Some *khalifa* (deputy) of a Shaykh was visiting this area and some devotees were with him. Some devotees made offerings of goats and sheep to him. When the deputy was crossing a particular area the customs officials arrested him and brought him to the check post.

Sufi Faujdar Khan *Raḥmatullāh Ꜥlayhi* was initially upset with the officers and told them that these were Darwish people who did not care much for worldly formalities. "Allah's earth is their earth. You have arrested him for nothing." When the deputy heard these words of encouragement, he tried to impress Sufi Faujdar Khan *Raḥmatullāh Ꜥlayhi* with his miracles although it is not a requirement of sainthood. It was cold weather and the deputy placed a sickle in the fire and

---

[122] Gorah
[123] Dangrot Sharif

96

when it became hot he placed it on his tongue. He wanted the audience to be impressed, to fear him and show remorse for arresting him.

Sufi Faujdar Khan *Rahmatullah Alayhi* states that, "I focused on Qibla Alam *Rahmatullah Alayhi* and when I felt that it was the right moment I placed my trust in Allah and took the same sickle and placed it on my tongue. Although the sickle was red hot, due to Allah's grace and my complete master's spiritual attention I was not burned. Then I reprimanded the deputy and said, "Are you trying to scare me with your spectacle? Show me if you have any more miracles? I showed you respect as I considered you as a Darwish but you mistook my kindness and gentleness as a weakness, I am not afraid of your miracles."

Hadrat Sahib narrates that, "Once I forced Sufi Faujdar Khan *Rahmatullah Alayhi* to repeat this action for me. He replied, "All of that happened due to the spiritual attention of Qibla Alam *Rahmatullah Alayhi*, but you will not rest until my tongue is burnt." Anyway upon my request he placed the hot sickle on his tongue and it did not burn." Hadrat Sahib remarked, "This is all due to the perfection of *tasawwar-e shaykh* (focus on the master)."

Qibla Alam *Rahmatullah Alayhi* had long hair which rested on his shoulders and following his example many *Sangis* kept long hair as well, but Sufi Faujdar Khan *Rahmatullah Alayhi* shaved his head. Once in the presence of Qibla Alam some *Sangis* expressed the desire that Sufi Faujdar Khan *Rahmatullah Alayhima* should also grow long hair but he declined because of his work. But the *Sangis* persisted and requested Qibla Alam *Rahmatullah Alayhi* to order him to keep long hair. In response Sufi Faujdar Khan *Rahmatullah Alayhi* replied, "There are many *Sangis* with long hair and if on the Day of the Judgement a need arose for a *kona Sangi* (head shaven) then you can present me." Qibla Alam *Rahmatullah Alayhi* stated, "He is an employee, let him be."

During the discussion of Sufi Faujdar Khan *Rahmatullah Alayhi* the custom inspector Labu Ram from Sialkot was mentioned. Hadrat Sahib narrates from Sufi Faujdar Khan *Rahmatullah Alayhi*. Labu Ram's job was to inspect the check posts and deal with any irregularities. In those days Sufi Faujdar Khan *Rahmatullah Alayhi* was stationed as the customs guard at the check post.[124] Labu Ram received a complaint that Sufi Faujdar Khan *Rahmatullah Alayhi* had taken a bribe and had let

---

[124] Shah Gazan

from some buffalo traders cross the border. Sufi Faujdar Khan *Rahmatullah Alayhi* was very bold about taking bribes. Once when Qibla Alam *Rahmatullah Alayhi* reprimanded him about taking bribes, his justification was that as his wage was so low he had no choice but to take bribes. Qibla Alam *Rahmatullah Alayhi* replied, "What if the situations do not allow you to take bribes, what will you do then?" Subsequently after Qibla Alam's remark, Sufi Faujdar Khan *Rahmatullah Alayhima* was stationed at the check post.[125] This area was populated by the Suddan tribe and there was no possibility of bribes. Nonetheless Labu Ram started proceedings of bribe taking against Sufi Faujdar Khan *Rahmatullah Alayhi* and summoned him to his office. Another person was to be stationed in his place, but this person knew Sufi Faujdar Khan's temperament and delayed taking over the post and only assumed his duty when Sufi Faujdar Khan *Rahmatullah Alayhi* had left.

The proceedings against Sufi Faujdar Khan *Rahmatullah Alayhi* began. Labu Ram personally came to the check post. In those days the government officials enjoyed a great deal of respect and a camp would be set up and dozens of employees would be present to serve them. Labu Ram was sat on his bed viewing the proceedings of the case. The witnesses were testifying against Sufi Faujdar Khan *Rahmatullah Alayhi,* but when he looked at one of the witnesses his testimony became muddled. At this point Labu Ram swore at Sufi Faujdar Khan *Rahmatullah Alayhi* and said, "What are you looking at?" Sufi Faujdar Khan *Rahmatullah Alayhi* became angry but he controlled his temper. Labu Ram swore at him again, now Sufi Faujdar Khan *Rahmatullah Alayhi* lost his temper as he was being insulted in front of the witnesses and the public. He tried to attack Labu Ram with his staff but the security guards took it away from him. So he began to beat Labu Ram with his bare hands. Consequently Sufi Faujdar Khan *Rahmatullah Alayhi* was charged with assaulting an officer. As Labu Ram was a claimant in the case the enquiry was handed over to the superintendent Khwaja Muhammad Abd Allah Ju *Rahmatullah Alayhi.*

Sufi Faujdar Khan would lose his temper very quickly and once mentioned it to Qibla Alam *Rahmatullah Alayhima* to request his help in this matter. Qibla Alam *Rahmatullah Alayhi* advised him, "When you become angry then look at your finger nails, if standing, sit down, if sitting, lie down, in this condition drink water. By using these methods your anger shall subside."

---

[125] Chachen

Khwaja Muhammad Abd Allah Ju *Rahmatullah Alayhi* was a Darwish like personality and greatly respected the saints and genuinely cared for the Muslim community. The state was ruled by the Hindus at the time. A Hindu official had been attacked. He wanted to appease Labu Ram and also protect Sufi Faujdar Khan *Rahmatullah Alayhi* from further harm. When the case was presented to him he initially reprimanded Sufi Faujdar Khan *Rahmatullah Alayhi*. He was a very wise person and politically astute. Sufi Faujdar Khan's behaviour in the court was aggressive so Khwaja Muhammad Abd Allah Ju *Rahmatullah Alayhi* softly said to him, "You claim to be a Darwish but your arrogance is still there." During the enquiry Sufi Faujdar Khan accused Khwaja Muhammad Abd Allah Ju *Rahmatullah Alayhima* of taking sides. He argued, "What type of justice is this that both Labu Ram and I are two claimants in the same case and yet he receives preferential treatment? He is given a chair and I am made to stand." The case continued and Sufi Faujdar Khan *Rahmatullah Alayhi* had to be present in the court. So he stayed at the mosque[126] in Pūnch city and recited his *waza'if* and *khatams* on a regular basis.

The clerk of Khwaja Muhammad Abd Allah Ju *Rahmatullah Alayhi* named Munshi Jamal al-Din[127] from Kakaza'i, was also a pious person and loved mystics. He had no sons and his daughter's son Malik Muhammad Muzaffar was the former principal of the Bagh Elementary College. Munshi Jamal al-Din also had Sufi Faujdar Khan's welfare at heart but Sufi Faujdar Khan's hot temper was his worst enemy and he was complicating matters. It was feared that Khwaja Muhammad Abd Allah Ju *Rahmatullah Alayhi* might sentence him. But he was so secretive that no one could tell for certain what he would decide.

The case continued and finally one day Khwaja Muhammad Abd Allah Ju gave Sufi Faujdar Khan *Rahmatullah Alayhima* a note for his son, Khwaja Sayf al-Din who was the jail warden. In the note it read, "Send two policemen with handcuffs to the court." It seemed that Sufi Faujdar Khan *Rahmatullah Alayhi* was to be sentenced. The next day Munshi Jamal al-Din presented the copies of the files before Khwaja Muhammad Abd Allah Ju *Rahmatullah Alayhi*, who wrote his decision, read it then tore it up, then wrote on a new piece of paper. When Munshi Jamal al-Din, who was standing beside Khwaja Muhammad Abd Allah Ju *Rahmatullah Alayhi* saw the decision, the colour on his face changed. Khwaja Muhammad Abd Allah Ju *Rahmatullah Alayhi* tore the second paper as well and tried to write his

---

[126] Bangyal
[127] He was a follower of Pir Sahib from Bakot Sharif

decision the third time and finally said, "*Allahu Ahad,* God is One," and then reclined in his chair. Addressing Munshi Jamal al-Din he said, "Munshi Sahib, If Allah wants to protect someone how can anyone harm him. I do not know if he has a Jinn or his Shaykh is a complete master as when I write guilty it reads not guilty. Therefore I reinstate him with full pay but first he should visit his master." Munshi Jamal al-Din praised the master of Sufi Faujdar Khan *Rahmatullah Alayhi* and stated, "These people are linked to a chain and one should not disturb them, as the pious people in the chain are supporting them." Sufi Faujdar Khan *Rahmatullah Alayhi* states that, "On the day of the decision I had no fear whatsoever. I was totally calm as wherever I looked in the court I could see the image of Qibla Alam *Rahmatullah Alayhi*."

After this incident Khwaja Muhammad Abd Allah Ju came to visit Qibla Alam *Rahmatullah Alayhima* in Checheyan Sharif with some colleagues. He mentioned to Qibla Alam *Rahmatullah Alayhi* that his eye sight was poor and the government wanted to make him redundant, but he wanted to continue in his post a few years longer and with this purpose he was going to Jammu and sought his prayers. When he went to Jammu his post was extended as he desired. Later Khwaja Abd Allah Ju *Rahmatullah Alayhi* sent his son Khwaja Sayf al-Din to Checheyan Sharif and drew a map of the area for his benefit. Hadrat Sahib states that he saw both Khwaja Sayf al-Din and the map.

There was another incident between Sufi Faujdar Khan *Rahmatullah Alayhi* and Labu Ram. When Sufi Faujdar Khan *Rahmatullah Alayhi* was released without charge Labu Ram was incensed and sought revenge. Sufi Faujdar Khan *Rahmatullah Alayhi* narrates that, "At one check post I had arranged to give a lesson on the *Maktubat* (Letters) of Hadrat Mujaddid *Rahmatullah Alayhi* to the other workers in our free time. Once Labu Ram came to inspect and Munshi Jamal al-Din was with him. Labu Ram was given all the files to inspect. When he saw the papers, he commented, "These papers smell (of corruption)." So I sat on the bed and began to focus on Qibla Alam *Rahmatullah Alayhi*. Suddenly Labu Ram had a severe pain in his stomach. He asked Munshi Jamal al-Din to carefully inspect the records. Again he felt a sharp pain in his stomach, so he shouted, "Forget the files, and worry about my life!" Magnesia was obtained from somewhere and he felt some relief from his pain. I went to sleep after reading the *khatam-e khawajgan* and *khatam* of Hadrat Shaykh Abd al-Qadir Jilani *Rahmatullah Alayhi*. Qibla Alam *Rahmatullah Alayhi* appeared in my dream and said, "The disbeliever has defiled the meeting place of *Maktubat Sharif.*" When I woke up I noticed that it was as I had been told in the dream. I cleaned that area from the filth and Labu Ram left without taking further action."

In Pūnch city there was an intoxicated mystic called Sain Manga who Labu Ram used to revere. Sufi Faujdar Khan *Rahmatullah Alayhi* narrates that, "I used to read all the *khatams* and *waza'if* as instructed by Qibla Alam *Rahmatullah Alayhi* but it had no affect on Labu Ram. Once when I was going to court I met Sain Manga on the way, he pointed and said, "Oh, oh, *khuda, khuda.*" Later that night I saw Qibla Alam *Rahmatullah Alayhi* in a dream and he said that, "Sain Manga is in charge of that place. The gun fires but he stops the bullets." Later I saw Sain Manga in the dream as well and he lifted his shirt and there were three bullet wounds on his back. Qibla Alam *Rahmatullah Alayhi* advised me, "When Labu Ram goes back to Sialkot, then read."

21) Tuesday 20ᵗʰ June 1989

Today the topic was Qibla Alam's simplicity, purity and humility. Hadrat Sahib stated that most of the *Sangis* narrate that the effect of Qibla Alam's spiritual gatherings was such that one's heart would turn cold towards the world, and the focus would turn to the hereafter. In his gathering there was no room for worldly conversation as it was filled with the remembrance of Allah. Some *Sangis* state that sometimes they went to his gathering with big worldly matters in their heads, but could not find the courage to mention them in such a blessed gathering. The whole atmosphere of the gathering was filled with the sense of total reliance upon Allah. His simple life was exemplary. In summer he would rest on the bed without a sheet cover or just cover his body with a shawl. He always stayed in the mosque. His gatherings were so simple it was difficult for a person to know who the master was. He had no special place reserved for himself. His humility was such that he personally used to wash the hands of the visitors and considered it an honour to serve the guests. He used to advise his *Sangis* that if anyone wanted to progress he should follow the path of the pious people. This was the easiest way to attain blessings.

22) Saturday 24ᵗʰ June 1989

Hadrat Sahib stated that Baba Faid Talab[128] was a relative of Ustad Muhammad Nazir Sahib *Rahmatullah Alayhima* and a tailor by profession. He was a sincere *Sangi* of Qibla Alam *Rahmatullah Alayhi*. Hadrat Sahib said, "When I went to meet him he was very feeble. He stood up to greet me and immediately started crying. He was always focused on the heart. He had a bench nearby for his worship. He asked someone to recite some poems of Miyan Muhammad Bakhsh *Rahmatullah Alayhi*; the person read the following couplets:

> *Dudh wajood teray vich sirin, rughan dar samani,*
> *Murshid laway jag param de jammey dudh pani.*

In your being is sweet milk with butter,
When the master uses the cream of love then milk and water merge.

> *Gal vich pah ghamay da gat ke zikrounh chick madani,*
> *Himmat nal Muhammad bakhsha makkan aya jaani.*

Put the noose of love and pain and then pull the cord with *dhikr*,
With effort Muhammad Bakhsh you shall attain the butter.

When Baba Faid Talab *Rahmatullah Alayhi* heard these couplets he went into ecstasy. In the same gathering someone said, "What can one say about Qadi Sahib from Checheyan Sharif, when he gave *dhikr* to someone it was stamped on the heart."

"When I set off from there Baba Faid Talab *Rahmatullah Alayhi* stood up to say farewell. I was riding a horse and he stood there until I disappeared from his sight. These people were the epitome of sincerity and devotion and were without any hint of show. The association with the master had turned them into an elixir, whosoever sat in their company benefitted?"

23) Sunday 2nd July 1989

Hadrat Sahib states that Qibla Alam *Rahmatullah Alayhi* was simple natured and very independently minded, hence he never had any contact with the rich

---

[128] Khadimabad area

and powerful. His outward state was adorned by the Shari'ah and inner state was free from all else but Allah. Once a Qari Sahib[129] visited Qibla Alam *Rahmatullah Alayhi* in Checheyan Sharif, and according to Qibla Mai Sahiba *Rahmatullah Alayha* he came with some students. When Qari Sahib entered the mosque one of his students picked up his shoes and brought them inside, Qibla Alam *Rahmatullah Alayhi* really liked this act of good manners from the student. Qibla Alam *Rahmatullah Alayhi* invited the Qari Sahib to lead one of the prayers. He recited the Holy Qur'an with the proper *tajwid*. Miyan Muhammad Alam[130] narrates that Qibla Alam *Rahmatullah Alayhi* enquired from Qari Sahib, "Do you recite the Holy Qur'an with such devotion in private or is it just to impress us?" Qibla Alam *Rahmatullah Alayhi* did not normally use this type of direct method of training. Qari Sahib began to cry and said, "We cannot recognize our faults and it is for this purpose that we come to you so you can correct us."

24) Sunday 9th July 1989

Hadrat Sahib states that once Qibla Alam *Rahmatullah Alayhi* was staying in the mosque[131] and Umm Abd al-Aziz came to visit him. She expressed her wish to meet Qibla Alam *Rahmatullah Alayhi* to the personal servant Sain Muhammad Ashraf Sahib. Sain Sahib informed her that when the *Sangis* left and it was time for Qibla Alam's siesta then he would call for her. Umm Abd al-Aziz narrates that, "When I went to the mosque to meet Qibla Alam *Rahmatullah Alayhi* as instructed by Sain Muhammad Ashraf, he was lying on a bed and perhaps about to go to sleep. When I stepped inside the mosque, he lifted the cloth from his face. There was so much light in his eyes that I could not look and I just sat down. After a few moments I paid my respects. He enquired about my welfare. Then I sought his permission to leave and I walked out backwards. Later whenever I had problems I would go and look at that place." Hadrat Sahib states that, "When Umm Abd al-Aziz was ill, I went to visit her. I went to her bed, she was very happy. At that moment she was focused on her heart. I asked her for prayers as she had directly benefitted from Qibla Alam *Rahmatullah Alayhi*. During that time I spent forty days at the above mosque. Like Umm Abd al-Aziz the paternal aunt of Professor Muhammad Tufail was a very pious lady who prayed *tahajjud*. She was instructed by the mother of Abd al-Aziz. Apart from her, the mother of

---

[129] Jand Sharif
[130] Kulla, Palandari
[131] Roli

Hajji Bustan Sahib also benefitted from her. Umm Abd al-Aziz had asked me to take care of her as she was dying. I was in Gulhar, Kotli when she passed away. I led her funeral prayers. She used to spin wool and also make *dhikr* constantly. She wove some wool and gave me some cloth. The women who were trained by her became pious and God fearing."

In this session Hadrat Sahib then mentioned the goldsmith family.[132] He maintained that first of all Sharfain Bi became a follower and afterwards her whole family became *Sangis*. This family had some land[133] that used to be farmed by Sain Umar Din and it is through him that the family came to Qibla Alam *Rahmatullah Alayhi*. It is necessary to explain Sain Umar Din's link with Qibla Alam *Rahmatullah Alayhi* before we discuss the family of goldsmiths.

It was Qibla Alam's practice to visit his maternal aunt for a short while in the evening. One day he suspected that he had been bitten by a snake, this news reached his master Khwaja Hafiz Muhammad Hayat[134] *Rahmatullah Alayhi*. An expert snake charmer called Umar Din who belonged to the Jat tribe and cured people from snake bites lived nearby to Khwaja Hafiz Muhammad Hayat- so he sent him to cure Qibla Alam *Rahmatullah Alayhima*. When he had cured Qibla Alam *Rahmatullah Alayhi* he was given a mountain goat as a gift. At the time Umar Din had a big moustache and an unusual appearance. He was very impressed with Qibla Alam's manners and became a *Sangi*. Afterwards he worked very hard and his heart began to make *dhikr*. Later Khwaja Hafiz Muhammad Hayat *Rahmatullah Alayhi* used to remark, "He went to cure him (Qibla Alam *Rahmatullah Alayhi*) and instead got cured himself." Sain Umar Din He was greatly transformed and he would offer *tahajjud* prayers and also meditated afterwards.

The head of village[135] was called Chaudary Ahmad Khan who was feared throughout the area and no one dared to go against his wishes. One day his horse went into Sain Umar Din's fields who humbly requested Chaudary Ahmad Khan to move the horse as it was destroying the crops. Instead of moving his horse from the field Chaudary Ahmad Khan scolded Sain Umar Din for such audacity. As a result Sain Umar Din was heartbroken and in that state of anguish he performed ablution and offered two units of prayer in the mosque,

---

[132] Hill Sanyaranh
[133] Chak Pathanah
[134] Dangrot Sharif
[135] Chak Pathanah

covered his face and started his *dhikr*. The horse which was grazing in his fields suddenly fell down and began to rubs its heels. Someone advised the family of Chaudary Ahmad Khan to go to the mosque and apologise to Sain Umar Din and to be careful in the future. In response to their pleas Sain Umar Din said, "Us poor people's plea is to Allah, take the horse out of my land, *assanh maskinah de faryad allah tak heh, ghori ke meri zamin vichun kad deo.*" As soon as the horse was taken from his field it recovered. Consequently the snake charmer became known as the mystic Umar Din.

Another interesting story of Sain Umar Din is as follows: Muhammad Husayn Chuwar had a watermill and Sain Umar Din went to him and requested him to grind the wheat quickly as it was needed for the *langar sharif*, Muhammad Husayn took no notice of him and instead made fun of him. It was now time for the sunrise prayer and after offering the prayers Sain Umar Din began to cry at the uncaring attitude of Muhammad Husayn and at his own helpless state. Soon afterwards the grinding stone began to produce blood instead of flour. Muhammad Husayn quickly stopped the grinding stone and begged forgiveness from Sain Umar Din. Later Muhammad Husayn also became a *Sangi* and became known as Sain Muhammad Husayn.

According to some *Sangis* when Qibla Alam *Rahmatullah Alayhi* was authorised to give *bay'a* at the age of forty, Sain Umar Din was the first person to become his follower. It was through Sain Umar Din that Mai Sharfain Bi and her family became followers of Qibla Alam *Rahmatullah Alayhi*. Mai Sharfain Bi's husband was called Sufi Ahmad Din and her son was named Ghulam Ahmad.[136] Mai Sharfain Bi's sister was married to Nawab Ali. All members of this family were Shi'a and they used to attend their gatherings.[137]. The first person to become a follower of Qibla Alam *Rahmatullah Alayhi* from this family was Mai Sharfain Bi thereafter her husband and his nephew Ghulam Haydar also became followers. Later her brother Sufi Muhammad Ismail ibn Nur Din ibn Nizam Din became a follower. In this way the whole family was linked with Qibla Alam *Rahmatullah Alayhi*. Both Sufi Ahmad Din and Ghulam Haydar were authorised deputies of Qibla Alam *Rahmatullah Alayhi* and went to Mandalay in Burma for business purposes.

---

[136] The family later moved to Bohraian in Sheikupura
[137] Sultanpura

The first large cooking pot for the Checheyan Sharif *langar* was brought by Sufi Ahmad Din *Rahmatullah Alayhi* from the Panjab. Sufi Ahmad Din and Ghulam Haydar were the first people to arrive during the *urs* ceremony and the last to leave. They invited Qibla Alam *Rahmatullah Alayhi* to Hill Sanyaranh before they set off for Mandalay in Burma, so they could have the honour of serving him. They requested that Sahibzada Sahib (Hadrat Sahib) be brought along as well. A date was set and Qibla Alam *Rahmatullah Alayhi* set off on the journey.

Hadrat Sahib relates that, "Sain Salāh al-Din, Khwaja Muhammad Akbar Ali and I accompanied Qibla Alam *Rahmatullah Alayhim* on the journey. I was very young so it was difficult for someone of that age to travel so far on foot. The *Sangis* insisted on carrying me on their backs but Qibla Alam *Rahmatullah Alayhi* said, "Let him walk for now and when he gets tired we shall take turns to carry him." During the journey a thorn pricked my foot so I could not walk any further. Qibla Alam *Rahmatullah Alayhi* borrowed a needle from a woman and personally took out the thorn and they took turns to carry me the rest of the journey. After walking for two miles we came across the cemetery where the grave of Khwaja Hafiz Muhammad Hayat is located, Qibla Alam *Rahmatullah Alayhima* gave his *salam* and made *du'a* there. Then we visited Qibla Mai Sahiba *Rahmatullah Alayha* (wife of Khwaja Hafiz Muhammad Hayat *Rahmatullah Alayhi*) and paid our respects. The people were so eager for our arrival that they were looking through binoculars to see where we were on the journey. They brought a horse along as well. In those days it was just this particular family that drank tea regularly otherwise it was not the custom. Perhaps because they had lived in Burma they were accustomed to it. Our lodgings were in the mosque and a bed was spread in the courtyard where all the *Sangis* had gathered. After *maghrib* prayer, Qibla Alam *Rahmatullah Alayhi* practically taught Sufi Ghulam Haydar how to pray *salatul tasbih*.

Mai Sharfain Bi *Rahmatullah Alayha* visited Checheyan Sharif every fifteen days and sometimes Qibla Alam *Rahmatullah Alayhi* would be on his travels so she would not be able to see him. He advised her that in his absence she should look at his daughter Rahmat Jan and that would be sufficient."

Mawlana Muhammad Zaman relates that, "Once after reciting *Fatiha* Qibla Alam was meditating at a grave[138] when Sain Mast Majdhub *Rahmatullah Alayhim*

---

[138] Dilyal shrine

came and conversed with him. We did not understand a word of the conversation. Later Qibla Alam explained that Sain Mast Majdhub *Rahmatullah Alayhima* was enquiring something about the saint who was buried at the shrine.

Hadrat Sahib mentioned another Majdhub, "Once during my travels I reached[139] at *dhur* time. And we (Mawlana Muhammad Zaman and Muhammad Hasan Suda'i) needed water to perform ablution. We found some clay pitchers under the shade of a tree and nearby was a raised platform, I either led or prayed behind someone, I cannot recall. After the prayer we talked to Sain Eido Majdhub *Rahmatullah Alayhi,* he was very old. He had a metal wire rosary and he used to throw it up in the air. His bone structure suggested that once he was a strong young man. I asked him, "Sain Sahib, do you know me and where my home is? He replied, "How do I know that you live?"[140] In those days these three places were the residence of this humble servant. Then I asked about Mawlana Muhammad Zaman *Rahmatullah Alayhi,* "Who is he?" Sain Eido replied, "There was a king called Sultan Khan and he is his slave." Mawlana Muhammad Zaman was the son in law and the authorised deputy of Qibla Alam *Rahmatullah Alayhima.* Then I asked him, "Have you been to Madinah Sharif?" He replied, "I cannot tell as the Pir Sahib[141] shall beat me." And he stated, "I have drunk the water of life once."

25) Tuesday 11ᵗʰ July 1989

25) Tuesday 11th July 1989

Hadrat Sahib related that Muhammad Buta, the wrestler from Jullundur stayed in Checheyan Sharif. He used to go with Mawlana Muhammad Zaman *Rahmatullah Alayhima* to get the wheat ground in the local village and then suddenly he disappeared. He reappeared four years after Qibla Alam's demise, which suggests that his earlier visit was in 1929. According to Mawlana Muhammad Zaman *Rahmatullah Alayhi,* "When he reappeared Muhammad Buta was wearing a loose shirt and a sarong around his waist and he had a shawl as well. He had lost so much weight that I did not recognize him. He was making ablution when I enquired as to where he came from. During the ablution he did not speak but afterwards he said, "Why would you recognize me?" I immediately recognized him and exclaimed, "Buta na'i (Barber)?" He replied, "When have I claimed to be a Sayyid?" Then he went to the shrine. He used to pray with the *Jama'at* and

---

[139] Chathro
[140] Kotli, Sai'nyala or Mirpur
[141] Bagham

afterwards stayed in seclusion. If the discussion was about religious matters he would listen, otherwise he hated talking about worldly matters. He hardly ate and would survive on a few morsels.

Once I asked him, "Where have you been and why are you in such a state?" He replied, "These are secret matters. Once Qibla Alam *Rahmatullah Alayhi* summoned me after *tahajjud* prayer and said, "Muhammad Buta, go away for nine years and do not go home." I kissed his feet and left crying. Nobody knew about my disappearance. I followed the spiritual instructions until I reached the jungles of Rangoon in Burma. There was a shrine in Rangoon where I had to perform my duty. There was an intoxicated mystic who lived nearby and he informed me that my master had passed away. But I was ordered to stay there for nine years. After nine years I came and stayed at the Jan Muhammad hotel, northern village, Jhelum and when I made enquires people told me that my master had indeed passed away four years earlier."

According to Qibla Mai Sahiba *Rahmatullah Alayha,* Muhammad Buta either stood near the water tank or strolled in the mosque. When Muhammad Buta returned to Checheyan Sharif Hadrat Sahib was not present. So he sought permission from Qibla Mai Sahiba *Rahmatullah Alayha* to return to his duty as of now, eventhough he did not even have permission to drink water here. So Qibla Mai Sahiba *Rahmatullah Alayhi* advised him to take something for blessing and he asked for a copy of the Holy Qur'an. He said, "Perhaps now my job shall be at the banks of the Ravi River. I have to return once more as I have to pass on a trust."

Hadrat Sahib mentioned that Sufi Faujdar Khan *Rahmatullah Alayhi* related to me that, "Once I was posted at the check post[142] as a Customs Officer. I met and had a long conversation with a woman magician and later she caused me a lot of trouble. At night I saw Qibla Alam *Rahmatullah Alayhi* and he poked me with his staff and said, "Get up and make ablution." When I woke up I could still feel the pain. I quickly made ablution with sand. And during this time it began to rain stones on the roof of my house. The next day the woman magician informed me that she saw a dark skinned person with long hair who hit her with a stick. When I came to visit Qibla Alam *Rahmatullah Alayhi* he enquired about the above incident that took place, on such a time and such a day and all of his information was correct."

---

[142]Sangot

Sufi Faujdar Khan *Rahmatullah Alayhi* related that, "Once I was posted [143]where I fell in love with a beautiful young girl and was tempted to commit sin. But one night I saw Qibla Alam *Rahmatullah Alayhi* in a dream and he picked me up and took me far away into the jungle and threw me into a well. The well was half full with blood and half full with pus and he told me that this is the punishment of the people who commit adultery. In this way Allah saved me from sinning. I saw the situation as described in the narration about committing adultery. For many days afterwards I could still smell the stench of the well.

Sufi Faujdar Khan *Rahmatullah Alayhi* stated that "My father Burhan al-Din Khan wanted to buy some land from a Hindu but before he could complete the transaction he died. Then one person from my tribe stated that he would now buy the land, his words really upset me. I immediately went to visit Qibla Alam *Rahmatullah Alayhi* and cried bitterly whilat relating the whole incident. Qibla Alam *Rahmatullah Alayhi* asked for full details, I mentioned that the Hindu wanted five hundred rupees and I did not have any money. Qibla Alam *Rahmatullah Alayhi* reassured me, "The money shall come and the Hindu will sell the land for three hundred (rupees)." Everything turned out as Qibla Alam *Rahmatullah Alayhi* had predicted.

Hadrat Sahib relates that Baba Lal Din personally mentioned the following incident to him and some other *Sangis*. He said, "My cousin Faqir Muhammad tried to harm me and had a warrant issued against me. I immediately went to Qibla Alam *Rahmatullah Alayhi* and informed him that this was to be my last visit as I intended to kill my cousin and as a result would be hanged to death. Qibla Alam *Rahmatullah Alayhi* enquired as to why I intended to take such a drastic action; I mentioned the whole incident and said, "At the least I shall chop off his hands." Qibla Alam *Rahmatullah Alayhi* enquired from Miyan Ghulam Din,[144] "What is the punishment for cutting off someone's hands?" He replied, "It is the same as killing someone and carries the same penalty." Qibla Alam *Rahmatullah Alayhi* stated, "When everyone beats him with their slippers then come." Then he enquired, "What is the source of his income?" I informed him that he received a pension. Incidentally his pension stopped that very month and his situation became such that he was disgraced.

---

[143] Palu La, Krayla Mahjan
[144] Kerhyi

Sain Muhammad Hasan[145] *Rahmatullah Alayhi* narrates that, "Once I came to Checheyan Sharif with Allah Ditta[146]. He told me on the way that he was going to eat meat that day. Coincidently that day Qibla Alam enquired from Qibla Mai Sahiba *Rahmatullah Alayhima* what she intended to cook, she replied, "Lentils." He said, "No, slaughter a chicken instead." Sain Muhammad Hasan states, Qibla Alam *Rahmatullah Alayhima* did not give us permission to return home that night and said, "Now we shall slaughter a goat as Allah Ditta has come to eat meat."

La'l Khan[147] relates that, "About six or seven years after the demise of Qibla Alam *Rahmatullah Alayhi*, I hired some builders to work on my house but they left without notice. So I was very upset and one day around midday I saw Qibla Alam *Rahmatullah Alayhi* near my house and he said, "Why are you worried? The builders shall return themselves." That is exactly what happened."

Some *Sangis* state that once whilst Qibla Alam *Rahmatullah Alayhi* was giving spiritual attention to the *Sangis,* Baba Khuda Bakhsh[148] kept opening his eyes and looking up. Qibla Alam *Rahmatullah Alayhi* warned him many times but to no avail. Finally Qibla Alam *Rahmatullah Alayhi* grabbed his head and placed it on his heart. Subsequently he could not move his head from that position for the rest of his life.

Qibla Alam *Rahmatullah Alayhi* enquired from Baba Rooda,[149] "How many children do you have?" He replied that both his wife and children had died. Qibla Alam *Rahmatullah Alayhi* advised him to get married again. He replied, "I am sixty/seventy years old, who shall marry me?" Qibla Alam *Rahmatullah Alayhi* replied, "Things will sort themselves out." Coincidently a lonely woman from the mountainous area came begging and ended up marrying Baba Rooda and they had two sons who are still alive.

Sufi Faujdar Khan *Rahmatullah Alayhi* narrates his own experience of how the masters of the spiritual chain came to his aid. "Once I was posted[150] in an area

---

[145] Potha
[146] Batli
[147] Kulla
[148] Chinar
[149] Sai'nyala, Sarota
[150] Darhal

where a woman lived who knew magic. In those days I was in seclusion (*itika'f*) and she brought milk for me but I did not open the door. Later that night insects began to trouble me and I started to get a fever and my whole body ached in pain. During the night as soon as I dreamt of Qibla Alam and Miyan Fath Muhammad *Rahmatullah Alayhima* all of my pain and fever went away as did the insects."

Sain Diwan Ali[151] relates his own tale. "I owed money to a Hindu money lender called Nand Lal. I had paid him the amount I borrowed from him plus interest but he kept adding more interest. So he had an injunction order against me for two thousand and five hundred rupees in the Kotli court. I paid him three hundred rupees to settle outside court and then went with Baba Lal Din to Checheyan Sharif.

Baba Lal Din explained the situation to Qibla Alam *Rahmatullah Alayhi*. Upon hearing the whole story he remarked, "Why did you pay him the settlement as you had already paid him above the actual debt." Then he mentioned that the *Sangis* had gone to get some jungle grass. He instructed me to sweep the mosque and advised me to bring the dust to one side and throw the 'disbeliever' down. I did not understand what wisdom lay behind that. But twenty four years have passed since that incident and Nand Lal cannot recognise me anymore and sometimes asks me, "Have you seen Sain Diwan Ali anywhere?"

Miyan Muhammad Alam[152] states, "Once I was stood next to Qibla Alam *Rahmatullah Alayhima* in Checheyan Sharif mosque when he said, "Miyan Sahib, if we could obtain this plot of land towards the east, then we could make guest rooms for the *Sangis* which would face the mosque." Qibla Alam *Rahmatullah Alayhi* passed away after this incident and later Hadrat Sahib bought that piece of land and despite the suggestion of most of the *Sangis* he did not build houses for his family but instead built guest rooms for the *Sangis* as Qibla Alam *Rahmatullah Alayhi* had desired.

Qibla Alam *Rahmatullah Alayhi* had a *Sangi* who did not know when to keep quiet. He would always intrude and make unnecessary comments. Qibla Alam *Rahmatullah Alayhi* warned him on numerous occasions but he could not give up his

---

[151] Khad Gujjaranh
[152] Kulla

bad habit. One day Qibla Alam *Rahmatullāh Alayhi* said, "May Allah block your throat." The *Sangis* can testify to the fact that after that incident he could not speak for the rest of his life.

Baba Lal Din[153] *Rahmatullāh Alayhi* relates, "My wife died and I did not get married again for twenty two years. However I fell in love with a woman but she would not agree to marry me. During the *urs* ceremony Qibla Alam *Rahmatullāh Aayhi* said to the *Sangis*, "Why do you not get Lal Din married?" One *Sangi* replied, "He loves a Gujjari women but she will not agree to the marriage." So I informed Qibla Alam *Rahmatullāh Aayhi* that the woman was a weaver and was tough as a rock and requested him to pray for her. He said, "Go and marry her." When I returned all the obstacles had been lifted and she agreed to marry me." It was during this time that Qibla Alam *Rahmatullāh Aayhi* visited his home.

According to the *Sangis*, on one occasion wheat was being threshed and it began to rain in the surrounding areas. Baba Faqir Muhammad Pahariyya came and requested Qibla Alam *Rahmatullāh Aayhima*, "Master, if it rains it might spoil the grain." Qibla Alam instructed Mawlana Hajji Baqa Muhammad *Rahmatullāh Aayhima* to go outside and write a particular word in the sky, which he did and by Allah's grace the rain clouds moved away.

Mawlana Ghulam Nabi from Bār relates, "I was the *imam* in our village mosque and I would often visit Qibla Alam *Rahmatullāh Aayhima* and the villagers did not approve of this. They complained that I went to meet some *pir* in Mirpur without their consent, and thus they decided to punish me on my return so that I would never go without their permission.

When I returned home from Checheyan Sharif and found out what had transpired I immediately returned to Qibla Alam *Rahmatullāh Aayhi*. He enquired as to why I had returned in such a manner and I explained my predicament. He said, "Stay here for fifteen days." After ten days I sought his permission to go back to the village and he said, "Go, and had you stayed for fifteen days it would have been better for you for many years to come. Even now things have turned upside down." When I returned back home I discovered that the local Shi'a community had fought amongst themselves and nobody was concerned about me anymore."

---

[153] Khad Gujjaranh

26) Wednesday 4th October 1989

Hadrat Sahib narrates from Sain Muhammad Hasan[154] *Rahmatullah Alayhi* who said, "We have not seen the Prophet ﷺ but whatever we have heard about him we have found those qualities in Qibla Alam *Rahmatullah Alayhi.*"

27) Monday 9th October 1989

Hadrat Sahib stated that Qibla Alam *Rahmatullah Alayhi* used to cover his knees whilst going to answer the call of nature, although he wore a *dhoti.*

Qibla Alam *Rahmatullah Alayhi* used to cultivate the land and encouraged other people also to seek lawful livelihood. Once Baba Faqir Muhammad Pothiyya was ploughing the field with two bulls; a black and white one (donated by Mawlana Ghulam Nabi *Rahmatullah Alayhi*) and another bull which was the source of his grievance. Qibla Alam came to inspect the new bull whilst Baba Faqir Muhammad *Rahmatullah Alayhima* had gone to get the harrow (to flatten the ground). In Baba Faqir Muhammad's absence, Qibla Alam *Rahmatullah Alayhima* took to ploughing despite the fact that Baba Faqir Muhammad had already predicted to Mawlana Muhammad Zaman that if Qibla Alam *Rahmatullah Alayhim* tried to plough the land he would end up breaking the plough and that is exactly what happened. Mawlana Muhammad Zaman narrates that, "One day Qibla Alam *Rahmatullah Alayhima* was busy working in the fields when I remarked, "Allah loves the worker, (*al-kasibu habibullah*)." He replied, "You exaggerate."

28) Thursday 12th October 1989

Hadrat Sahib stated that Qibla Alam *Rahmatullah Alayhi* used to stay and pray in the village[155] in the home of Sain Muhammad Husayn known as Sain Mandu. His neighbour was a Sikh called Subhan Singh and everyday he used to read the *Granth* (Sikh holy book) early in the morning. He often came to meet Qibla Alam *Rahmatullah Alayhi* and this association had such an impact on him that he was transformed. He left worldly matters and just wore a pair of boxer shorts and would travel to Kashmir and other areas. Hadrat Sahib relates, "Once I was

---

[154] Potha
[155] Agro

saying farewell to some *Sangis* when I noticed Subhan Singh walking on the public path on his own wearing a blanket as the local villagers walked in front of him. So I went and embraced him and enquired, "Sardar Ji why are you walking behind on your own whilst your colleagues are going ahead?" He replied, "It is better to stay away from such company, *is jagat nalunh turati hi balli*."

Similarly Bakhshi Moti Ram[156]almost left the worldly matters in his last days. He also used to visit Qibla Alam *Rahmatullah Alayhi*. In the same manner a Hindu used to come from Mirpur to visit Qibla Alam *Rahmatullah Alayhi*. He used to dress like a Muslim and read *wazifa* as well. Some *Sangi* complained to Qibla Alam *Rahmatullah Alayhi* and he said, "These people have strong beliefs, they even put their faith in stones and if they become Muslim then they are very strong in *tawhid* (belief in one God).

29) Monday 30th October 1989

Hadrat Sahib said that Qibla Alam *Rahmatullah Alayhi* never criticised anyone and accepted everyone as they came. He never told anyone to keep a beard or reprimand anyone for not following the Shari'ah. In fact he would use his spiritual focus by which the weaknesses of people would be removed and they would begin to correct themselves.

30) Tuesday 31st October 1989

Hadrat Sahib states that, "My uncle Qadi Muhammad Fadal narrates that Qibla Alam *Rahmatullah Alayhima* used to send mustard seeds and have them pressed then put in containers and in the evening the oil would be used to burn the lamps."

31) Wednesday 8th November 1989

Hadrat Sahib states that Hadrat Mirza Mazhar Jan-e Janan Delhawi gave initiation to the wife of his deputy Hadrat Qadi Thana Allah Panipati and in the same way Qibla Alam *Rahmatullah Alayhim* gave initiation to some women followers.

---

[156] Chief of Siyakh

32) Thursday 9th November 1989

Hadrat Sahib states that Sain Muhammad Hasan *Zulfain Wallay* narrates that Qibla Alam *Rahmatullah Alayhima* said, "He who runs after the world, the world runs away from him. And he turns away from the world it chases him. This is what we have witnessed."

33) Tuesday, 14th November 1989

Hadrat Sahib mentioned that as a *Sangi* was near death he advised his children, "I have met many holy people but I was never content, finally I met Qibla Alam *Rahmatullah Alayhi*. So after my death do not stop visiting him as I have found him after a great deal of difficulty."

34) Tuesday, 21st November 1989

Hadrat Sahib said that Khwaja Muhammad Akbar Ali stated, "We did not understand who Qibla Alam *Rahmatullah Alayhima* was and what spiritual station he occupied."

Neyu laya nal pathanah,
Owh maran pashtu teh samaj na janah,
Samaj aie teh kooch sadanah.

I have become friends with the Pathan,
They speak Pashtu which I do not understand,
When I was able to understand they moved on.

35) Thursday 23rd November 1989

Hadrat Sahib narrates from the *Sangis* that when the seekers of spirituality used to come and visit Qibla Alam *Rahmatullah Alayhi* he would be delighted. He said, "When the *Sangis* come my heart opens like a rosebud and when they leave I am heartbroken and become sad."

36) Monday 4th December 1989

Hadrat Sahib states that once Qibla Alam *Rahmatullah Alayhi* was staying in a small mosque[157]. Many *Sangis* had gathered and he passionately related the stories of the pious people. Everyone was moved by these accounts when suddenly one person shouted, "I have been bitten by a snake." A snake had fallen from the ceiling onto a person and had bitten him. Qibla Alam *Rahmatullah Alayhi* placed his finger on the spot where the person had been bitten and said, "*Sangiyya*, Friend, you have ruined our gathering as we were talking about the pious people. Never mind, do not make any noise." The person was cured. And Qibla Alam *Rahmatullah Alayhi* moved on.[158]

Hadrat Sahib states that Qibla Alam *Rahmatullah Alayhi* said, "If a person loses his way he should recite *sura Ya-Sīn* or give the call to prayer and God willing he will find his way."

37) Tuesday 19th December 1989

Hadrat Sahib states that once Sain Muhammad Ya'qub *Rahmatullah Alayhi* met a religious scholar who was carrying a bundle of books. He said to him. "You are carrying all these books, go and visit Qibla Alam *Rahmatullah Alayhi* as he changes the barren land into a garden." The religious scholar went and met Qibla Alam and informed him what Sain Muhammad Ya'qub *Rahmatullah Alayhima* had said. Qibla Alam *Rahmatullah Alayhi* replied, "You are a learned and a pious person; do not pay heed to the words of an intoxicated mystic."

Hadrat Sahib states that Qibla Alam *Rahmatullah Alayhi* never drank tea or milk at home. He might have drunk tea at[159] as those people regularly drank tea. His temperament was cold and he used to eat roasted chickpeas. Qibla Alam *Rahmatullah Alayhi* used the mixture called Lului' made by Hakim Nawab Ali, the brother in law of Mai Sharfain. Hakim Nawab Ali was a Shi'a and a student of Hakim Ajmal Khan from Delhi in medicine. Once Hakim Nawab Ali mentioned the virtues of the Lului' mixture and so he was asked to prepare some. He said, "Bring me the expensive ingredients and I shall add the other ingredients myself." Hakim Nawab Ali later repented from the Shi'a beliefs and became a follower of Qibla Alam *Rahmatullah Alayhi*. He used to say:

---

[157] Pallathi, Kandor
[158] Beyli Batar

[159] Hill Sanyaranh

Munh nikka tey gal vadairi, nah kar, matt koi hassay,
Azam, shafi', malik, hanbal eh maslay neyunh dassay.

Small mouth and big talk, do not speak, people might laugh,
Imam Azam, Shafi,' Malik and Hanbal have not mentioned these matters.

Hadrat Sahib said that Raja Pahinda Khan narrates that he was getting married[160] and Qibla Alam *Rahmatullah Alayhi* was invited. He came and as there was music in the wedding and his pious nature did not approve of this, he immediately left the gathering. However in order to keep our hearts he came to visit us later but the marriage proved unsuccessful.

38) Thursday 1st February 1990

Hadrat Sahib narrates that Khwaja Ahmad Ji,[161] Hadrat Chanan Shah[162] and Khwaja Muhammad Khan Alam *Rahmatullah Alayhim* from Bawali Sharif were brothers in the spiritual path. All three were followers and deputies of Hadi Namdar[163] *Rahmatullah Alayhi*. These three are also listed as the deputies of Hadrat Nur Muhammad Tehrahi, the reason for this is that before Hadi Namdar *Rahmatullah Alayhima* died he instructed these three that, "My master is still alive therefore all of my followers and deputies should go to him and remember 'Allah,' 'Allah'." These three heeded the advice of their master and that is why they are listed as the deputies of Hadrat Nur Muhammad Tehrahi *Rahmatullah Alayhi*.

Hadrat Sahib then mentioned Bawali Sharif. He stated that Mai Sahiba *Rahmatullah Alayha* from Bawali Sharif expressed her impression of Qibla Alam *Rahmatullah Alayhi* in these words, "Outwardly he seemed a very simple man but inwardly he was a very intelligent and thoughtful person. He used to wear his *dhoti* above his ankles and served his master's residence with the utmost devotion. He used to warm the clay oven and bring the trays of flour to us so we could make roti. He used to massage his master but never stepped on his bed. He would stand or sit and massage his master. During summer nights he would fan his master. The master would tell him to rest and sleep but he would say, "It

---

[160] Dilyal
[161] Rupar Sharif
[162] Alu Mahar Sharif
[163] Nethyal Sharif

is very hot and there are many mosquitoes, master please rest." Sometimes this practice would continue until early dawn. Mai Sahiba *Rahmatullah Alayha* commented that, "We used to think this person was not human but an angel."

39) Sunday 4th February 1990

In this session the discussion was about the dome built over the graves in the *dargah* of Hadrat Shah Abu al-Khayr Delhawi *Rahmatullah Alayhi* as the Khanqah-e Fathiyya had the good fortune to provide some monetary assistance in this project.

Then the conversation turned to Mawlana Ghulam Nabi's account of Sufi Ghulam Muhyi al-Din. Hadrat Sahib stated that Sufi Ghulam Muhyi al-Din[164] used to make combs and rosaries, these rosaries were made with big beads. Even now some of these rosaries are preserved in the homes of the old *Sangis*. One of these rosaries was used by Qibla Alam *Rahmatullah Alayhi* and is preserved with his other relics. Sufi Ghulam Muhyi al-Din's whole family belonged to the Ahl-i Hadith. When Allah willed, a desire grew in his heart to meet Qibla Alam *Rahmatullah Alayhi*. Sufi Ghulam Muhyi al-Din mentioned this desire to Mawlana Ghulam Nabi from Bār *Rahmatullah Alayhima* and they both set off for Checheyan Sharif. When they were a short distance from Checheyan Sharif they saw a holy person from afar. Sufi Ghulam Muhyi al-Din remarked, "If this is the holy person that we have come to visit then my heart testifies that he is a friend of Allah." That holy person they saw from afar was none other than Qibla Alam *Rahmatullah Alayhi*.

Afterwards Sufi Ghulam Muhyi al-Din had a lengthy discussion with Qibla Alam *Rahmatullah Alayhi*. He was so impressed with Qibla Alam's good manners and piety that he became a follower and began to practise the teachings of the Path. After Qibla Alam's demise Sufi Ghulam Muhyi al-Din would come to visit his shrine to recited the whole Qur'an and then sought permission from Qibla Mai Sahiba *Rahmatullah Alayha* to leave.

Hadrat Sahib relates that once I was staying at the home of Mawlana Ghulam Nabi of Bār when I met Sufi Ghulam Muhyi al-Din *Rahmatullah Alayhima* and we made a programme to visit Sirhind Sharif. Hence Sufi Ghulam Muhyi al-Din travelled with us to Sirhind Sharif. During that time Mawlana Ghulam Nabi

---

[164] Dadhla, Jalab Pind Dad Khan, Jhelum

mentioned that, "Qibla Alam *Rahmatullah Alayhima* had informed me that, "We shall send you to Sirhind Sharif but first we need to find someone to accompany you." And today Qibla Alam's words have been realised as we are able to visit Sirhind Sharif with you."

40) Missing

41) Thursday 15ᵗʰ February 1990

Hadrat Sahib said, "Once Qibla Alam *Rahmatullah Alayhi* was staying at the house of Baba Lal Din, and he asked Saifu Malik for his daughter's hand for Sufi Bahadur Ali[165] and he agreed. On the joyous occasion dried dates were distributed but later Saifu Malik broke his promise and gave his daughter to someone else. When Qibla Alam *Rahmatullah Alayhi* was informed of this situation he said, "He shall not leave with this face." Eventually Saifu Malik committed suicide and died a forbidden death. Later Sufi Bahadur Ali got married in the Domal family and had a son named Qari Muhammad Bashir from his wife."

There was a severe famine[166]. Hadrat Sahib mentioned that Sain Muhammad Ashraf, the personal attendant of Qibla Alam *Rahmatullah Alayhima* narrated this incident to him. "From the beginning the communal food was served to all the *Sangis* and this tradition continues to the present day. Due to the famine when there was shortage of wheat, someone suggested that because of the shortage some criteria should be set to feed people. Qibla Alam *Rahmatullah Alayhi* replied, "Put your trust in Allah." At that very moment the news arrived that the last batch of grain had been sent to be ground into flour and there was no grain left in the house. He said, "Look perhaps there is still some grain left in the containers." Mai Fath Begum *Rahmatullah Alayha* (Hadrat Sahib's maternal grandmother) was a very intelligent person and understood what he alluded, so she said to her daughter, "Sajjaddah Begum go and see if there is any wheat left in the containers." She replied, "Please mother you go." So when she looked, she found the containers full of grain. Sahibzada Muhammad Maruf heard this story directly from Qibla Mai Sahiba *Rahmatullah Alayha*."

42) Saturday 24ᵗʰ March 1990

---

[165] Domal, Khad Gujjaranh
[166] 1978 Bikrami

Hadrat Sahib narrates that once Qibla Alam *Rahmatullah Alayhi* went to the village[167] and stayed in the home of Umm Bustan. Many *Sangis* came to gain spiritual benefit. When he was about to set off Umm Bustan complained that her (female) buffaloes never became pregnant. He stroked the buffaloes' backs with his walking stick. He had not reached the pond when the buffaloes were overwhelmed by the passion to mate.

43) Sunday 25th March 1990

Hadrat Sahib said that in the gatherings of Qibla Alam *Rahmatullah Alayhi* if anyone criticised or belittled someone he would stop them by saying, "Worry about death, leave other people, worry about yourself. Death is chasing you. You will find out later. Just mind your own business and do not talk about other people." Qibla Alam *Rahmatullah Alayhi* always thought about the welfare of his *Sangis*. If he did not meet a *Sangi* for some time, he would send him a message to visit him. And when he said farewell to the *Sangis*, he would say, "One cannot trust these breaths, therefore visit often, *Sah da wasaha nahin, jildi milaney kohsish karya karo.*" He never gave any importance to money or gifts and in his view the real criteria of love was sincerity and performing deeds purely for Allah's sake.

44) Monday 26th March 1990

Hadrat Sahib briefly mentioned two people: Sain Nawab Din,[168] Qibla Alam *Rahmatullah Alayhi* said about him that he was a man of Allah. He would spend the long severe nights of winter by just listening to the tune of a one stringed instrument. (Due to his intoxicated spiritual state he managed to survive the long and severe nights of winter without any warm clothing).

The second person was Sain Sultan Bakhsh whose love was extraordinary and who had great devotion for Qibla Alam *Rahmatullah Alayhi*. A few days before the *urs* ceremony he would be excited and joyful and his state was worth watching. He would go to the houses of the *Sangis* and give the good news about the *urs* ceremony; this he did of his own accord. He had a powerful voice. And when the group of *Sangis* were nearing Checheyan Sharif he would shout with excitement, "Allah, Allah." Qibla Alam *Rahmatullah Alayhi* would smile and

---

[167] Parothi,Kotli
[168] Kharand near Kulla

remark, "Sultan Bakhsh is here." Hadrat Sahib said, "I have seen the cracked feet of Sain Sultan Bakhsh myself."

45) Sunday 1ˢᵗ April 1990

Hadrat Sahib narrates that it was the practice of Qibla Alam *Rahmatullah Alayhi* to recite *sura Mulk* and *sura Sajda* (21ˢᵗ Para) every night.

46) Monday 2ⁿᵈ April 1990

Hadrat Sahib mentioned Mawlana Sayyid Ahmad[169] *Rahmatullah Alayhi* who was known as *Kassriyain Wallay Maulvi Sahib*. He used to teach people 'Allah', 'Allah' in this area. Khwaja Muhammad Akbar Ali *Rahmatullah Alayhi* was also in the same area and he was known as the *Kashmir Wallay Pir Sahib*. Once Mawlana Sayyid Ahmad came to visit Khwaja Muhammad Akbar Ali *Rahmatullah Alayhima* and afterwards when his followers asked about him he said, "He is a holy person but lacks knowledge." That night Mawlana Sayyid Ahmad saw Qibla Alam *Rahmatullah Alayhima* in a dream and he said, "You think he lacks knowledge but there are many lamps burning inside him." In the morning Mawlana Sayyid Ahmad *Rahmatullah Alayhi* set off for Checheyan Sharif. However when he arrived he found out that Qibla Alam *Rahmatullah Alayhi* had passed away, he was devastated and cried uncontrollably. Later he completed his spiritual training of the Mujaddidiyya path under Khwaja Muhammad Akbar Ali *Rahmatullah Alayhi* and he had thousands of followers.

47) Tuesday 10th of April 1990

Hadrat Sahib mentioned the loyalty and chivalry of Sain Muhammad Hasan who was present when Qibla Alam *Rahmatullah Alayhima* was on his deathbed. He expressed his anxiety and stated that, "I am an illiterate person and with your guidance I have led my life but after your demise what will become of me?" Qibla Alam *Rahmatullah Alayhi* replied, "Say, Allah, Allah, establish prayer and everything shall be fine." Consequently Sain Muhammad Hasan's last words were the Creed of Faith. Sain Muhammad Hasan's death took place in the following circumstances: He was helping to build a mosque (in those days the mosques were made of mud), by taking out rocks from the earth when the area collapsed and he was trapped under the soil. The villagers came to rescue him

---

[169] Campbellpur

and when they took him out of the soil, it seemed as if he was already dead, as there was no sign of breathing, his pulse was not beating and there was no outward sign of life. Suddenly his lips moved and he began to recite the 'Creed of Faith.' The villagers carried him on the bed and began to recite the first 'Creed of Faith' out loud. At that time Sain Muhammad Hasan *Rahmatullah Alayhi* gave two messages: "Firstly give my greetings to Qibla Mai Sahiba *Rahmatullah Alayha* and ask her to forgive my shortcomings. Secondly call Sahibzada Sahib (Hadrat Sahib) and request him to come wherever he is."

Hadrat Sahib states, "By a coincidence I was at home and set off as soon as I heard the news. However, when I reached the banks of the Pūnch River, I heard that he had passed away. Maulvi Qutb al-Din asked me to walk in front of the funeral procession and said, "This is the benefit of associating with pious people." A large crowd attended the funeral."

In this area[170] there were many followers of Qibla Alam *Rahmatullah Alayhi* and hence the Shari'ah was practised, and most people avoided innovations at the time of birth and death. They avoided local customs that were contrary to the Shari'ah.

Diwan Ali Sahib states that Nigha Ali[171] was a follower of Golra Sharif but he said that, "Qibla Alam's personality had an immediate impact on a person for example Habib Allah still read *tahajjud* prayer."

Hadrat Sahib narrates that Maulvi Muhammad Ibrahim[172] *Rahmatullah Alayhi* was a great scholar and a teacher. Once he met Qibla Alam *Rahmatullah Alayhi* at the funeral of Hashmat Ali Sahib[173] and humbly said, "As you were here, you should have led the prayer." He continued, "If a person has read a few books he becomes arrogant but the funeral prayer is a supplication that requires humility."

48) Wednesday 18th April 1990

Hadrat Sahib narrates that Muhammad Alam Rajka in his old age requested Qibla Alam *Rahmatullah Alayhi* to teach him the Qur'an, he replied:

---

[170] Potha Bungash
[171] Chakwal
[172] Siyakh
[173] Potha

Batin da ik sansh mubarak betar sal hazarunh,
Su, su khatam kalam allah da ik, ik sa'at parunah.

One blessed breath from the inner self is better than a thousand years,
It is like finishing hundreds of Qur'ans in each breath.

*"If a person becomes a hunchback through worship then this dhikr is still
better."*

Brother Muhammad Zaman *Rahmatullah Alayhi* once saw a *Majdhub* and
wanted to be like him. When Qibla Alam *Rahmatullah Alayhi* found out he said, "Eat
well, take the middle path and occupy yourself in acts that please Allah." Then
he recited the following couplet:

Nah chandain bekhur kaz dahnat bar ayad,
Nah chandain ke az dhof janat ayad.

Do not over eat that it spills out from your mouth,
Nor so little that you starve yourself to death.

The *Sangis* of Qibla Alam *Rahmatullah Alayhi* had a great passion for worship.
For example Sain Muhammad Hasan *Zulfain Wallay* used to apply mustard oil
to his eyes to stay awake. And Khuda Bakhsh[174] performed a seclusion for nine
months and during which he used to tie his hair to the ceiling to stay awake.

49) Wednesday 2ⁿᵈ May 1990

Hadrat Sahib mentioned that Qibla Alam *Rahmatullah Alayhi* used an umbrella
during the rainy season and during the heat he would use a cotton shawl. If he
forgot anything he would keep on reciting the salutations on the Prophet ﷺ until
he remembered.

50) Saturday 5ᵗʰ May 1990

---

[174] Mehnder

Hadrat Sahib mentioned some of Qibla Alam's practices. He stated that Qibla Alam *Rahmatullah Alayhi* normally changed and washed his clothes on a Wednesday. He also used to patch his clothes. Once a *Sangi* complained about poverty and Qibla Alam *Rahmatullah Alayhi* advised him, "Wash your clothes and have a bath on Wednesday. Keep the intention in your heart that you are doing this to remove poverty. If for some reason you cannot wash your clothes then just partially wash any piece of cloth or a handkerchief."

Then the conversation turned to the teacher of teachers, Hadrat Mawlana Muhammad Abd Allah *Rahmatullah Alayhi* from Ladar, Hadrat Sahib stated that, "He was an unrivalled scholar and a great mystic. Before Qibla Alam's demise he came to visit him. During that time Qibla Alam *Rahmatullah Alayhi* was often in the state of absorption with Allah and would not converse with anyone. Baba Faqir Muhammad Pahariyya *Rahmatullah Alayhi* would help him to make *wudu*, he had not washed the feet when Hadrat Mawlana Muhammad Abd Allah walked in, brother Muhammad Zaman informed Qibla Alam *Rahmatullah Alayhima* that Ustad Sahib had come. Qibla Alam *Rahmatullah Alayhi* lifted his feet and sat on his knees and shook his hands with Ustad Sahib and said a few words. Ustad Sahib was on his way back home when Qibla Alam *Rahmatullah Alayhi* passed away. It was Ustad Sahib who led the funeral prayer of Qibla Alam *Rahmatullah Alayhi*."

51) Sunday 6th May 1990

Hadrat Sahib states that Baba Nadir[175] once mentioned to Qibla Alam *Rahmatullah Alayhi* that he wanted to build a house, and asked him which direction the doors should face. Qibla Alam *Rahmatullah Alayhi* replied, "Towards South." Then he mentioned the benefits of this action.

52) Tuesday 5th June 1990

Hadrat Sahib narrates that most of the *Sangis* maintained just looking at Qibla Alam *Rahmatullah Alayhi* removed laziness and negligence. As a result a person inclined towards Allah and constant prayer.

53) Monday 11th June 1990

---

[175] Thanpal

Hadrat Sahib states that Us man Ali Tahthi from Gujjar Khan was a follower of Golra Sharif; in addition he often visited and took some spiritual lessons from Qibla Alam *Rahmatullah Alayhi*.

Hadrat Sahib also stated that, "We have inherited some *waza'if* from the Qadiriyya order, such as:

1) *Astagfirulla hil alladhi la ilaha illahu al-hayyu al-qayyum wa atubu ilahi.*

2) *La ilaha illallahu* and after every hundredth *muhammadur rasulullah sallallahu alayhi wasalam*

3) *Illallahu* 1000 times daily

4) *Haq Allah Hu* 1000 times daily

5) *Hu wallah* 1000 times daily

6) *Antal hadi antal haqq laysal hadi illahu* 1000 times daily

7) *Allahuma salli ala muhammadin wa alayhi wa itratihi be-a'dad-e kulli ma'lumin lak* 1000 times daily."

54) Sunday 17th June 1990

Hadrat Sahib stated that Qibla Alam *Rahmatullah Alayhi* used to perform precautionary *dhur* prayer after *jum'a*. This was in line with the practice of Hadrat Mujaddid Alf Thani *Rahmatullah Alayhi* who prayed in a similar manner during the rule of the tyrant Akbar, who set out to destroy Islamic identity. Qibla Alam *Rahmatullah Alayhi* lived during the British and Hindu rule in which the situation was similar to Akbar's rule.

55) Monday 18th June 1990

Hadrat Sahib narrates from Sain Muhammad Hasan *Zulfain Wallay* that once Qibla Alam *Rahmatullah Alayhima* was addressing the gathering of the *Sangis* and said, "*Sangiyu*, absolute power is in the hands of the King (God) and unity of God means that one totally relies on Allah."

56) Thursday 21st June 1990

Hadrat Sahib stated that Qibla Alam *Rahmatullah Alayhi* used to advise, "Work hard and do not seek gifts or presents."

57) Wednesday 4th July 1990

Hadrat Sahib said that Qibla Alam *Rahmatullah Alayhi* did not permit any *Sangi* to criticise anyone and if anyone did this he would immediately stop them. He would advise them to worry about their own salvation as they did not have any guarantee that they were saved. In his view everyone was under threat before death and therefore one should value these precious moments and not waste them.

58) Saturday 14th July 1990

Hadrat Sahib states that it was Qibla Alam's practice never to pass a graveyard without giving spiritual attention. He would recite the *Fatiha* and send the merit to the deceased. However, once he passed a graveyard[176] in without reciting *Fatiha*. He turned back and stood near a particular grave and then sat down and meditated. When one *Sangi* enquired as to the reason for this action, Qibla Alam *Rahmatullah Alayhi* replied, "She was being punished and the blazes of fire were visible."

59) Thursday 19th July 1990

Hadrat Sahib narrates from Sain Muhammad Hasan[177], "When Qibla Alam *Rahmatullah Alayhima* was touring this area,[178] I met him and he advised me, "Sain Sahib, visit this place[179] twice a week," but I forgot which days in particular."

60) Wednesday 1st August 1990

Hadrat Sahib said that Baba Allah Ditta was the uncle of Sain Muhammad Hasan *Zulfain Wallay* *Rahmatullah Alayhi*. He was a handsome and wealthy land owner, who had five sons. Each son had his own house that was

---

[176] Dullar
[177] Rada
[178] Rajur
[179] Ashab-e Rada

built with cedar wood. Baba Allah Ditta was linked with another Shaykh before he became a follower of Qibla Alam *Rahmatullah Alayhi*.

Baba Allah Ditta's previous Shaykh came to this area and some detractors misinformed him that his followers were being misled. This was mere accusation. Indeed, Qibla Alam *Rahmatullah Alayhi* had so much integrity that he did not know how many followers he had as he never kept a record. His sole purpose in guiding anyone was to attain Allah's pleasure. The Shaykh was very upset that Baba Allah Ditta had become a follower of Qibla Alam *Rahmatullah Alayhi* and therefore expressed his desire to meet and challenge or debate with Qibla Alam *Rahmatullah Alayhi* who was staying in the local mosque.

So the Shaykh came with a large procession, perhaps these people had joined in to witness the debate. Qibla Alam *Rahmatullah Alayhi* was reading with his rosary. Someone informed him that the Shaykh was coming to him with such an intention. Qibla Alam *Rahmatullah Alayhi* did not respond and remained quiet. Finally the Shaykh went past the local mosque and carried on walking to some other follower's house. Sain Muhammad Hasan *Rahmatullah Alayhi* said that, "If the Shaykh had come to the mosque he would have been treated with the utmost respect and we would have offered him some gifts as this is the etiquette of the path."

Baba Allah Ditta continued to perform his *dhikr* and meditation under the supervision of Qibla Alam *Rahmatullah Alayhi* and he designated a room in his house for worship. Although he was illiterate, he read *salatul tasbih* and *durud tunajjina* on a regular basis. Hadrat Sahib states that, "I attended the funeral of Baba Allah Ditta and the prayer was led by Mawlana Ibrahim Sahib.[180] The children of Baba Allah Ditta distributed one and a half *mann* of dates (68 kg) at his funeral."

61) Thursday 2nd August 1990

Hadrat Sahib said that once a person from[181] came to meet Qibla Alam *Rahmatullah Alayhi*. He mentioned how impressed he was with the large gatherings at Data Darbar in Lahore. He said, "I wonder what *wazifa* Hadrat Data Ganj Bakhsh *Rahmatullah Alayhi* read?" Mawlana Ghulam Nabi *Rahmatullah Alayhi* from Bār

---

[180] Siyakh
[181] Pind Dad Khan

narrates that when this person mentioned this matter many times Qibla Alam *Rahmatullah Alayhi* said, "Come again and we shall send you there and you can speak to Data Sahib *Rahmatullah Alayhi* and ask him yourself."

Once a person from Mawlana Ghulam Nabi's *Rahmatullah Alayhi* village of Bār came to visit Checheyan Sharif and he was neither impressed with the simple lifestyle of Qibla Alam *Rahmatullah Alayhi* nor the simple mud built mosque. Addressing Mawlana Ghulam Nabi *Rahmatullah Alayhi*, he said, "Oh, Maulvi! What attraction did you see here? *Oh, Maulvi! murr kai'an teh bullaya hain?"* Mawlana Ghulam Nabi *Rahmatullah Alayhi* replied, "Mister, you came of your accord, if you want to take some benefit do so, why criticise me?" The next day when the *Sangis* sat in the mosque in the company of Qibla Alam *Rahmatullah Alayhi*, this person covered himself with a sheet and went to sleep. Mawlana Ghulam Nabi *Rahmatullah Alayhi* felt very embarrassed by his behaviour and wondered what Qibla Alam *Rahmatullah Alayhi* would think of this person who had come with him. During the conversation Qibla Alam *Rahmatullah Alayhi* looked in the direction of the sleeping man. A few moments later that person woke up and said in his Chakwali dialect, "Shaykh you are a really deep person, *pir murr tunh teh bara dunga adami hain."* Qibla Alam *Rahmatullah Alayhi* angrily said, "Be silent." And the person remained quiet.

After the session Qibla Alam *Rahmatullah Alayhi* left and Mawlana Ghulam Nabi *Rahmatullah Alayhi* said to him, "What way is this to address the Shaykh?" The man replied, "Maulvi, first of all listen to what happened to me, *Maulvi, wat tudh nunh gal das hain meray nal ki hoya.* I dreamt that it was the Day of Judgement and Qibla Alam's face was full of light, he had a crown on his head and held a walking stick. He was gathering his followers and said, "The people from the Path of Hadrat Siddiq-e Akbar ﷺ shall cross the bridge first." Then I woke up and foolishly uttered those words."

62) Monday 1ˢᵗ October 1990

Hadrat Sahib said that Qibla Alam *Rahmatullah Alayhi* knew the graves of his ancestors in Mirpur. Once he told Qadi Muhammad Fadal *Rahmatullah Alayhi* the location of the graves, but unfortunately he could not remember. This cemetery was near the Mirpur locality. Hadrat Qadi Fath Allah Qadiri Shattari *Rahmatullah Alayhi* had donated some land in that area for the graves of his family. When Qibla

128

Alam *Rahmatullah Alayhi* used to visit these graves he used to kiss the feet of his great ancestor Hadrat Qadi Fath Allah Qadiri Shattari *Rahmatullah Alayhi* and then he would sit facing the west and recite *Fatiha* and meditate.

Once, Maulvi Ghulam Nabi *Rahmatullah Alayhi* came with his son Muhammad Hanif to visit the shrine of Hadrat Qadi Fath Allah Qadiri Shattari *Rahmatullah Alayhi*. Muhammad Hanif went into a mystical state and when he regained consciousness both father and son left. On the way back Muhammad Hanif mentioned to his father that in his mystical state he felt as if Hadrat Qadi Fath Allah Qadiri Shattari *Rahmatullah Alayhi* wanted them to stay. Mawlana Ghulam Nabi *Rahmatullah Alayhi* said, "If you had told me that earlier then we would have stayed." Mawlana Ghulam Nabi *Rahmatullah Alayhi* used to maintain that his son Muhammad Hanif was able to experience the unveiling of the graves.

63) Tuesday 9th October 1990

Hadrat Sahib states that the builder called Muhammad was a student of Qibla Alam *Rahmatullah Alayhi*. "He informed me that Qibla Alam *Rahmatullah Alayhi* taught him to say *jalla jallaluhu* when the *mu'adhin* said, *Allahu Akbar*." He continued that, "Qibla Alam *Rahmatullah Alayhi* also taught him how to pray and especially how to keep the space between the belly and the thighs during prostration. In addition he taught him to say 🕌 when the blessed name of the Prophet 🕌 was uttered."

64) Thursday 11th October 1990

Hadrat Sahib said that Qibla Alam *Rahmatullah Alayhi* always used to recite, "*In the name of Allah the most Gracious most Merciful*," before starting anything and he always gave and took with the right hand. In the beginning of ablution, supplication and at the end he would recite *durud sharif* three times. "He taught me how to sweep up; he said to grip the handle firmly and open the face of broom at the front and then sweep."

65) Sunday 14th October 1990

Hadrat Sahib states that Qibla Alam *Rahmatullah Alayhi* used to advise that if you do not know the ruling or have not researched the matter then you should not discuss it as it can harm your faith. Similarly he did not like to talk about miracles and mystical states. Instead he would advise, "Remember Allah and obey the Shari'ah. Lest miracles and mystical states delude you into thinking you have attained perfection."

66) Wednesday 17th October 1990

Hadrat Sahib narrates that, "Qibla Alam *Rahmatullah Alayhi* instructed me to tie the turban by reciting *durud sharif* on every layer and to unravel it in the same manner and to keep it with the utmost respect."

67) Thursday 18th October 1990

Hadrat Sahib states that Qibla Alam *Rahmatullah Alayhi* would recite *ayatul kursi* (Verse of the Thorne) three times before going to sleep and then blow on his chest. At *tahajjud* time he would recite, *"And those who believe."* He maintained that if a person makes a firm intention then Allah makes it possible for him to wake up.

68) Saturday 3rd November 1990

Hadrat Sahib states that Qibla Alam *Rahmatullah Alayhi* used to say if a person reads, *"Ya Hadrat Jafar Sadiq Rahmatullah Alayhi,* when he feels sick (nauseous) then by Allah's grace he shall be cured."

69) Tuesday 6th November 1990

Hadrat Sahib states that as long as the Zubayriyya spiritual connection was dominant Qibla Alam *Rahmatullah Alayhi* experienced ecstasy in mystical states. For example, once in this state, he looked at Baba Ismail who went into ecstasy. However, when the Sayfiyya spiritual connection became dominant, then Qibla Alam *Rahmatullah Alayhi* became like an ocean and subsequently there were no signs of ecstasy. It is said that Sain Muhammad Hasan *Zulfain Wallay Rahmatullah Alayhi* experienced spiritual ecstasy before his death.

70) Wednesday 7th November 1990

Hadrat Sahib mentioned some of Qibla Alam's practices. He stated that Qibla Alam *Rahmatullah Alayhi* wore both woollen and leather socks in winter, but he only considered it permissible to wipe over leather socks. Some *Sangis* gave him gloves but there is no evidence to suggest that he wore them. Qibla Alam *Rahmatullah Alayhi* used to cover his head and both sides of his face with a shawl. He would not pray if his shirt buttons were open. He preferred to burn oil rather than have a lamp in the mosque. He always addressed the *Sangis* with dignity and respect; he would refer to them as '*Sufi*', '*Miyan*', '*Hajji*' or '*Sangi*'. In food he liked *sujana* beans, *kerla* and dried chapatti, brown bread, egg and *mung* lentils. He did not drink milk or *lassi* and did not eat rice. He would have a sweet dish made of starch or shrub roots.

71) Sunday 11th November 1990

Hadrat Sahib narrated from Sain Muhammad Hasan Suda'i, that Qibla Mai Sahiba stated that Qibla Alam *Rahmatullah Alayhi* used to recite *ayatul kursi* 11 times after *fajr*, 9 times after *dhur*, 7 times after *asr*, 5 times after *maghrib* and 3 times after *isha*.

72) Monday 12th November 1990

Hadrat Sahib states that Qibla Alam *Rahmatullah Alayhi* used his shawl like a *niqab* (face cover). His method of offering *namaz* was in line with the practice of Hadrat Mujaddid Alf Thani *Rahmatullah Alayhi*. For example he did not raise his index finger during the second or final sitting, nor did he advise anyone else to do this.

73) Saturday 26th June 1993

Today Sain ibn Sultan Ali died, his funeral was held at 6 p.m. at the Khanqah-e Fathiyya. When Hadrat Sahib heard about his death he said, "When Qibla Alam *Rahmatullah Alayhi* first came to Kotli he stayed at Sain ibn Sultan Ali's house."

74) Friday 14th January 1994

Hadrat Sahib stated that throughout his life Qibla Alam *Rahmatullah Alayhi* never attributed any greatness to himself. He lived a simple and humble life.

The following testimony from Hadrat Mawlana Muhammad Abd Allah *Rahmatullah Alayhi* from Ladar is sufficient, he said, "I have had the good fortune of associating with many of the great scholars of Hindustan and some scholars of Arabia but I have not met anyone more humble than Qadi Sahib."

75) Sunday 3rd April 1994

Yesterday Sain Muhammad Hasan[182] came to Khanqah-e Fathiyya, Gulhar, Kotli; he suffered from arthritis. He mentioned that he had taken *bay'a* with Qibla Alam *Rahmatullah Alayhi* along with Sain Muhammad Husayn. He said, "Qibla Alam *Rahmatullah Alayhi* gave him *bay'a* in the mosque[183] on the request of Sain Muhammad Husayn. He said that he prayed and wrote down the date when he completed the Holy Qur'an. "Despite my illness I recite two to four chapters every day. And when I think of Qibla Alam *Rahmatullah Alayhi*, his wide forehead, his long tresses and his long shirt come to mind. Apart from that I see him performing *wudu*."

76) Wednesday 15th June 1994

Hadrat Sahib mentioned the poetry of Baba Ghafuri a *Sangi* of Qibla Alam *Rahmatullah Alayhima*. Hadrat Sahib stated that amongst Baba Ghafuri's *waza'if* was the *khatam* of Hadrat Mujaddid *Rahmatullah Alayhi*, *dhikr* of the breath and 4 units of *tahajjud* prayer. Baba Ghafuri is buried in Kotli.[184]

77) Wednesday 29th June 1994

Hadrat Sahib narrated that Sain Muhammad Husayn owed money to Bakhshi Diwan Chand. Although he had paid the original amount the interest upon interest was too much for him to pay. So Bakhshi Diwan Chand took him to court. Sain Sahib mentioned the situation to Qibla Alam *Rahmatullah Alayhi*. Ghulam Muhyi al-Din[185] who knew legal matters, was there as well and advised Sain Sahib to hire a solicitor and reduce the amount of payment. However after Qibla Alam *Rahmatullah Alayhi* was convinced that the original amount had been paid, he told Sain Sahib that there was no need to hire a solicitor. He advised him,

---

[182] Rajur
[183] Gorah
[184] Baliyah
[185] Kheri Suchani

"When you go to court remember Allah, Allah." Sain Sahib did as he was instructed and for some unknown reason the case was dismissed. Despite further appeals by Bakhshi Diwan Chand to the Jammu court the original verdict stood.

78) Friday 18th November 1994

Hadrat Sahib mentioned a favourite verse of Qibla Alam *Rahmatullah Alayhi* which he had read in a particular gathering and stated that by practising this poem one would be saved from many difficulties.

Halq-e khudra dur dar az har maz-e,
Ta nayafti dar bala wa dar baz-e

Keep your throat away from all tastes,
So that you do not fall into trouble.

79) Friday 13th January 1995

Hadrat Sahib states that Qibla Alam's view on matters of jurisprudence was that those issues that had been resolved by the earlier jurists should not be debated again; as those jurists were nearer to the period of Prophet hood and today centuries later there was agreement in the Muslim *ummah* on those matters. However, it was permissible to use independent judgement on new issues but there were strict measures in this field and not everyone could exercise this right. Therefore it was vital to avoid dispute in religious matters.

Regarding matters of difference Qibla Alam *Rahmatullah Alayhi* had a clear viewpoint. He used to tell the *Sangis* to worry about themselves. "Once you are safe then you can dispute about others, an important trial lies ahead."

Qibla Alam *Rahmatullah Alayhi* had advised *Sangis* to honour elder *Sangis*. When a tree becomes old it is viewed with respect, so how can one neglect to honour and respect the elders?" Despite being a master Qibla Alam *Rahmatullah Alayhi* expressed a great deal of respect towards people in general and the *Sangis* in particular.

80) Saturday 11th March 1995

Hadrat Sahib states that the *Sangis* of Qibla Alam *Rahmatullah Alayhi* had great love for one another. They served their master with exemplary love and sincerity. Hadrat Sahib said, "I have personally witnessed the good manners of Miyan Fath Muhammad *Rahmatullah Alayhi*. Once at the occasion of the *urs* ceremony Miyan Fath Muhammad *Rahmatullah Alayhi* came with some of his followers walking in front of his horse. The horse was saddled but out of respect for Qibla Alam *Rahmatullah Alayhi* he would not ride it. In old age when he became very weak by Qibla Alam's permission and constant order he would ride his horse. "That particular day I was going to get some tablets from Ladar. Miyan Fath Muhammad *Rahmatullah Alayhi* was silent as were his followers. All of his followers were walking barefoot. He enquired as to why I was going to Ladar and when I informed him about the tablets, he took care of the matter. Miyan Fath Muhammad *Rahmatullah Alayhi* came and placed his cap on Qibla Alam's feet and kissed his hands, who tried to stop him but without success. Miyan Fath Muhammad *Rahmatullah Alayhi* sat down with complete humility before his master.

81) Saturday 11th March 1995

Today Hadrat Sahib talked about the Naka Kurti mosque which is presently known as the University Campus mosque. Hadrat Sahib mentioned Hajji Mawlana Muhammad Baqa who narrated that Qibla Alam *Rahmatullah Alayhima* said to him, "If you build a mosque then build it better than your home."

Then Hadrat Sahib talked about the old mosque in Checheyan Sharif. He stated that the old mosque was built with mud and it used to be plastered. *Sangi* Muhammad Ramadan was of the view that it should be made of bricks. A builder was consulted and he estimated that about 22,000 bricks were needed. In those days one could purchase 1000 bricks for 22 rupees. The bricks were ordered but the work did not begin on the mosque. So *Sangi* Muhammad Ramadan sent the money to Mawlana Muhammad Zaman *Rahmatullah Alayhi* although it took a while for the money to arrive.

Qibla Alam *Rahmatullah Alayhi* was not keen on demolishing the old mud built mosque. However the *Sangis* decided that the old mosque should be martyred and a new one constructed. According to this decision, *Sangi* Muhammad Ramadan began to demolish the ridge of the wall. The foundation was laid with uncut stones and mud. The building consisted of a hall 12ft by 24 ft, a door, two cupboards and a window in the north side measuring 3ft by ½ ft. It was decided to build the roof with timber. Miyan Ghulam Muhyi al-Din pledged to bring wood for the walls and the roof. Miyan Sahib was a very well informed person hence it was thought he would purchase the best type of wood for the money. But for some reason he was unable to fulfil his pledge.

So Qibla Alam *Rahmatullah Alayhi* personally went to the mosque.[186] That particular day Sain Muhammad Hasan was not in at home.[187] When Qibla Alam *Rahmatullah Alayhi* reached the area [188] the women *Sangis* came running from their homes. At that point Sain Muhammad Hasan *Zulfain Wallay* arrived as well, he pleaded with Qibla Alam *Rahmatullah Alayhi* to go back to his village otherwise this area would suffer calamity. Qibla Alam *Rahmatullah Alayhi* rested in the Sain Muhammad Hasan Suda'i mosque. An old lady called Mai Rasul Bi invited Qibla Alam *Rahmatullah Alayhi* to her house and she gave her daughter's gold block (nose ring) for the mosque.

Consequently the *Sangis* found out that Miyan Ghulam Muhyi al-Din was unable to keep his promise. Later Sain Muhammad Husayn known as Sain Mandu found out that Qibla Alam *Rahmatullah Alayhi* had visited this village and was now near the area.[189] He was upset with Mawlana Muhammad Zaman for taking Qibla Alam *Rahmatullah Alayhima* to that area.[190] He then said, "These kings (pious people like Qibla Alam *Rahmatullah Alayhi*) are simple people, we are here to serve." He recommended that plywood should be used for the beams in the mosque.

Unfortunately a few days later Miyan Ghulam Muhyi al-Din's home was robbed and the thieves took everything and they were never caught. His wife, Gul Begum who used to come to Checheyan Sharif with an entourage became penniless. After a prolonged illness Miyan Sahib died in a state of poverty. The mosque was completed after Qibla Alam's demise. The roof was set up under the supervision of Hadrat Qibla Mai Sahiba *Rahmatullah Alayha*. However, the minaret could not be built. *Sangi* Muhammad Ramadan later went to Iran where he burned his ears in an accident. When, he finally returned to his homeland there was no one who recognised him.

---

[186] Kheri
[187] Potha
[188] Mast Khan pond
[189] Bohri
[190] Keri

135

82) Wednesday 31st January 1996

Hadrat Sahib narrates that sometimes Qibla Alam's conversation outwardly seemed to be about *dunya* but even then it was done to correct someone. Consequently the person in question would feel a change in his condition.

Regarding some of the *waza'if* that Qibla Alam *Rahmatullah Alayhi* gave to the *Sangis*, Hadrat Sahib states that Qibla Alam *Rahmatullah Alayhi* did not always give *waza'if* from the books. However, *waza'if* such as *durud mustaghas* and *shajarah tariqat* (spiritual genealogy), were given to most of the *Sangis* as were the *khatam* of Hadrat Mujaddid Alf Thani and Hadrat Shaykh Abd al-Qadir Jilani *Rahmatullah Alayhima* and he instructed that these be read regularly. Similarly he told some of the *Sangis* to read *durud tunajjina* 313 times, *durud hazara* 1100 times, *durud khidri* 1100 times and greatly stressed the importance of *ism-e zat* (Allah) and said, "One should keep this in mind in every situation: sitting, standing and walking. This is the only *wird* that does not require ablution and it is very beneficial to purify the heart." In addition Qibla Alam *Rahmatullah Alayhi* preferred the *Sangis* to practice *tassawwar-e Shaykh,* the *khatams* and continuous *dhikr*. Sometimes his deputies would be told to practise a particular lesson for weeks and he would give them his spiritual attention as well. After his demise his deputies propagated these teachings to their respective followers.

Khwaja Muhammad Akbar Ali, the authorised deputy of Qibla Alam *Rahmatullah Alayhima* narrated to Hadrat Sahib that, "Once I was alone with Qibla Alam *Rahmatullah Alayhi* in his private chamber in Checheyan Sharif, and when he gave me his spiritual focus, I could see a light which spread from my heart and make a shining circle on the wall." This was due to the greatness of Qibla Alam's *Rahmatullah Alayhi* focus and this light of the heart is greatly desired by people of the path.

When Qibla Alam *Rahmatullah Alayhi* used to say farewell to the visitors he would recite *ayatul kursi* three times and wish them a safe journey. He had advised the *Sangis* to recite *ayatul kursi* three times and then blow on the people as they were leaving.

Qibla Alam *Rahmatullah Alayhi* was an avid reader. He read the *Risala-e Munawwar* in which the Qura'nic verses are translated into poetry. Hadrat Sahib narrates that once a group started to read the 'Creed of Faith' out loud. Some *Sangis* reprimanded them. However, Qibla Alam *Rahmatullah Alayhi* said, "*Sangiyu*, some people mention Allah's name loudly and some silently, perhaps their master has taught them this method. Keep busy with your own duties and do not create discord."

Hadrat Sahib narrates that, "Once I was waiting for a train at the Lala Musa train station with Hajji Ali Dad[191]. A person approached us and introduced himself as Qari Ghulam Nabi and said that he was linked with the shrine.[192] He enquired as to where we were from. I told him that we came from Mirpur in the state of Jammu and Kashmir." He said, "There was a Sultan in the Mirpur area, he was a great saint. There were four 'Sultans': firstly Hadrat Sultan Bahu, secondly Hadrat Sultan Mahmud and thirdly Hadrat Sultan Alam *Rahmatullah Alayhim* and I cannot remember the fourth one." He invited Hadrat Sahib to his home and Hadrat Sahib thanked him for the invitation but politely declined the offer.

83) Monday 11th November 1996

Hadrat Sahib narrates that Sufi Faujdar Khan *Rahmatullah Alayhi* used to state that, "Although both types of *dhikr* are important, silent *dhikr* is more beneficial than loud *dhikr*. He used to stress the importance of silence by giving the following example, "If one is ill on the inside then putting ointment on the outside is of little benefit but if one were to eat one seed of *jipal* (laxative) then that flushes out all the dirt." He said, "Every type of worship is fine but *dhikr* is the only worship that is linked to the breath. As long as a person is alive he can make *dhikr* it does not have conditions such as ablution and clean clothes." Therefore Sufi Faujdar Khan *Rahmatullah Alayhi* used to train the *Sangis* to perform silent *dhikr* to the extent that it became second nature to them.

Hadrat Sahib narrates that Pir Nigh Ali Shah *Rahmatullah Alayhi* once said to Miyan Diwan Ali [193] that, "I have seen many great *pirs* but there is no comparison with the impact Qibla Alam *Rahmatullah Alayhi* had on people. Due to his

---

[191] Kurti
[192] Lillah Sharif
[193] Dullar

association the rebellious and wicked people became obedient servants. They left their evil ways and became practising Muslims.

84) Monday 25th November 1996

Hadrat Sahib stated that once Qadi Muhammad Fadal *Rahmatullah Alayhi* ate more than usual on the day of *eid* and felt sick. So he went into the cornfield and put his finger in his mouth to make himself vomit but without any success. During this time the call for *dhur* started and so in this condition he went to the mosque to make ablution. Qibla Alam *Rahmatullah Alayhi* was already there and had a water jug from which he was making ablution. He said to Qadi Muhammad Fadal *Rahmatullah Alayhi*, "You must take care in the beginning, what is the benefit of putting your finger in your mouth afterwards?"

Chapter Three

The Deputies of Qibla Alam *Rahmatullah Alayhi*

A fruit is a good indicator of the tree and from a student one can measure the greatness of the teacher. Similarly to assess the greatness of a Sufi master one has to examine his followers and in particular his deputies. It is these spiritual offspring of the master, followers and especially the deputies who present the living embodiment of their master. It is they who revive his teachings for the future generations. Without knowing the followers and deputies one cannot fully understand the virtues of the master. Therefore this section of the *Tazkira-e Sultaniyya* is devoted to the *Sangis* and deputies of Qibla Alam *Rahmatullah Alayhi*. The exact number of Qibla Alam's deputies is not known as there is no written record of these people, because he did not consider this necessary. Some of his *Sangis* and deputies kept close contact with him and following his demise they stayed loyal to his successor Hadrat Sahib. Through various sources, information has been gatherd about these *Sangis* and deputies. What follows is a summary of these accounts.

1) Hadrat Miyan Fath Muhammad (d.1935) *Rahmatullah Alayhi*

His blessed name was Fath Muhammad,[194] he was tall, slim had a brown complexion and used Henna. He wore a long loose shirt and a *dhoti*. His *dhoti* always rested above his ankles and he wore customary shoes. He also wore a five pointed skull cap and a light turban.

By proffesion he was a farmer and all of his family were practicing Muslims. Once he went to the animal market and was bringing a buffalo home and on the way back he spent the night in the Checheyan Sharif mosque. At early dawn he recited some verses from the *Sayf al-Muluk* of Miyan Muhammad Bakhsh with great love and passion, which Qibla Alam *Rahmatullah Alayhima* overheard. After the sunrise when Qibla Alam lifted his shawl from his face the first person his gaze fell on was Miyan Fath Muhammad *Rahmatullah Alayhima*. This single glance was to change the course of Miyan Fath Muhammad's life. He was a young man at the time and had not previously met Qibla Alam *Rahmatullah Alayhi*. Qibla Alam *Rahmatullah Alayhi* sat down in the mosque and conversed with him for a few moments. This brief meeting with Qibla Alam *Rahmatullah Alayhi* sowed the

---

[194] Chinar,Thub,Dadyal

seeds in his heart. Afterwards he went back to his village but his heart became restless. As a result, many questions came to his mind and his world view began to change. His previous interests no longer held any attraction for him. His days and nights passed in this troublesome state. The Divine Hand was at work and he was torn between his home and his heart. He was eager to go back and meet Qibla Alam *Rahmatullah Alayhi*. Suddenly an incident took place that made things clear for him.

In order to avoid repercussions from the above mentioned incident Miyan Fath Muhammad decided to migrate to Checheyan Sharif. Sometime later Qibla Alam *Rahmatullah Alayhima* sent a message to Miyan Fath Muhammad's noble wife that, "Either come and join your husband here in Checheyan Sharif or forgive him the obligations he owes you." She was a very wise lady and instead of accepting the offer she laid some conditions of her own. She said she was willing to forgive Miyan Sahib her rights on the condition that she would receive her share of the spirituality from Qibla Alam *Rahmatullah Alayhi*. Following this correspondence Qibla Alam delegated the *khadim* Baba Faqir Muhammad Pothiyya *Rahmatullah Alayhima* to bring the noble lady and her son named Miyan Fadal Ilahi to Checheyan Sharif. Baba Faqir Muhammad *Rahmatullah Alayhi* carried the young boy Miyan Fadal Ilahi on his shoulders. In the meantime the sister of Miyan Fath Muhammad *Rahmatullah Alayhi* had also arrived in Checheyan Sharif with her two daughters searching for her lost brother. Subsequently the families of Qibla Alam and Miyan Fath Muhammad *Rahmatullah Alayhima* were united through marriage.

After receiving his spiritual training Hadrat Miyan Fath Muhammad emerged as the greatest deputy of Qibla Alam *Rahmatullah Alayhima*.[195] Afterwards his son Miyan Fadal Ilahi *Rahmatullah Alayhi* continued this spiritual legacy.

Hadrat Miyan Fath Muhammad *Rahmatullah Alayhi* used to perform the *dhikr* of *nafi-asbat* by holding his breath, and he would perform the *dhikr* of 'Allah' 25000 times daily on *saba' lataif* (the seven subtle spiritual centres). He read the *khatam* of Hadrat Mujaddid Alf Thani and Hadrat Shaykh Abd al-Qadir Jilani *Rahmatullah Alayhima* every day. In addition he read *Dalail al-Khayrat*, *Hizb al-Azam*, *durud mustaghas* and *shajarah tariqat* daily. He regularly performed *tahajjud*,

---

[195] The people of Pūnch Mehnder, Tehkyala and Parawa became his followers and greatly benefited from him

ishraq awwabin and *salatul tasbih*. He also performed his meditations on a regular basis. His supplications were often accepted by Allah Almighty.

Hadrat Sahib narrates that, "Before his demise Hadrat Miyan Fath Muhammad *Rahmatullah Alayhi* was ill and would sit near the northern window in the mosque and recite the Holy Qur'an. In those days he used to recite from a Qur'an with a red cover. His temperament was somewhat intense but he was totally absorbed in his master."

Many miracles are related about Hadrat Miyan Fath Muhammad *Rahmatullah Alayhi*. It is stated that once a Qadiani Mullah named Maulvi Ruda came to meet him. At that time many people were taking *bay'a* from Miyan Fath Muhammad *Rahmatullah Alayhi* and in jest Maulvi Ruda said, "Give me *bay'a* as well, *meki ve bait karo.*" Hadrat Miyan Fath Muhammad *Rahmatullah Alayhi* said, "Okay, come on, *ajj aie ja.*" He then gave *bay'a* to Maulvi Ruda and gave him spiritual attention and hit his heart with the beat of 'Allah Hu'. Maulvi Ruda went into ecstasy and jumped from one place to another and ended up in the stables with his clothes covered in dung. When the *Sangis* tried to control him Hadrat Miyan Fath Muhammad *Rahmatullah Alayhi* said, "Let his internal filth be washed away." The spiritual attention also had an impact upon the horse in the stable as it began to jump up and hit the floor forcefully with its hooves.

Qibla Alam *Rahmatullah Alayhi* gave a copy of *Dalail al-Khayrat* to Maulvi Ruda which he used to recite throughout his life. After his death that copy of *Dalail al-Khayrat* was discovered in a mosque, and with his daughter's permission it was brought back to Khanqah-e Sultaniyya.

Hadrat Miyan Fath Muhammad *Rahmatullah Alayhi* passed away on 23rd Rajab 1354 AH and was buried in Checheyan Sharif. Approximately 62 years later on 5th March 1993 his body was transferred to the Khanqah-e Sultaniyya, Jhelum. His son Miyan Fadal Ilahi *Rahmatullah Alayhi* passed away on 3rd November 1992; both graves are next to one another. Miyan Fadal Ilahi had the good fortune of being the son in law of Qibla Alam *Rahmatullah Alayhima* as he was married to Qibla Alam's beloved daughter Rahmat Begum *Rahmat Allah Alayha*. Miyan Fadal Ilahi *Rahmatullah Alayhi* had three sons: Sahibzada Muhammad Mahbub, Muhammad Arshad and Muhammad Aqsad and two daughters.

2) **Hadrat Qadi Muhammad Alam** (d.1934) *Rahmatullah Alayhi*

(NB, For the benefit of the readers, this section has been reformatted, Translator)

Family Background: Qibla Alam's grandfather Qadi Muhammad Akbar Ali *Rahmatullah Alayhima* was greatly traumatised by many tragedies he faced, especially the brutality of the Sikh rulers. He lost all interest in matters of the world and wanted to live a life of celibacy. His pain and anguish would not let him settle anywhere. During this traumatic period he came to Dina[196] where he led a *namaz* in the local mosque. The local people loved his recitation of the Qur'an and pleaded with him to stay in the village. Subsequently Qadi Muhammad Akbar Ali *Rahmatullah Alayhi* spent most of his life as the *imam* of the mosque.[197] Qadi Muhammad Akbar Ali *Rahmatullah Alayhi* was *hafiz* of the Holy Qur'an and used to recite it completely every day. This practice of Qadi Muhammad Akbar Ali is attested by Maulvi Ghulam Ali Sahib *Rahmatullah Alayhima* from Bawali Sharif. It was in this area that Qadi Muhammad Akbar Ali *Rahmatullah Alayhi* got married to a lady from the Kokkhar tribe, who had also memorised the Holy Qur'an. Both Qadi Fadal Ahmad and Qadi Muhammad Rukn Alam *Rahmatullah Alayhima* were born in this village.

One day Qadi Muhammad Akbar Ali's eldest son Qadi Fadal Ahmad *Rahmatullah Alayhi* went to the local well to fetch some water. The boys from the village taunted him that the well was theirs and he had no right to fill the water. Qadi Fadal Ahmad *Rahmatullah Alayhi* was deeply upset by this behaviour of the village boys and pleaded with his noble father to return to their ancestral home in Checheyan Sharif, which he did.

Qadi Muhammad Akbar Ali had five sons: Qadi Fadal Ahmad, Qadi Muhammad Rukn Alam, Qadi Faid Alam, Qadi Nur Alam and Qadi Chirag Alam *Rahmatullah Alayhim*. Qadi Faid Alam and Qadi Nur Alam *Rahmatullah Alayhima* lived in different hamlets. Qadi Fadal Ahmad had two sons Qadi Muhammad Alam and Qadi Muhammad Fadil. Qadi Muhammad Rukn Alam had only one child, Qadi Muhammad Sultan Alam (Qibla Alam) *Rahmatullah Alayhim*.

---

[196] Morah Maldeh
[197] Mohra Maldeh Mahal

Qadi Muhammad Alam was the eldest son of Qibla Alam's uncle Qadi Fadal Ahmad *Rahmatullah Alayhim*. He had a brother called Qadi Muhammad Fadil *Rahmatullah Alayhi*. In addition to being a cousin of Qibla Alam, Qadi Muhammad Alam *Rahmatullah Alayhima* was his follower and authorised deputy as well. In the beginning Qibla Alam *Rahmatullah Alayhi* used to live with him in the ancestral home. The ancestral home was divided by a wall which was not fully built. Later Qibla Alam *Rahmatullah Alayhi* built a house near the mosque. It was this house and the mosque that became the centre of guidance.

Qadi Muhammad Alam *Rahmatullah Alayhi* was tall, of medium build and his beard was grey. When he walked, he used to take long steps. He wore a long shirt and his *dhoti* was above his ankles. He wore a four or five pointed skull cap over which he wore a turban; he had long hair, used to carry a walking stick and preferred to wear white clothes. Apart from farming he also taught students, Sawan Shah[198] *Rahmatullah Alayhi* and Ghulam Muhammad[199] were two his students. He was authorised to guide people. He also had an interest in natural medicine and used natural herbs to cure people. His recitation of the Holy Qur'an was very beautiful and he read with proper *tajwid*. When he recited the Holy Qur'an people's hearts would be filled with joy. He learned the Holy Qur'an from Khwaja Hafiz Muhammad Hayat *Rahmatullah Alayhi* and would recite in his style.

Qadi Muhammad Alam obtained the Mujaddidiyya spiritual path from Qibla Alam *Rahmatullah Alayhima* and later became his deputy. He had ample opportunities to associate with Qibla Alam *Rahmatullah Alayhi* at home and on his travels. Often Qibla Alam *Rahmatullah Alayhi* would trust him with many responsibilities. Once he was instructed along with Mullah Muhammad Ramadan to go to Lahore and read *durud tunajjina* in order to locate a lady who had been kidnapped. Due to the blessing of the *durud tunajjina* the kidnapped lady was found safe and well. Similarly once on a visit to Bawali Sharif Qibla Alam *Rahmatullah Alayhi* instructed him to teach Sain Ranjah the name of Allah which he did and consequently he became a saint. In the early days, he used to grind the wheat for the *langar sharif* and sometimes he would prepare food for Qibla Alam *Rahmatullah Alayhi* as well.

Qadi Muhammad Alam *Rahmatullah Alayhi* prayed *tahajjud, ishraq, awwabin* and *salatul tasbih* every day. Between *maghrib* and *isha* he stayed inside the

---

[198] Fathpur
[199] Jabr

mosque and read *durud tunajjina* 313 times daily. In addition he read the *khatam* of Hadrat Mujaddid Alf Thani and Hadrat Shaykh Abd al-Qadir Jilani *Rahmatullah Alayhima*, *Dalail al-Khayrat, durud mustaghas* and the *shajarah tariqat*. He would eat food after *isha*. He would give *ta'wiz* and also blew on people. He had a son and a daughter, his son was called Qadi Muhammad Latif who had the good fortune of being the son in law of Qibla Alam *Rahmatullah Alayhi*, as he was married to his beloved daughter Manzur Begum Sahiba. Qadi Muhammad Latif *Rahmatullah Alayhi* had three sons Sahibzada Muhammad Masum, Muhammad Maruf, Muhammad Faruq and three daughters.

Qadi Muhammad Alam *Rahmatullah Alayhi* passed away on 7th *Muharram* 1352 A.H, about two weeks prior to Qibla Alam's demise. He was buried in the family cemetery in Checheyan Sharif and on 7th May 1993 his body was transferred to the Khanqah-e Sultaniyya, Jhelum, where he is buried next to his noble father Qadi Fadal Ahmad towards the western side of Qibla Alam's grave *Rahmatullah Alayhim*.

Hadrat Sahib narrates that, "Hadrat Qadi Muhammad Alam went to visit Baba Muhammad Ramadan *Rahmatullah Alayhima* in Gurdaspur and the day he came back I saw him make ablution near the *dehrak* tree. I enquired about his health and he said he had a fever. A few days later he passed away."

Miyan Muhammad Yusuf[200] who was in the state of intoxication dearly loved Qadi Muhammad Alam *Rahmatullah Alayhima* and they were good friends. Miyan Muhammad Yusuf had made a will that when he died Qadi Muhammad Alam *Rahmatullah Alayhima* should bathe him and lead his funeral. In this regard Miyan Muhammad Yusuf *Rahmatullah Alayhi* had given thirty rupees, one suit and a pair of shoes. One day Miyan Muhammad Yusuf sent Qadi Muhammad Alam *Rahmatullah Alayhima* to visit a *Majdhub* in Lahore. Qadi Muhammad Alam stated that, "When I met the *Majdhub* he instructed me to return straight away and I obeyed his order. When I arrived home, Miyan Muhammad Yusuf was on his death bed, thus his will was carried out."

3) **Mawlana Ghulam Nabi** (d.1954) *Rahmatullah Alayhi*

---

[200] Gorsian

Mawlana Ghulam Nabi[201] later migrated to the village[202] in the Sind province. Due to the civil unrest in Sind one of his grandsons, named Ghulam Murtada bin Muhammad Hanif, wrote a letter to Hadrat Sahib in 1992 in which he mentioned the wretched state of his household and sought his permission to relocate to Gujjar Khan in the Panjab. Hence Ghulam Murtada Sahib, who was a calligrapher moved to Tehsil Gujjar Khan, however the rest of his family remained[203]. In recent times Ghulam Murtada Sahib has left Gujjar Khan and moved back.[204]

Qibla Alam's cousin Qadi Muhammad Fadil introduced Mawlana Ghulam Nabi to Qibla Alam *Rahmatullah Alayhim.* Qadi Muhammad Fadil was the son of Qadi Fadal Ahmad and the younger brother of Qadi Muhammad Alam *Rahmatullah Alayhim.* He had studied in Lahore under Mawlana Nabi Bakhsh Halawa'i and was later appointed[205] as the *imam* and it was here that he met Mawlana Ghulam Nabi *Rahmatullah Alayhima.*

Mawlana Ghulam Nabi had heard a lot about Qibla Alam from Qadi Muhammad Fadil *Rahmatullah Alayhim.* Incidentally Qadi Muhammad Fadil's elder brother Qadi Muhammad Alam came to visit him and Mawlana Ghulam Nabi *Rahmatullah Alayhim* also met him. When Mawlana Ghulam Nabi compared that information he had about Qibla Alam with the characteristics of Qadi Muhammad Alam *Rahmatullah Alayhim,* he found him to be a perfect reflection of his master. As he conversed with Qadi Muhammad Alam it increased his longing to meet Qibla Alam *Rahmatullah Alayhima.* Although Mawlana Ghulam Nabi had previously taken *bay'a* from some other *Pir Sahib,* nonetheless he went to visit Qibla Alam *Rahmatullah Alayhima* in Checheyan Sharif. After observing Qibla Alam's impeccable manners, piety, and observance of the Shari'ah, he asked for *bay'a,* which was accepted. Under Qibla Alam's supervision he completed the Mujaddidiyya spiritual path and was appointed a deputy and given authorisation to guide people.

Mawlana Ghulam Nabi *Rahmatullah Alayhi* gave *bay'a* and guided people with the utmost care and affection. Some of his notable followers include Fadal

---

[201] Pind Dad Khan and Chak Hakimanh No: 18, Tehsil Pahliya District, Mandi Baha al-Din
[202] Dur
[203] Dur
[204] Dur
[205] Havali Mikanah, Tehsil Pahliya

Ahmad[206] Imam Din[207] and Muhammad Mirza.[208] Mawlana Ghulam Nabi had great love for Qibla Alam *Rahmatullah Alayhima* and often visited Checheyan Sharif on foot. Everything he possessed was dedicated to his master. He would personally take part in the *langar sharif* activities and showed great concern in this area. In order to fulfil the need for milk in the *langar sharif* he would sometimes bring a cow or a buffalo. When he realised that there was a shortage of fire wood for the kitchen fuel and that the wood had to be brought from a jungle faraway, he bought two camels, one after the other, to carry the fire wood for the *langar sharif.* One of the she camels produced four calves. In this way the process of bringing fire wood became much easier. If Mawlana Ghulam Nabi *Rahmatullah Alayhi* felt that the mosque needed prayer mats he would buy good quality mats from the Panjab and then spread them out in the mosque. Hence he was always keen to perform some sort of service for his master or the *langar sharif*. Sometimes he would bring books for the religious and spiritual benefit of the *Sangis*.

Mawlana Ghulam Nabi *Rahmatullah Alayhi* was of medium height, plump, his hair reached his ear lobes and later he used to shave his head. His long shirt was below his knees, his shirt would have open sleeves and he wore a *dhoti*. He liked white cotton clothes. In winter he would wear a woollen cap and in summer a cotton cap. He wore a turban on top. He wore customary shoes. Mawlana Ghulam Nabi's daily practice consisted of: *tahajjud, ishraq, awwabin,* 25,000 times 'Allah', *dhikr* of *nafi-asbat*, meditations and *khatam*. He used a middle range rosary which had 10 and 25 counters. His reading consisted of one and a quarter *para* of the Holy Qur'an, daily section of the *Dalail al-Khayrat, Hizb al-Azam, durud mustaghas* and *shajarah tariqat*.

Although Mawlana Ghulam Nabi *Rahmatullah Alayhi* was a pious person he was obsessed with the art of alchemy. He formed an alchemist's group which included some prominent *Sangis*. In order to achieve his objective of obtaining the secret formula he travelled from place to place to try out new experiments. Qibla Alam *Rahmatullah Alayhi* did not approve of his obsession with alchemy and often reprimanded him on the subject. Consequently this obsession with alchemy caused many problems for Mawlana Ghulam Nabi *Rahmatullah Alayhi* but despite this his piety was worthy of praise.

---

[206] Khatyala near Malikwal
[207] Pahjranh
[208] Mandi Baha al-Din

Mawlana Ghulam Nabi's noble wife used to spend a great deal of time in Checheyan Sharif. Hadrat Sahib used to call her Auntie. She was a very pious and caring person. Every day she recited five *paras* and in old age it was reduced to one and a quarter *para*. She used to grind the wheat for the *langar sharif* and during this process she would recite *sura Ya-Sīn*. She also had some other *wird* from the books and she read them regularly. She used to teach the village children. She used to state that, "So much wheat is produced and every seed goes through my hands." She would grind the wheat on her own grinding stone as her husband would not eat flour from the machine as he was of the view that such machines were kept outside and impure animals licked them.

Mawlana Ghulam Nabi *Rahmatullah Alayhi* had five sons: Muhammad Hanif, Nur Ahmad, Muhammad Husayn, Muhammad Siddiq and Ghulam Sarwar. It is well known that Muhammad Hanif was able to unveil the graves. Muhammad Husayn was linked with Qibla Alam *Rahmatullah Alayhi*. Some years ago Muhammad Hanif came to Khanqah-e Sultaniyya to attend the *urs* ceremony and later visited Khanqah-e Fathiyya in Gulhar Sharif; he brought his son with him and joined the noble path.

Mawlana Ghulam Nabi *Rahmatullah Alayhi* often prayed not to die in Sind. Allah accepted his supplications and as he was staying with his follower Muhammad Salih[209]he fell ill and soon passed away. His date of death is 14th Jamadi' al-awwal 1373 AH. He was buried in Rukn and for some time his followers knew the location of the grave. However as time passed and the graveyard was extended, his grave was neglected by his children and it could no longer be located. Many attempts were made by various *Sangis* as directed by Hadrat Sahib to locate Mawlana Ghulam Nabi's grave but without success. When all seemed lost Allah provided such proof of the grave that no doubts remained. One person mentioned that when Mawlana Ghulam Nabi *Rahmatullah Alayhi* was buried a special stone was placed over his grave. When the grave was located by this person and after digging the grave the same stone was found. Later the body of Mawlana Ghulam Nabi *Rahmatullah Alayhi* was transferred near the University Campus Mosque, Kotli.

Mawlana Ghulam Nabi's account cannot be complete without the mention of Jummah. Jummah was a *mussali* by caste and a student of Mawlana Ghulam Nabi *Rahmatullah Alayhi* who used to come with him to Checheyan Sharif,

---

[209] Rukn, Tehsil Pahliya, Mandi Baha al-Din

where he died and was buried. Mirpur is an arid area and it is not possible to have green pastures throughout the year. So on Mawlana Ghulam Nabi's request Qibla Alam *Rahmatullah Alayhi* sent his horse to graze.[210] According to Mawlana Ghulam Nabi, "Qibla Alam *Rahmatullah Alayhima* instructed Jummah to take care of the horse as Maulvi Sahib was going to go into seclusion. Jummah was a peculiar character."

When Jummah arrived[211] with the horse he said to Mawlana Ghulam Nabi *Rahmatullah Alayhi*, "You take care of the horse I am going home to Chakwal for a few days." Mawlana Ghulam Nabi informed him that he was instructed by Qibla Alam *Rahmatullah Alayhima* to perform seclusion and had told Jummah to look after the horse. "Both of us should do our duties," said Mawlana Ghulam Nabi *Rahmatullah Alayhi*. But Jummah was intent on going to Chakwal, so Mawlana Ghulam Nabi *Rahmatullah Alayhi* went into the seclusion. Jummah tied the horse and sat in the corner of the mosque. He began to read *durud tunajjina*. Qibla Alam *Rahmatullah Alayhi* had informed Jummah that whenever he had a problem or was faced with difficulty he should read *durud tunajjina* 1000 times and Allah would make matters easier. During this time Jummah addressed Mawlana Ghulam Nabi *Rahmatullah Alayhi* and said, "It will not be good for you." Then Jummah began to read *durud tunajjina* and cried uncontrollably. Mawlana Ghulam Nabi *Rahmatullah Alayhi* states that "At Midnight I had a panic attack and I had to abandon my seclusion."

Mawlana Ghulam Nabi states, "Later when I brought the horse back to Checheyan Sharif Qibla Alam *Rahmatullah Alayhima* enquired about the seclusion. I mentioned the whole incident. Qibla Alam *Rahmatullah Alayhi* said, "Go to the Duliya area in the mountains and practise your spiritual exercises." As always Jummah was there to irritate me. One day Jummah said he was missing Qibla Alam *Rahmatullah Alayhi* and wanted to go Checheyan Sharif. So he went to visit Qibla Alam *Rahmatullah Alayhi* who enquired about my seclusion from him, Jummah said. "Maulvi Sahib eats tons of food then goes to sleep! So who remembers Allah! *kah kar man anaj so jatey hain, Allah, allah koun karta hai.*" Mawlana Ghulam Nabi states *Rahmatullah Alayhi*, "It is because of this and other such incidents that I labelled Jummah as a 'wise enemy'."

---

[210] Chak No: 18
[211] Chak No: 18

Mawlana Ghulam Nabi states that when he was with Qibla Alam *Rahmatullah Alayhima* Jummah used to massage him, and when Qibla Alam *Rahmatullah Alayhi* said, "*Jazak Allah,*" he would say, "Janab please pray for my teacher although he is an arrogant person and does not think anyone is his equal in knowledge."

Mawlana Ghulam Nabi *Rahmatullah Alayhi* states that once in Checheyan Sharif the *Sangis* gave food to Jummah and him in the same plate. Jummah said, "Do not give Maulvi Sahib food in the same plate as me as he is a learned person and is offended as I am a low caste." These words of Jummah were mentioned to Qibla Alam *Rahmatullah Alayhi* who was very upset, as he never treated any *Sangi* with less respect due to his caste. Qibla Alam stated *Rahmatullah Alayhi,* "It is regrettable that Jummah talks of high and low caste here, in fact he is like a member of our household."

A guard dog was kept for the protection of livestock.[212] Qibla Alam *Rahmatullah Alayhi* had instructed the guard dog not to bark at the *Sangis* and so he never barked at any *Sangi* after that. But due to Jummah's complaint against Mawlana Ghulam Nabi to Qibla Alam *Rahmatullah Alayhi* it seemed that the protection was lifted. Subsequently one night when Mawlana Ghulam Nabi *Rahmatullah Alayhi* woke up, the dog began to bark at him. Hadrat Sahib's grandmother who lived there enquired, "Who is the dog barking at? *Kutta keynh nal ahy.*" Mawlana Ghulam Nabi *Rahmatullah Alayhi* replied, "He is barking at me, *kutta mein nal ayh.*" Hadrat Sahib's grandmother said in astonishment, "But he does not bark at the *Sangis*. Mawlana Ghulam Nabi *Rahmatullah Alayhi* replied, "Perhaps today I am outside the fold of the *Sangis* as Jummah has gone to Checheyan Sharif."

During this period Qibla Alam *Rahmatullah Alayhi* was in Mirpur for some reason and Mawlana Ghulam Nabi *Rahmatullah Alayhi* pleaded with him that, "Jummah grew up in our household, gained his education and became a young man there. He has lived as a member of our family and has participated in every family event. Indeed he sometimes prepared food with his own hands and fed us. We have never shown any discrimination towards him. And how of all the places, would I have the audacity to show discrimination against him in the sacred place as my Master's residence? He requested Qibla Alam *Rahmatullah Alayhi,* "Please master if you hear any complaint against me with regards to the Shari'ah and the mystical path then use your inner vision so that it appears in its true light."

---

[212] Duliya Jattain

Qibla Alam *Rahmatullah Ûlayhi* replied, "We do not like to spy on our *Sangis*. Allah might expose some *Sangis* to us of whom we have a good opinion and this would result in us not praying for that *Sangi* and we want to continue to sincerely pray for our *Sangis*."

Maulvi Akbar Husayn narrates from both Muhammad Salih and Nur Muhammad, that Mawlana Ghulam Nabi *Rahmatullah Ûlayhi* could treat a person with epilepsy even if he was at an acre's distance away. When a person came to Mawlana Ghulam Nabi *Rahmatullah Ûlayhi* and mentioned that someone suffered from epilepsy, he would merely rub his thighs and blow and the person would be cured. Nur Muhammad said, "I was a young man at the time and not interested in spiritual matters otherwise Mawlana Ghulam Nabi *Rahmatullah Ûlayhi* was a very gifted person and one could have learned a lot from him."

Hadrat Sahib narrates that, "Once I was staying at the house[213] of Mawlana Ghulam Nabi *Rahmatullah Ûlayhi*. The son of Chaudary Habib came running and said his sister had a painful toothache, and invited Mawlana Ghulam Nabi *Rahmatullah Ûlayhi* to his house. However he told him to go home and report back about the condition of his sister. When the boy left, Mawlana Ghulam Nabi *Rahmatullah Ûlayhi* began to rub his thighs forcefully and the boy came back and said his sister was fine. So I asked Mawlana Ghulam Nabi about this practice. He explained, "I focus on Qibla Alam *Rahmatullah Ûlayhima* and then think about the illness and then try to move it away. Mostly Allah grants a cure through the means of His chosen servant, it is simply this action and nothing else."

4) **Mullah Muhammad Ramadan** *Rahmatullah Ûlayhi*

Mullah Muhammad Ramadan[214] *Rahmatullah Ûlayhi* showed extreme respect for holy people. Whenever he heard of any holy person he would visit them. He had a great desire to achieve nearness to Allah. In Lahore he often prayed in the mosque of Mawlana Nabi Bakhsh Halawa'i *Rahmatullah Ûlayhi,* who was a staunch Sunni scholar. Indeed, he did not let anyone pray in his mosque if he did not agree with the beliefs of *Ahl-e Sunnat wa al-Jama'at*. In those days Qibla Alam's cousin Qadi Muhammad Fadil was studying with Mawlana Nabi Bakhsh Halawa'i in Lahore, and often his elder brother Qadi Muhammad Alam *Rahmatullah Ûlayhim* had to visit him in Lahore and take care of him. In this very

---

[213] Chak No: 18
[214] Baghwanpur,Tehsil Batala, Gurdaspur and worked in Lahore

mosque Mullah Muhammad Ramadan met Qadi Muhammad Alam *Rahmatullah Alayhima*. He was already impressed by the good conduct of the younger brother, Qadi Muhammad Fadil, so he was greatly impressed by Qadi Muhammad Alam *Rahmatullah Alayhim*. Consequently, a desire grew in his heart to meet the master of Qadi Muhammad Alam *Rahmatullah Alayhi* in Checheyan Sharif who had trained people to become such pious individuals.

Mullah Muhammad Ramadan *Rahmatullah Alayhi* was a humble and well mannered person. When he stopped at a hotel in Jhelum on his way to Checheyan Sharif, he took off his shoes and walked barefoot to Checheyan Sharif. This became his life practice, he would not wear any shoes during his stay there. In Checheyan Sharif he would help serve the *langar sharif*. Once due to extreme cold weather there was ice on the ground. Qibla Alam *Rahmatullah Alayhi* had to go for the call of nature and Mullah Ramadan *Rahmatullah Alayhi* thought that the master would need water so he took a water jug and waited outside. It was freezing weather and he could not bear the cold on his naked feet, so he put one foot on top of the other to fight off the cold. When Qibla Alam *Rahmatullah Alayhi* saw him in that state, he said, "Mullah Muhammad Ramadan who told you to bring the water, quickly leave the water jug and go inside?"

When Mullah Muhammad Ramadan was convinced that he had found the perfect guide, he requested Qibla Alam *Rahmatullah Alayhima* for spiritual guidance and eventually completed the Mujaddidiyya spiritual path under him. He attained such a level of piety, purification and worship that he was granted authorisation to guide the seekers of the truth. Afterwards he went to work in Iran. The exact duration of his stay in Iran is not known. The number of people who became his followers in Iran is also unknown. He was the first *Sangi* to have the table spread made in Allahabad and brought to Checheyan Sharif. He had the opportunity to travel with Qibla Alam *Rahmatullah Alayhi* on short journeys. In addition he had the good fortune of holding the reins of Qibla Alam's horse, but he made sure that his back was not towards his master in the process. During the journey he would also hold the staff of Qibla Alam *Rahmatullah Alayhi* and he would never put it on the floor but carry it instead.

Hadrat Sahib narrates that, "Once Qibla Alam told Mullah Muhammad Ramadan *Rahmatullah Alayhima* to carry out some task in Mirpur. I wanted to go with him but he said he could not take me without the consent of Qibla Alam *Rahmatullah Alayhi*. Qibla Alam *Rahmatullah Alayhi* stated that, "Mullah Muhammad Ramadan is going to Mirpur to carry out some task. What business does he (Hadrat Sahib) have there? He rides the horse very fast and might hurt himself." Permission was obtained from Qibla Alam *Rahmatullah Alayhi* by my grandmother on the condition that Mullah Muhammad Ramadan would hold the reins of the horse. When we reached,[215] I asked Mullah Muhammad Ramadan to let go of the reins so I could race the horse. He replied, "God forbid if anything should happen to you, both my worlds shall be ruined." After I had raced the horse and came back to him safely he said, "*Masha Allah.*"

Hadrat Sahib narrates that a friend of Mullah Muhammad Ramadan named Hafiz Sahib worked as a tailor in Lahore, and his wife was kidnapped. So Hafiz Sahib requested prayer and focus from Qibla Alam via Mullah Muhammad Ramadan *Rahmatullah Alayhima*. Hence Qadi Muhammad Alam was sent with Mullah Muhammad Ramadan *Rahmatullah Alayhima* to Lahore, to read *durud tunajjina* to retrieve the kidnapped lady. By the blessing of the *durud sharif,* she was found safe in the Ambala Camp and it transpired that a soldier had kidnapped her.

Mullah Muhammad Ramadan *Rahmatullah Alayhi* was tall and stocky, had a big bushy beard and shaved his head. He wore a long shirt and *dhoti* which was above the ankles. He wore a turban and wore customary pointed shoes. His practices consisted of; *tahajjud, ishraq, awwabin* and *dhikr* of *nafi asbat.* His reading consisted of the Holy Qur'an, *Dalail al-Khayrat, durud mustaghas* and *shajarah tariqat.*

During the partition in 1947, according to the boundary commission's decision, District of Gurdaspur was included in Hindustan. Hence Mullah Muhammad Ramadan *Rahmatullah Alayhi* had to migrate.[216]He settled in[217] where he was given some land and later died and was buried there.

Hadrat Sahib narrates that, "Once I went at the invitation of some *Sangis* to celebrate the *urs* of Qibla Alam,[218] where I met the son of Mullah Muhammad Ramadan *Rahmatullah Alayhima* called Abd al-Majid."

5) **Mawlana Muhammad Zaman** (d.1967) *Rahmatullah Alayhi*

---

[215] Mera Fathpur
[216] From Baghwanpura
[217] Narowal in Ramanh Wali
[218] Narowal

Mawlana Muhammad Zaman[219] *Rahmatullah Alayhi* was tall and well built, he neither looked slim nor fat. His hair was up to his ears. He was handsome and well dressed. In the beginning he was very particular about his appearance and wore expensive soft quality shoes. But when he began to follow the spiritual path his focus moved to other things. Thereafter he was always busy trying to adorn his inner self.

He gained his education from various teachers. For example in Lahore he studied with Mawlana Abd al-Aziz, in Gujjar Khan he studied[220] at the *madrasa* and he studied[221] under Mawlana Ghulam Nabi *Rahmatullah Alayhima*. Mawlana Muhammad Zaman was an excellent orator and he used to recite the poems from Mawlana Rumi's *Mathnawi*, Hafiz Shirazi and Miyan Muhammad Bakhsh *Rahmatullah Alayhim* in his speeches. He had a nice voice and recited the poems in an endearing manner. The mystical poetry coupled with the sweet voice of Mawlana Muhammad Zaman *Rahmatullah Alayhi* had a great impact and would make his audience cry. They would listen with great attention. Later due to his other duties Qibla Alam *Rahmatullah Alayhi* stopped him from preaching.

Khushi Muhammad and his brother lived near Mawlana Muhammad Zaman *Rahmatullah Alayhi* and had relatives in the Underhill, Dadyal area whom he used to visit often. These relatives of Khushi Muhammad were *Sangis* of Qibla Alam *Rahmatullah Alayhi* and through them he also became a follower. It was through Khushi Muhammad that Mawlana Muhammad Zaman became a *Sangi* of Qibla Alam *Rahmatullah Alayhima*. At that time Mawlana Muhammad Zaman was a student and would visit Qibla Alam *Rahmatullah Alayhima* whenever it was possible, this process continued throughout his education. Qibla Alam *Rahmatullah Alayhi* visited[222] on numerous occasions and many people became *Sangis,* including Khushi Muhammad's brother Nur Muhammad, and also Muhammad Ibrahim, Hayat Ali and so forth.

After completing his studies Mawlana Muhammad Zaman mostly spent his time with Qibla Alam *Rahmatullah Alayhima*. He would carry out the duties of the *langar sharif* and looking after the *Sangis* in Checheyan Sharif with great hardship. Miyan Ghulam Nabi was so impressed with the good manners and

---

[219] Mehta Losar, Dina, District Jhelum
[220] Aheer
[221] Padandori
[222] Mehta Losar

153

hard work of Mawlana Muhammad Zaman that he suggested to Qibla Alam *Rahmatullah Alayhima* that this young man would be good for the duties at Bawali Sharif and hence he should be sent there. This matter was discussed with Mawlana Muhammad Zaman *Rahmatullah Alayhi* and he stated that he wanted to stay with his master but on Qibla Alam's order he went to Bawali Sharif. He could only spend one night there, and with apologies he set off back to his master in Checheyan Sharif.

Mawlana Muhammad Zaman completed the Mujaddidiyya spiritual path with Qibla Alam *Rahmatullah Alayhima* and was authorised to guide people. He taught the name of Allah to many people including Hafiz Feroze al-Din *Kamili Wallay*, Muhammad Habib[223] and Master Abd al-Ghani.[224] Mawlana Muhammad Zaman's daily practice consisted of *tahajjud, ishraq, awwabin, khatam* of Hadrat Mujaddid and Hadrat Shaykh Abd al-Qadir Jilani *Rahmatullah Alayhima,* contemplation, *dhikr* of Allah, *nafi asbat* and meditations. His written *waza'if* included the Holy Qur'an, *Dalail al-Khayrat, durud mustaghas* and *shajarah tariqat*. He used to stay awake at night and would be awake especially before dawn and he encouraged the *Sangis* to do likewise.

After Qibla Alam's demise Mawlana Muhammad Zaman *Rahmatullah Alayhima* was married to the eldest daughter of his master named Hadrat Maqbul Begum. Hence Mawlana Muhammad Zaman *Rahmatullah Alayhi* was the brother in law of Hadrat Sahib and that is why he always used to call him, "Bahai Muhammad Zaman." Mawlana Muhammad Zaman, had three sons; Zahur Ahmad, Mushtaq Ahmad, Aftab Ahmad and a daughter.

Due to Mawlana Muhammad Zaman many incidents and saying of Qibla Alam *Rahmatullah Alayhima* have been preserved, most of which have been mentioned earlier. Mawlana Muhammad Zaman *Rahmatullah Alayhi* narrates that, "Once, after performing my tiring duties in Checheyan Sharif, I was about to get some much needed rest when Hadrat Qibla Mai Sahiba *Rahmatullah Alayha* told me to light the clay oven. I was really upset and thought to myself, "What have I let myself into, as I cannot have a moment of rest?" Qibla Alam *Rahmatullah Alayhi* was in his room having his siesta, suddenly the door opened and he addressed me and said, "We also used to do service for our master's residence." I was really embarrassed as Qibla Alam *Rahmatullah Alayhi* had read my thoughts." Mawlana

---

[223] Potha
[224] Dina

Muhammad Zaman *Rahmatullah Alayhi* passed away on Saturday 27ᵗʰ March 1967 in his ancestral village.[225] He was buried inside the chamber of the mosque. He had reserved this spot for his grave during his life time. Now that chamber has been turned into a shrine with a beautiful dome.

6) **Miyan Sattar Muhammad** (d.1956) *Rahmatullah Alayhi*

He lived in Amb in Dadyal where he was the *imam* and teacher at the local mosque. Even today a group of students learn *hifz* in this particular mosque under the supervision of Darbar Sharif. His house was a few yards from the mosque and he would take advantage of this, by offering his *tahajjud* prayers in the mosque. He often stayed in the mosque, as this is the speciality of Qibla Alam's *Sangis*.

After performing *ishraq* prayer he would start to teach his lessons, which normally continued until *dhur* time. He was well versed in both Arabic and Farsi. He was a good calligrapher and some examples of his writings are preserved in the Khanqah-e Sultaniyya. He recited the Holy Qur'an with proper *tajwid* however, his dialect suggested a heavy influence from the local language.

Miyan Sattar Muhammad and Sain Muhammad Halim *Rahmatullah Alayhima* were best friends. Indeed, Sain Muhammad Halim *Rahmatullah Alayhi* spent about sixty years of his life in the above mentioned mosque. He spent all of his time fasting during the day and praying at night. He had no other preoccupation. He was ill for a few months in this mosque and died there as well. Sain Muhammad Halim *Rahmatullah Alayhi* is buried in the Khidri mosque in Gulpur.

Miyan Sattar Muhammad *Rahmatullah Alayhi* was of slim stature, light complexion, had long hair and a beard according to the Sunnah. He used henna. He wore a long shirt and a *dhoti* which was above the ankles. He wore a four pointed cap with a soft cotton turban. He wore pointed shoes and liked to dress in white clothes.

Once Qibla Alam was visiting the Underhill area and Miyan Sattar Muhammad *Rahmatullah Alayhima* heard about the visit, and came to pay his respects to him. Prior to this they had never met. As Miyan Sattar Muhammad *Rahmatullah Alayhi* was a religious person he was impressed by Qibla Alam's way of living.

---

[225] Metha Losar

Although he was already a follower of a Naqshbandi Shaykh, upon seeing Qibla Alam's piety he became his devout follower. He completed his spiritual training of the Mujaddidiyya path under the supervision of Qibla Alam *Rahmatullah Alayhi,* and was granted authority to guide people.

Qibla Alam had great affection for Miyan Sattar Muhammad *Rahmatullah Alayhima* as he was sincere and dedicated to the observance of Shari'ah. Qibla Alam often visited Amb and during his stay he would hold special sessions with Miyan Sattar Muhammad *Rahmatullah Alayhima,* in which he would discuss the finer points of Shari'ah and the spiritual path.

Miyan Sattar Muhammad *Rahmatullah Alayhi* loved Qibla Alam's mystical commentary on some verses of the Holy Qur'an and would mention them in his own gatherings. Miyan Sattar Muhammad's household was religious and everyone was steeped in religious observance. Hadrat Sahib narrates that, "Once I went to Amb and went to Miyan Sattar Muhammad's house on his invitation. His daughter had a high fever. I overheard that her mother was instructing the girl to perform *tayyamumm* (ablution from dust) and read her prayers. The mother explained that as long as she was conscious, then the prayer was an obligation and this obligation continued until death. At the same time the mother encouraged her daughter and told her she would hold her and give her support whilst she did *tayyamumm* and read the prayer. From this one can deduce that all the members of the family were deeply religious people."

Miyan Sattar Muhammad's daily practice consisted of; *durud tunajjina* 313 times after *fajr, salatul tasbih* after *maghrib, ism-e zat, nafi asbat* and meditations. His written *waza'if* included one quarter *para* of the Holy Qur'an, *Dalail al-Khayrat* after *dhur* prayer and also *durud mustaghas* and *shajarah tariqat.* He also regularly read the *khatam* of Hadrat Mujaddid and Hadrat Shaykh Abd al-Qadir Jilani *Rahmatullah Alayhima.* He practiced *qaylula* (siesta) everyday.

Miyan Sattar Muhammad *Rahmatullah Alayhi* had a generous nature. He would greet the *Sangis* with love and embrace them with affection. He would consider it his good fortune to serve them. Jum'a Gul Afghani was his follower. Miyan Sattar Muhammad had permission to give *ta'wiz* from Qibla Alam *Rahmatullah Alayhima,* in fact sometimes he would write the *ta'wiz* for Darbar Sharif.

Miyan Sattar Muhammad had two sons, Muhammad Sadiq and Abd al-Haqq. Muhammad Sadiq was the son in law of Sain Abd al-Halim[226]in occupied Kashmir, as he was married to the daughter of Sain Sahib *Rahmatullah Alayhima* called Salima. Nowadays she is very weak. Before 1947 Abd al-Haq went to study with Sain Abd al-Halim's son, Kalu.[227] After partition Kalu went to occupied Kashmir whilst Abd al-Haq stayed with his teacher Mawlana Hafiz Mukam Din *Rahmatullah Alayhi* in Faisalabad and served him through his life. Miyan Sattar Muhammad *Rahmatullah Alayhi* passed away on 3rd September 1956 after *ishraq* prayer in Amb, and his grave is situated near the mosque.

7) Miyan Muhammad Ji (d.1949) *Rahmatullah Alayhi*

He lived in Dadyal,[228] where he was the local *imam*. He was a religious scholar and had a good understanding of matters of jurisprudence. He had studied with a learned jurist in his local area. He became a follower of Qibla Alam *Rahmatullah Alayhi* and completed his spiritual training under him. He obtained *waza'if* from Qibla Alam *Rahmatullah Alayhi* and was steadfast upon them throughout his life. It is related that in old age his eye sight was very weak. For this reason Sufi Faid Alam Sahib asked him to give him the copy of the *Dalail al-Khayrat,* but he refused saying that he was going to have an operation and Allah willing his sight would get better.

Miyan Muhammad Ji *Rahmatullah Alayhi* was a simple person with a keen sense of humour. He was also a man of integrity. Sufi Faid Alam narrated to Hadrat Sahib that, "Once Miyan Muhammad Ji *Rahmatullah Alayhi* was asked to perform a marriage ceremony but for some reason he refused. As a result the Chief of the village was incensed and said, "Miyan lives here and how dare he not perform the marriage ceremony." When this was related to Miyan Muhammad Ji *Rahmatullah Alayhi* he left the village straightaway and settled in the nearby village[229] and never went back. Miyan Muhammad Ji *Rahmatullah Alayhi* passed away[230] on 25th August 1949 was buried there.

8) Miyan Ghulam Muhammad (d.1933) *Rahmatullah Alayhi*

---

[226] Wangat
[227] Pathankot
[228] Thanpal
[229] Mera
[230] Thanpal

He lived belonged to the Kashmiri family.[231] He had relatives in Dadyal[232] and married from there. As a result he often visited that area and Qibla Alam *Rahmatullah Alayhi* often toured this area. After hearing the virtues of Qibla Alam *Rahmatullah Alayhi* he desired to meet him. When he met Qibla Alam *Rahmatullah Alayhi* he became a follower, took the *wazifa*, completed his spiritual training and was given permission to guide people.

Afterwards Miyan Ghulam Muhammad *Rahmatullah Alayhi* went to Kenya where he worked in the postal service. He had so much love for his master that as soon as he arrived back from Kenya, he went straight to Checheyan Sharif and stayed there for many days. It was his wish to sacrifice everything for his Master's family. In his view the pleasure of the master was better than anything else. Once he sent a parcel from Kenya which contained: a chandelier for the mosque, three watches, a pocket watch, wrist watch, a wall clock for Qibla Alam *Rahmatullah Alayhi*, a pen, an ink pot, and a velvet waistcoat for Hadrat Sahib who was a young boy at the time. Qibla Alam *Rahmatullah Alayhi* was free from desires and he gave one of the watches to a land steward, who used to come and meet him with respect. The other watch he gave to Mawlana Ghulam Nabi *Rahmatullah Alayhi* from Bār, and the third to the special servant Baba Faqir Muhammad Pothiyya *Rahmatullah Alayhi*. The wall clock was put up in the mosque but due to the simplicity and the lack of knowledge of *Sangis* it was soon ruined by misuse. The chandelier was hung up in the mosque. Miyan Ghulam Muhammad's wife had died and he only had one daughter named Hidayat Begum. It was his wish that his daughter would be raised and educated in the environment of Checheyan Sharif. But his mother-in-law did not agree with this idea as she gained monetary benefit from Miyan Ghulam Muhammad *Rahmatullah Alayhi* for looking after the girl, so she took the girl back home.[233]

Qibla Alam gave a normal winter shawl to Miyan Ghulam Muhammad *Rahmatullah Alayhima* as a present. Once on his way to Kenya he forgot his shawl in a hotel in Bombay which caused him great pain. In one of his letters to Qibla Alam *Rahmatullah Alayhi* he mentioned the pain he felt at the loss of the shawl.

Miyan Ghulam Muhammad *Rahmatullah Alayhi* was of medium stature with good limbs. He wore a *shalwar*, a *qamis* and a brown turban. He always dressed

---

[231] Suhawa
[232] Samlotha
[233] Samlotha

simply. It is said that he had some followers in Africa as he was an authorised person who spent a considerable time there. When he returned from Kenya he built a small mosque[234] and spent the rest of his life remembering Allah. His grave is situated on the northern side of the mosque.

When Hajji Abd al-Aziz[235] was appointed as the tax collector of Suhawa in Mangla Dam, the location of Miyan Ghulam Muhammad's grave was traced. According to Hajji Abd al-Aziz, Miyan Ghulam Muhammad's brother took him to the grave. The headstone had the date of death as 2nd March 1933 and two Panjabi verses were written which he read with great difficulty.

Aye mazar Ghulam Muhammadi ya rabb tahian khasmana,
Barkat Nabi Muhammad howey jannat vich takana.

Oh Lord, take care of this shrine of Ghulam Muhammad,
By the blessing of the Prophet Muhammad 鬒, may he reside in Paradise.

Wafat vich march unni so tehti, march doh mehina,
Aye mazar tayar mukammal rahmat nur khazina.

He died on the second of March 1933,
Shrine is completed and may it be the treasure house of mercy.

9) **Miyan Shah Wali** (d.1924) *Rahmatullah Alayhi*

He had the honour of being the first deputy of Qibla Alam *Rahmatullah Alayhi.*[236] Through him most members of his family became followers of Qibla Alam *Rahmatullah Alayhi.* One of his followers was disabled, but he had such passion for the *din* that he would walk on his crutches and go door to door to teach women to read the Holy Qur'an. It is related that both the son of Miyan Fath Muhammad, Miyan Fadal Ilahi and the disabled person were students of Miyan Shah Wali *Rahmatullah Alayhim.*

---

[234] Suhawa
[235] Chaksawari
[236] Kandor,Dadyal

159

Miyan Shah Wali was a well mannered and sincere follower of Qibla Alam *Rahmatullah Alayhima* He was steadfast upon his *wazifa* and worship. His forehead was very luminous. Once he became ill in Checheyan Darbar Sharif. Due to the high fever he was in agony and Qibla Alam could not bear to see his pain and began to massage Miyan Shah Wali *Rahmatullah Alayhima* in the dark. When Miyan Shah Wali realised that the person massaging him was none other than Qibla Alam *Rahmatullah Alayhima*, he immediately sat upright and said, "Sire, what if the river begins to flow in the opposite direction?" Qibla Alam *Rahmatullah Alayhi* replied, "It is our duty to serve."

It is said that later in life for some reason Miyan Shah Wali did not have the same type of connection with Qibla Alam *Rahmatullah Alayhima,* and subsequently his visits to Checheyan Sharif were less frequent.

Miyan Shah Wali *Rahmatullah Alayhi* passed away on Wednesday 24th Jeayth 1982 Bikrami and was buried in the village.[237] After his death Qibla Alam *Rahmatullah Alayhi* coincidently went to that area and one *Sangi* pointed to the grave of Miyan Shah Wali to him, Qibla Alam *Rahmatullah Alayhima* stopped at the grave and stood there quietly and then read the customary *Fatiha* and lifted his hands for prayer. Miyan Shah Wali *Rahmatullah Alayhi* used to wear white clothes. In the beginning he used to have long hair but later he shaved his head. He used to wear a cap. His temperament was somewhat intense.

10) **Mawlana Abd al-Aziz** (d. 1969) *Rahmatullah Alayhi*

The Qur'an reciters of Jand Sharif were well known in the Panjab and their form of recitation was distinctive. Many people who graduated from there spread its brand of Qura'nic recitation. Mawlana Abd al-Aziz[238] *Rahmatullah Alayhi* also started learning in this institution and recited in the same manner throughout his life. He was very confident and proud of his recitation.

Some of the teachers from whom Mawlana Abd al-Aziz learnt Arabic, Farsi and jurisprudence   included Mawlana Muhammad Abd Allah *Rahmatullah Alayhima* from Ladar who also happened to be the teacher of Hadrat Sahib. After completing his studies Mawlana Abd al-Aziz *Rahmatullah Alayhi* began to teach, give

---

[237] Kandor
[238] Kerhi Afghanan, District Jhelum

sermons and lead the prayers in a mosque in Sharqpur Sharif. He later performed these duties in Rawalpindi.[239]

In spirituality Mawlana Abd al-Aziz was a follower of Khwaja Ghulam Muhyi al-Din *Rahmatullah Alayhima* of Bawali Sharif, who was a renowned scholar and Sufi master of the time. Coincidently Mawlana Muhammad Abd Allah from Ladar was also a follower and a deputy, of Khwaja Ghulam Muhyi al-Din *Rahmatullah Alayhima* from Bawali Sharif. There is evidence to suggest that the father of Mawlana Abd al-Aziz was also a follower of Khwaja Ghulam Muhyi al-Din *Rahmatullah Alayhima*.

However, after the demise of Khwaja Ghulam Muhyi al-Din, Mawlana Abd al-Aziz became a follower of Qibla Alam *Rahmatullah Alayhim*. He completed the Mujaddidiyya spiritual path under him and became an authorised deputy. Mawlana Abd al-Aziz's following was based in Rawalpindi.

Mawlana Abd al-Aziz *Rahmatullah Alayhi* was a fanatical Sunni and was steadfast upon his beliefs. He would have no dealings with those people who did not have the beliefs of *Ahl-e Sunnat wa-al-Jama'at*.

Mawlana Abd al-Aziz completed the *Dalail al-Khayrat* with Qibla Alam *Rahmatullah Alayhima*. Apart from *Dalail al-Khayrat* he had permission to read other *waza'if* of the Mujaddidiyya path from Qibla Alam *Rahmatullah Alayhi*. Mawlana Abd al-Aziz was given authorisation at the same time as Mawlana Baqa Muhammad *Rahmatullah Alayhima* and hence he used to say that, "Hajji Sahib and I were born on the same day. Real life is the spiritual life and that life we began on the same day."

Mawlana Abd al-Aziz *Rahmatullah Alayhi* had an interest in natural medicine as he had studied some books on this subject. About *mooli* he stated, "This is dry and hot and removes phlegm (*har-un ya-bis qata' balgham*). He used to drink salted *lassi* (yoghurt) at night.

Mawlana Abd al-Aziz *Rahmatullah Alayhi* was tall and slim. He had a brown complexion and long hair up to his ears. He was well dressed, handsome and well built. He wore a long shirt, *dhoti* and a turban on top of his cap. He paid great attention to the postures in prayer. He would only leave the distance of

---

[239] Pajra

161

four fingers between his feet. He passed away in his village. His shrine is located near the road. His devotees have built a dome over his grave and hold an annual ceremony. On his gravestone the date of death is written as 1st *Muharram* 1389, AH/ 20th March 1969.

11) **Miyan Manzar Husayn** (d.1945) *Rahmatullah Alayhi*

He belonged to the learned Hashmi Qureshi family.[240] From the beginning this family had called the people to Islam. His early education was at home. It was not possible to find out from whom he gained further education. However it is evident from his knowledge that he had studied with some learned people. He became a follower of Qibla Alam *Rahmatullah Alayhi* in the Mujaddidiyya way and with hard work and self discipline he reached the rank of authorisation. He had extreme love for Qibla Alam *Rahmatullah Alayhi*. During the travels in the Underhill area he often accompanied Qibla Alam *Rahmatullah Alayhi*.

Miyan Manzar Husayn *Rahmatullah Alayhi* was a good poet of the Panjabi language. He was more proficient in poetry than prose. He could compose poetry instantly. When the mosque in Amb was rebuilt he composed some verses. In those days the mosques in the village were made of clay and so the first mosque in Amb was also built from mud. Baba Nawab Din *Rahmatullah Alayhi* from Amb had gone to work in some European country. He had the mosque rebuilt from bricks with his own money. The poems that Miyan Manzar Husayn *Rahmatullah Alayhi* composed were written inside the hall. These poems remained until the third re-building of the mosque. These verses were as follows:

Bakhshy rabb sawab nawab tahian,
Pasa kharch benam ghafar kita.

May the Lord grant the merit to Nawab,
Who spent his wealth in the way of Allah.

Changey mistri, neyk, sharif ānday,
Naqshajat mishal gulzar kita,

He brought good pious and noble builders,
And made it like a garden.

---

[240] Kajlani,Tehsil Kotli

Manzar Husayn vich amb nawab changja,
Andar zindigi āh didar kita.

Manzar Husayn in Amb the good Nawab,
In his own lifetime he saw Paradise.

Miyan Manzar Husayn *Rahmatullah Alayhi* through his poetry beautifully painted the picture of injustice and brutality of the Dogra rulers, during the independence movement of 1931 in the State of Jammu and Kashmir. These poems raised the morale of the freedom fighters. Unfortunately these poems were not published. However some of these poems have been transferred from generation to generation.

As he belonged to a religious family, Miyan Manzar Husayn *Rahmatullah Alayhi* was already a practising Muslim but the association with Qibla Alam *Rahmatullah Alayhi*, gave him greater depth and hence he was always in the state of the remembrance of Allah. Currently, Maulvi Ghulam Qadir from this family manages the local mosque. Miyan Manzar Husayn *Rahmatullah Alayhi* passed away on 9th September 1945 and was buried in his ancestral village.

Miyan Manzar Husayn *Rahmatullah Alayhi* was big and strong, had brown a complexion and long hair. He wore white clothes. He had a slight lisp but this did not affect his reading and daily practices. His daily practice consisted of the Holy Qur'an, *Dalail al-Khayrat, durud tunajjina, ism-e zat* 25000 times, *la illaha ill lallah*, the *khatam* and meditations. In addition he read *tahajjud, ishraq* and a*wwabin* daily.

12) **Miyan Fath Muhammad** (2nd) *Rahmatullah Alayhi*

He was one of the oldest *Sangis* of Qibla Alam *Rahmatullah Alayhi*.[241] He often stayed in the company of his master. He completed his spiritual training under Qibla Alam *Rahmatullah Alayhi* and was given authorisation. Many people benefitted from him and many miracles are attributed to him.

---

[241] Ganjpur, Dadyal

Miyan Fath Muhammad the 2nd *Rahmatullah Alayhi* was a great devotee of Qibla Alam *Rahmatullah Alayhi*. He held a high status in the local area. He was a well built young man and due to his handsome features he was often the cause of temptation but by the grace of Allah he was protected. Finally one day he castrated himself to prevent himself from sinning. When Qibla Alam *Rahmatullah Alayhi* found out what Miyan Fath Muhammad *Rahmatullah Alayhi* had done he was extremely upset, as this action was against the noble Shari'ah. Qibla Alam *Rahmatullah Alayhi* told him, "Although there was good intention behind this act nonetheless it is an act that is against the Shari'ah and fortitude, which is the soul of the Mujaddidiyya path."

Mawlana Baqa Muhammad *Rahmatullah Alayhi* the deputy of Qibla Alam *Rahmatullah Alayhi* narrates, "My first meeting with Qibla Alam *Rahmatullah Alayhi* in Amb was by a coincidence. Later I went to Chinar to become a follower, where Qibla Alam *Rahmatullah Alayhi* taught me how to perform *ism-e zat.* During the *dhikr* at night Miyan Fath Muhammad *Rahmatullah Alayhi* hit my heart so intensely with *Allah hu* that despite my heavy body, I bounced up many feet like a football. Afterwards I began to feel the taste and passion (for Allah) in my heart."

According to the narration of the local people, Miyan Fath Muhammad *Rahmatullah Alayhi* was the *imam* of a mosque the land of which had been donated by Master Sabir Sahib. Miyan Fath Muhammad *Rahmatullah Alayhi* died and was buried in the local cemetery, which is located at a distance from the main road.[242]

13) **Qadi Karam Din** known as **Qadi Kammah** *Rahmatullah Alayhi*

The village in which he lived is situated at the border between Azad Kashmir and occupied Kashmir.[243] This village is often the target of firing from Indian forces. During the Dogra rule this area was deprived of education but nowadays by the grace of Allah the people in this area are literate and politically well informed. People from this region have occupied the posts of president and prime minister of Azad Kashmir.

During the Dogra rule the Muslims in this area were not even aware of the basic tenets of Islam. The presence of Qadi Karam Din *Rahmatullah Alayhi* in this area was a godsend. He was better educated and more religious than other

---

[242] Ganjpur
[243] Lanjut,Tehsil Nekyal, before 1947 this village was a part of the Tehsil Mehnder in District Pūnch

people in this area and hence he would guide them. Qadi Karam Din *Rahmatullah Alayhi* came to the spiritual path via Baba Lal Din known as 'Lala'. Baba Lal Din was not literate and he was a rebellious and bad-tempered person. He had no interest in religion and instead loved taking part in fights and mischief. Most of the local people were aware of his unruly behaviour. Qibla Alam appointed his deputy Miyan Fath Muhammad *Rahmatullah Alayhima* in charge of the area[244] in order to guide the Muslims there. Due to the efforts of Miyan Fath Muhammad *Rahmatullah Alayhi* Baba Lal Din became his follower. Baba Lal Din already possessed the quality of determination and courage, and the very features which caused him to make mischief were now utilised for good actions. The news spread of Baba Lal Din's transformation throughout the area.

When Qadi Karam Din *Rahmatullah Alayhi* heard of Baba Lal Din's spiritual transformation he said, "I shall become the follower of that holy person who has converted 'Lala'." Therefore Qadi Karam Din *Rahmatullah Alayhi* became a follower of Miyan Fath Muhammad and was later given authorisation. Due to the influence of Qadi Karam Din, Khuda Bakhsh[245] also became a follower of Miyan Fath Muhammad *Rahmatullah Alayhima*. Later Khuda Bakhsh moved and is buried in occupied Kashmir.[246] Khuda Bakhsh accompanied Miyan Fadl Ilahi on his visit to Sirhind Sharif.

Due to the efforts of Qadi Karam Din *Rahmatullah Alayhi* there was a religious and spiritual awakening amongst the local populace. The effect of that work is still present, as most of his family is linked to the Khanqah-e Fathiyya and are carrying out their duties to guide the local people. Qadi Karam Din *Rahmatullah Alayhi* was physically a strong person; he had a thick beard and a brown complexion. He wore a white long shirt and a *dhoti*. His daily routine consisted of reciting the Holy Qur'an, *Dalail al-Khayrat*, daily section, *durud tunajjina*, the *khatam* of Hadrat Mujaddid and Hadrat Shaykh Abd al-Qadir Jilani *Rahmatullah Alayhima* and *ism-e zat* 25000 times daily. He loved to read the third *kalima* and many *Sangis* narrate that Qadi Karam Din *Rahmatullah Alayhi* would read it in his sleep as well. His love and dedication for his master was exemplary. Qadi Karam Din *Rahmatullah Alayhi* passed away in his village and his grave is situated inside a garden. According to Qibla Alam's instructions Qadi Karam Din's only son Ghulam Muhammad regularly performed his annual *khatam* in a simple manner. Ghulam

---

[244] Mehnder
[245] Chota Nar
[246] Chajla,Mehnder

Muhammad narrates, "Once I complained to Qibla Alam *Rahmatullah Alayhi* that I had pain in my knees. Qibla Alam *Rahmatullah Alayhi* advised me that, "Whenever you go into the *ruku* position in your prayers than grip your knees tightly and read *subhana rabbi al-Azim* at least seven times." By obeying his instructions my pain was gone."

14) **Miyan Abd al-Haqq** (d.1963) *Rahmatullah Alayhi*

He lived in Kartot, and he died in Tehsil Kotli. His date of birth could not be traced but the date of his death is 1963, he is buried in his village.[247] He belonged to a religious family. Presently the family continues on the path of learning. Most members of this family had studied at the *dar al-ulum* Deoband. In those days there was no centre of learning or provision for religious education in this area. Hence most of the students used to go to Deoband which offered some concession for the students from the state of Kashmir.

One branch of this family moved to Kulla and performed a great service for Islam in that area. Miyan Abd al-Haqq *Rahmatullah Alayhi* was a very learned person and was an expert in the Farsi language. He often used to teach Farsi books to his students. In addition he would teach the Holy Qur'an with its translation. Poetry is a major feature of this family and every member of the family has composed some poems, although they have not preserved or published their poetry. Nonetheless some people have memorised some of their poems. Miyan Abd al-Haqq *Rahmatullah Alayhi* performed the duties of the *imam* and orator in the central mosque.[248]

Miyan Abd al-Haqq met Qibla Alam *Rahmatullah Alayhima* by accident. He had set out to meet Qadi Sultan Mahmud *Rahmatullah Alayhi* from Awan Sharif but on the way the weather became extremely hot. When Miyan Abd Al-Haqq *Rahmatullah Alayhi* reached the Kharri Sharif area a hot wind began to blow. He panicked and decided to turn back. On the way back he reached the mosque[249] and decided to spend the night there. This mosque is still standing and has become a part of New Mirpur and is still known by the old name. The local people realised he was a stranger and enquired where he had been or where he was going. When Miyan Abd al-Haqq *Rahmatullah Alayhi* explained his situation the local people said,

---

[247] Kartot,Tehsil Kotli
[248] Samwar Sarohta
[249] Chati Hattainh

"There is a Qadi Sahib nearby in Checheyan Sharif, and he is a very pious person and you should meet him on your way back."

Miyan Abd al-Haqq narrates that, "When I arrived in Checheyan Sharif Qibla Alam *Rahmatullah Alayhi* had come out to say farewell to some *Sangi*, I did not know him so I enquired, "Where does Qadi Sahib live?" He replied, "This humble servant is addressed by this name." I explained my predicament and asked for his special spiritual attention. Qibla Alam *Rahmatullah Alayhi* replied, "This humble servant does have that ability but if you are interested and willing then we have received some things from our masters that we can tell you." Then Qibla Alam *Rahmatullah Alayhi* instructed me to make *dhikr* on the rosary and said, "If within fifteen days you feel an increase in your desire and passion (for Allah), then come again. The condition is that you are mindful of the etiquette of *dhikr*." After this I had a permanent connection with Qibla Alam *Rahmatullah Alayhi*."

Miyan Abd al-Haqq *Rahmatullah Alayhi* completed his spiritual training in the Mujaddidiyya path and was granted authorisation. Both the appearance and dress of Miyan Abd al-Haqq *Rahmatullah Alayhi* was according to the Shari'ah. He also had the distinction of being the first *Sangi* of Qibla Alam *Rahmatullah Alayhi* from his own family. Seeing his progression on the spiritual path, other members of his family also became attached to Qibla Alam *Rahmatullah Alayhi*. Miyan Abd al-Haqq *Rahmatullah Alayhi* was proud of the fact that he had guided his family to the source of guidance and turned them into real people. It is not an exaggeration to state that due to the link and training of Qibla Alam *Rahmatullah Alayhi* most members of this family have love for knowledge and observe the commands of the Shari'ah.

15) Sayyid Asghar Ali Shah (d.1983) *Rahmatullah Alayhi*

He came from a religious family and according to the family records he was born around 1910.[250] He studied up to Middle in his local village and then pursued his religious studies. Although he read *Kanz ud- Daqa'iq* and other religious books, he was unable to complete his studies. However, he did benefit from numerous teachers and became well acquainted with the essential matters of faith. In spiritual matters he was a follower of Hadrat Sayyid Muhammad Husayn [251] *Rahmatullah Alayhi*. In addition, he associated with Hadrat Sayyid

---

[250] Panj Garain, District Sialkot
[251] Alu Mahar Sharif

Muhammad Ismail *Karamanh Wallay,* and Sayyid Nur al-Hasan Shah[252]; both were followers of Hadrat Miyan Sher Muhammad Sharqpuri *Rahmatullah Alayhim* and were great masters of the period.

For thirty years Sayyid Ashgar Ali Shah *Rahmatullah Alayhi* performed the duties of the *imam* and orator at the central mosque.[253] One farmer from his village named Muhammad Taj, who perhaps had a spiritual connection with Sayyid Asghar Ali Shah *Rahmatullah Alayhi,* went to work as a harvest cutter where Qibla Alam's loyal *Sangi* Mawlana Ghulam Nabi *Rahmatullah Alayhi* from Bār lived.[254] Mawlana Ghulam Nabi *Rahmatullah Alayhi* could not stop talking about his master, so Muhammad Taj often heard discussions about Qibla Alam *Rahmatullah Alayhi* and became familiar with his personality.

Due to his previous link with Muhammad Taj, Sayyid Asghar Ali Shah came to visit him in and in the local mosque he met Mawlana Ghulam Nabi *Rahmatullah Alayhi.* Sayyid Asghar Ali Shah had heard some things from Muhammad Taj, about Qibla Alam and when he heard further information from Mawlana Ghulam Nabi a desire grew in his heart to visit Qibla Alam *Rahmatullah Alayhim.* So he quickly went to Checheyan Sharif, where he was very impressed with the lifestyle and spirituality of Qibla Alam *Rahmatullah Alayhi* and became his follower. He already had an interest in spirituality and so Qibla Alam *Rahmatullah Alayhi* made him go through the stages of the Mujaddidiyya path and at completion he gave him permission and authorisation. So Sayyid Asghar Ali Shah *Rahmatullah Alayhi* became a regular visitor to Checheyan Sharif.

It is related that Sayyid Asghar Ali Shah had a five pointed cap made for Qibla Alam *Rahmatullah Alayhima,* which he liked very much and it became the tradition amongst the *Sangis* and Hadrat Sahib to wear the cap.

Around 1928/9 there was a great flood in the state of Jammu and Kashmir and it affected its link with the Panjab province. During these days Sayyid Asghar Ali Shah was in Checheyan Sharif with Qibla Alam *Rahmatullah Alayhima.* So Qibla Alam *Rahmatullah Alayhi* advised him to go back home via Dangrot Sharif which was situated at the crossing where the Pūnch and Jhelum rivers met. A boat would take people across the river. He was also advised to stay the

---

[252] Kilyanh Sharif
[253] Burj Atari in Baigpur
[254] Chak Hakimanh

night with the *Sangis*,[255] coincidently that very day Miyan Sher Muhammad Sharqpuri *Rahmatullah Alayhi* passed away. The next day he had to catch a train from Dina to Sialkot. Chaudary Ali Akbar[256] was a follower of Sayyid Asghar Ali Shah *Rahmatullah Alayhi*, and apart from him other people also took benefit from him as well.

Hadrat Sayyid Nur al-Hasan was one of the benefactors of Sayyid Asghar Ali Shah *Rahmatullah Alayhima*. Once, he was staying with Hadrat Sayyid Nur al-Hasan *Rahmatullah Alayhi*, who recited the Holy Qur'an out loud and made a few mistakes in his recitation either intentionally or unintentionally. Sayyid Asghar Ali Shah *Rahmatullah Alayhi* was educated at the Numaniyya Institute and was well aware of the rules of recitation but out of respect he did not say anything. After the recitation Hadrat Sayyid Nur al-Hasan *Rahmatullah Alayhi* enquired, "Did I make any mistake in the recitation?" Sayyid Asghar Ali Shah *Rahmatullah Alayhi* replied with complete respect, "It seemed so on numerous occasions." He said, "Why did you not correct me?" Sayyid Asghar Ali Shah *Rahmatullah Alayhi* replied, "With respect, I am not here as a teacher but as a servant." At that point Hadrat Sayyid Nur al-Hasan *Rahmatullah Alayhi* stated, "I have not learned the Holy Qur'an from a teacher but through a supplication. One day I was in the company of Hadrat Miyan Sahib Sharqpuri *Rahmatullah Alayhi* and he asked me if I had read the Holy Qur'an or not? I replied, "I have not." Hadrat Miyan Sahib Sharqpuri *Rahmatullah Alayhi* then said, "Say I have read it." After that moment I was able to read the Holy Qur'an due to his supplication."

Hadrat Sayyid Nur al-Hasan mentioned that, "Before I became a follower of Hadrat Miyan Sher Muhammad Sharqpuri *Rahmatullah Alayhima*, I was a well known Shi'a speaker." Sayyid Asghar Ali *Rahmatullah Alayhi* enquired, "When you were a Shi'a speaker, you would have addressed many gatherings and brought them into frenzy. To make people laugh and cry is your expertise. So how was this possible without knowing the Holy Qur'an?" Hadrat Sayyid Nur al-Hasan *Rahmatullah Alayhi* replied, "Allah had granted me a powerful voice and I took full advantage of that. For example, once the Shi'a community invited a famous singer and speaker from Chakwal, who had a nice voice but when I recited poetry of lament his heart sank."

---

[255] Hill Sanyaranh
[256] Malla Warkanh

Sayyid Asghar Ali Shah *Rahmatullah Alayhi* was the epitome of integrity and had complete trust in Allah. He never asked anyone for anything throughout his life and would not express his needs to anyone, as he was content with what he had. He did not write or give *ta'wiz,* however he would recite the Holy Qur'an and blow on people. A month prior to his demise Sayyid Asghar Ali Shah *Rahmatullah Alayhi* became ill, and as his condition worsened he had to perform his prayers with signs. At the last moment his family relatives arrived without anyone informing them of his critical condition. At the time of his death he was reciting the 'Creed of Faith' and passed away on Monday 21st January 1983. His funeral prayer was led by Mawlana Hafiz Muhammad Alam from Sialkot, and he was buried in the family graveyard inside the raised platform along with his father and brother. Whenever Sayyid Asghar Ali Shah used to visit Miyan Nazir Ahmad[257] who was also a *Sangi* of Qibla Alam *Rahmatullah Alayhim,* he has since passed away. When Miyan Nazir Ahmad *Rahmatullah Alayhi* moved to Gujranwala this connection between the two *Sangis* continued, as he had played a part in introducing Checheyan Sharif to Sayyid Asghar Ali Shah *Rahmatullah Alayhi.*

16) **Miyan Muhammad Alam** (d. 1968) *Rahmatullah Alayhi*

Miyan Muhammad Alam *Rahmatullah Alayhi* lived in Kulla and his family came from Kotli[258] where most members of his family still reside. In order to spread the knowledge of the religion, his ancestors decided to move to Kulla. Apart from other matters it has been the tradition of this family to teach people about Islam. Miyan Muhammad Alam *Rahmatullah Alayhi* tried to increase the awareness of Islamic teachings amongst the local people and hence became well respected.

The leading elder and political and social activist Raja Karim Dad Khan was greatly impressed by the services rendered by Miyan Muhammad Alam *Rahmatullah Alayhi* in Kulla and requested him to move to village[259] so that the local people could benefit from his knowledge. Upon the constant requests of Raja Karim Dad, Miyan Muhammad Alam *Rahmatullah Alayhi* moved and was given land and a mosque was built for him. Miyan Muhammad Alam *Rahmatullah Alayhi* began his duties as the *imam* of the mosque and teaching children.

---

[257] Malla Warkanh
[258] Chowki Mung
[259] Manor

When Qibla Alam *Rahmatullah Alayhi* visited, Miyan Muhammad Alam *Rahmatullah Alayhi* was the *imam* of the mosque.[260] During those days Sayyid Ata Allah Shah Bukhari came to this village on the invitation of Raja Karim Dad. During the meal at Raja Karim Dad's home, Qibla Alam *Rahmatullah Alayhi* met Sayyid Ata Allah Shah Bukhari. This period was the beginning of the political awakening against the tyrannical rule of the Dogras in the state of Jammu and Kashmir. Sayyid Ata Allah Shah Bukhari made a speech and the brief meeting he had with Qibla Alam *Rahmatullah Alayhi* during the meal had a pleasant impact upon him. Qibla Alam *Rahmatullah Alayhi* mostly remained silent during the meal. Sayyid Ata Allah Shah Bukhari said, "We believe in saints on the condition that a person is a saint." After the meal when Qibla Alam *Rahmatullah Alayhi* went to the mosque, Sayyid Ata Allah Shah praised him as a saint.

Miyan Muhammad Alam's family environment was religious and he had a great interest in spiritual matters. His family's spiritual link was with Qibla Alam *Rahmatullah Alayhi*. For example, Miyan Abd al-Haqq from this family was a deputy of Qibla Alam *Rahmatullah Alayhima*, Miyan Muhammad Alam became a follower of Qibla Alam *Rahmatullah Alayhima* and completed his spiritual training under him and was granted authorisation.[261] Some of his followers include: Subedar Feroze Khan[262], Subedar Din Muhammad Khan son of Burhan Khan[263], Faqir Muhammad[264] and Jamal Din[265] the builder. Although Miyan Muhammad Alam's son, Azam Din had taken *bay'a* with Qibla Alam *Rahmatullah Alayhi* he completed his spiritual training under his father and became his deputy.

Azam Dim *Rahmatullah Alayhi* worked in the hotel of Baba Abd Allah Hindustani in Jhelum; this hotel is located near the courthouse. Hadrat Sahib visited this hotel on many occasions in order to meet Azam Din *Rahmatullah Alayhi*. It was from this hotel that Hadrat Sahib went to see *Amir-e Hizb Allah* Pir Fadal Shah Jalalpuri *Rahmatullah Alayhi,* who had come to address a gathering in Jhelum.[266]

Hadrat Sahib narrates that, "Azam Din's practice was to delay his *isha* prayer until he had finished all of his duties, after the prayer he would read the

---

260 Manor
261 The people from Pūnch,Palandari and Manor benefited from him
262 Kulla
263 Hillah Buryuyanh
264 Bobra
265 Manor
266 Jada

khatam of Hadrat Mujaddid *Rahmatullah Alayhi*." It was in this hotel that Azam Din *Rahmatullah Alayhi* met Muhammad Buta [267] the wrestler who later became the 'intoxicated Buta', his story has been mentioned earlier. Muhammad Buta had come to Jhelum to participate in a wrestling match and was staying in the same hotel. When Azam Din *Rahmatullah Alayhi* saw the sinful life of Muhammad Buta, he reprimanded him saying, "There was a Muhammad Buta in Gujarat from whose poetry people gain guidance and then there is this Muhammad Buta who has no thought about the afterlife. He thinks that the purpose of this life is fun and games and wastes his energies in useless activities." As a result Muhammad Buta became very emotional and asked Azam Din *Rahmatullah Alayhi* to guide him to a complete master. Azam Din suggested that he visit Qibla Alam *Rahmatullah Alayhima* and subsequently Muhammad Buta became Sain Muhammad Buta the 'intoxicated'.

Once Qibla Alam ordered both Qadi Muhammad Alam and Miyan Muhammad Alam to attend the *urs* ceremony in Bawali Sharif and also instructed them to visit Thani Sahib *Rahmatullah Alayhim* who would be there. Miyan Muhammad Alam *Rahmatullah Alayhi* narrates that, "There were many masters at Bawali Sharif and so we went out in search of Thani Sahib *Rahmatullah Alayhi*. We saw many guestrooms of the masters and each one contained things of comfort. But when we went to the guestroom of Thani Sahib *Rahmatullah Alayhi* we found it locked and there were some devotees waiting outside. Later Thani Sahib *Rahmatullah Alayhi* came out and walked towards the fields and sat on the earth under the shade of a tree. Thani Sahib *Rahmatullah Alayhi* shook hands with everyone and asked about their welfare. He asked us as well and expressed his surprise that we were namesakes, he said, "Both are Muhammad Alam."

Miyan Muhammad Alam *Rahmatullah Alayhi* passed away on 4th March 1968 in Manor and was buried on the western side next to the mosque. The real brother of Miyan Muhammad Alam *Rahmatullah Alayhi* was called Miyan Muhammad Rukn Alam; [268] he graduated from Deoband and held a post in the State Education Department. Miyan Muhammad Rukn Alam was handsome, well dressed and possessed a nice voice. He passed away in his village. According to Faqir Muhammad[269], Miyan Muhammad Rukn Alam also had taken *bay'a* from Qibla Alam *Rahmatullah Alayhi* and one of his sons named Sahibzada Muhammad

---

[267] Jullundur
[268] Chowki Mung
[269] Kulla, Kulla is situated between Palandari and Kotli

Tayyib was also a *Sangi*. Miyan Muhammad Alam's other brothers were Faid Alam and Abd al-Karim, who died during his studies at Deoband and was buried there. On the occasion of Abd al-Karim's death his brother Miyan Muhammad Rukn Alam wrote a very touching poem of lament.

17) **Miyan Fadal Ilahi** *Rahmatullah Alayhi*

He belonged to the same family as Miyan Muhammad Alam *Rahmatullah Alayhi* and was part of the family who migrated from Chowki Mung to Kulla, in Palandera. Like most members of his family Miyan Fadal Ilahi *Rahmatullah Alayhi* was both a poet and a preacher. The Friday prayers were not held in the villages, so one Friday he would lead the *jum'a* in the central mosque[270] and the following week at the central mosque in Kotli.

Miyan Fadal Ilahi took *bay'a* from Qibla Alam *Rahmatullah Alayhima*, and completed his spiritual training under his supervision and was finally granted authorisation.[271] At the request of the local people, during the month of Ramadan he would lead the *taraw'ih* prayer.[272] The famous leader of the Kashmir Independence Movement and the founder of The Suddan Educational Conference, Captain Khan Muhammad Khan known as 'Bare Khan Sahib' belonged to the Suddan tribe, and was a great devotee of Miyan Fadal Ilahi *Rahmatullah Alayhi* and would often invite him for a meal in his house. Both wives of Bare Khan Sahib were followers of Miyan Fadal Ilahi *Rahmatullah Alayhi*. Bare Khan Sahib was very impressed with the noble characteristics of Miyan Fadal Ilahi *Rahmatullah Alayhi* and greatly revered him.

Due to this close link with Miyan Fadal Ilahi *Rahmatullah Alayhi*, Bare Khan Sahib invited Miyan Fath Muhammad *Rahmatullah Alayhi*.[273] When Miyan Fath Muhammad *Rahmatullah Alayhi* was leaving Bare Khan Sahib and his father personally walked with the *Sangis* to bid them farewell. Indeed Bare Khan Sahib made his father carry the *Sangi's* bag in the hope that perhaps by carrying the load of the people of Allah, Allah would forgive his father's sins.

Miyan Fadal Ilahi *Rahmatullah Alayhi* had only one son Miyan Alf Din and would proudly state that his son was a '*sahib-e tartib*', which meant he had not

---

[270] Palandari
[271] He had followers in Kartot, Bang Duwara (Kharri), Uday Chathi and Kara
[272] Uday Chathi
[273] from Chinar to Chachen

missed more than five prayers in a row in his life. This is considered such a great virtue that many holy people desire to be '*sahib-e tartib*'. Miyan Fadal Ilahi's daily practice consisted of 25000 times *ism-e zat, la ilaha ill lallah*, daily section of *Dalail al-Khayrat,* the two *khatam* and so forth.

He was a sincere devotee of Qibla Alam *Rahmatullah Alayhi* and was peerless in his love for his master. This love was highlighted during the journey to the *urs* ceremony. For many years before and after the partition in 1947, there were no roads in the Kotli area. However, during the 1950s for military purposes a dirt track was made between Rawalpindi and Kotli. Due to the floods and the destruction of the bridges and erosion, this road became useless. For this reason the caravan of people going to *urs* ceremony in Checheyan Sharif would walk on foot and they had designated places for rest.[274] Along the way other *Sangis* would join the caravan. Then this big caravan would continue the journey whilst praying in congregation and making *dhikr*. It seemed as if it was a caravan of angels who had no other interest than to praise and reflect upon Allah's favours. This caravan was led by Miyan Fadal Ilahi *Rahmatullah Alayhi* and he was also the *imam* of the congregation. He would travel steeped in the love of his master to Checheyan Sharif. From this one can only imagine what a lofty position he occupied amongst the *Sangis*.

The demise of Miyan Fadal Ilahi *Rahmatullah Alayhi* was very enlightening. When his time of death approached and his family knew that he was about to die, his nephew Miyan Muhammad Alam *Rahmatullah Alayhi* began to cry. Miyan Fadal Ilahi *Rahmatullah Alayhi* enquired, "Why are you crying, I have handed all the people in my family over to Qibla Alam *Rahmatullah Alayhi* and I have no fear that you shall go astray?" Miyan Muhammad Alam *Rahmatullah Alayhi* replied, "Uncle, I used to share my problems with you, what shall happen after your death?" Miyan Fadal Ilahi *Rahmatullah Alayhi* answered, "Do not consider me dead, come to my grave and tell me your problems, I shall hear and understand everything you say." He instructed the people around him to make a circle of *dhikr*. He became unconscious, and when he regained his consciousness Miyan Muhammad Alam *Rahmatullah Alayhi* enquired, "Did you faint?" Miyan Fadal Ilahi *Rahmatullah Alayhi* replied, "Yes, I was unconscious but also a little intoxicated." In his last moments he remembered his dear *Sangi* Sain Ranjah from the Kokkhar area. According to

---

[274] The *Sangis* of Kulla would stop at Rajur, Saru'ah, Amb and Dadyal on their way to Checheyan Sharif

the family account Miyan Fadal Ilahi *Rahmatullah Alayhi* passed away at the age of 90, however his actual date of birth or death could not be traced.

Miyan Fadal Ilahi *Rahmatullah Alayhi* had great love for Hadrat Sahib so it was only fitting that he should be there at his funeral. By a divine coincidence Hadrat Sahib was travelling to visit Sufi Faujdar Khan who was posted there as a customs officer.[275] Incidentally Hadrat Sahib had to spend the night[276] and that very night Miyan Fadal Ilahi *Rahmatullah Alayhi* passed away. Hadrat Sahib was informed and went to the funeral. When Miyan Muhammad Alam *Rahmatullah Alayhi* saw Hadrat Sahib at the funeral, he remarked, "If the deceased knew you were coming he would have asked the Angel of Death to give him one extra day to live."

Miyan Fadal Ilahi *Rahmatullah Alayhi,* had travelled to Delhi where he visited the shrine of Khwaja Muhammad Baqi Billah *Rahmatullah Alayhi,* and he wrote about his travels and experiences in his dairy. Miyan Fadal Ilahi's son Alf Din was a simple natured person who had great love for Islam. He followed the spiritual path and his daily practice consisted of 25000 time *ism-e zat*, Qur'an Sharif, daily section of *Dalail al-Khayrat*, mediations and *khatams.* He would repeat each meditation for a week, and in order to earn lawful earnings he worked as a farmer.

Miyan Alf Din was the nephew of Qibla Alam's deputy Mawlana Hajji Baqa Muhammad. The wife of Bashir Husayn, Miyan Alf Din's son was the granddaughter of Mawlana Hajji Baqa Muhammad *Rahmatullah Alayhima.* Miyan Fadal Ilahi's other brother was called Miyan Ghulam Nabi *Rahmatullah Alayhima.* Both brothers were the brother-in-laws of Mawlana Hajji Baqa Muhammad *Rahmatullah Alayhim.* Miyan Ghulam Nabi had a son called Sufi Abd al-Qadir, who was married to the eldest daughter of Mawlana Hajji Baqa Muhammad *Rahmatullah Alayhima.*

Hadrat Sahib was married to the second daughter of Mawlana Hajji Baqa Muhammad *Rahmatullah Alayhi* who gave birth to the eldest son, Hadrat Hafiz Muhammad Abd al-Wahid known as 'Hajji Pir Sahib'. Mawlana Hajji Baqa Muhammad's third sister was the grandmother of Qadi Muhammad Rafiq[277]. It

---

[275] Chachen
[276] Lammiyan Pattiyan, Panjera
[277] Kurti

seems from these relationships that the Qureshi families are interlinked. [278] Miyan Ghulam Nabi *Rahmatullah Alayhi* is buried in his village. [279] Hadrat Sahib mentioned one of his supplications, "O Allah Almighty populate this house with your servants and engage your servants in Your remembrance."

18) **Mawlana Abd al-Khaliq Chachi** (d.1968) *Rahmatullah Alayhi*

Mawlana Abd al-Khaliq Chachi *Rahmatullah Alayhi* lived in District Attock.[280] His son Muhammad Ghawth narrates from his uncle who narrates from his father Gul Ahmad that Mawlana Abd al-Khaliq was born on a Friday in February 1878. Coincidently he passed away on Friday as well, at 4 am 26th April 1968. On the same day at 4 pm, and the funeral prayer was led by a famous religious scholar and spiritual master Mawlana Abd al-Ghafur[281] *Rahmatullah Alayhi*, he was buried in the local cemetery.

Mawlana Abd al-Khaliq *Rahmatullah Alayhi* was a pious scholar; he performed the duties of *imam*, teacher and orator in India.[282] Later he migrated and continued his duties as *imam*, teacher and orator.[283] Some *Sangis* of Qibla Alam *Rahmatullah Alayhi* lived in the same village and used to pray at Mawlana Abd al-Khaliq's mosque. Mawlana Abd al-Khaliq *Rahmatullah Alayhi* was very impressed with their good conduct. Through these *Sangis* he became aware of Qibla Alam *Rahmatullah Alayhi* and a desire grew in his heart to meet him. Mawlana Abd al-Khaliq was a follower of Hajji Sahib Targzai', who was a deputy of Akhund Sahib *Rahmatullah Alayhim* in the Qadiriyya order.

Mawlana Abd al-Khaliq narrates that, "Due to the *Sangis*, I wanted to visit Qibla Alam *Rahmatullah Alayhima*. I asked for directions to Checheyan Sharif from the *Sangis* and set off on my own. When I arrived at Checheyan Sharif Qibla Alam *Rahmatullah Alayhi* was sat amongst the *Sangis* in the mosque. I spent the night in the mosque and in the morning when I sought Qibla Alam's permission to return home, I was informed that he had gone to Mirpur on some important business. So I set off from Checheyan Sharif in the hope that I would meet Qibla Alam *Rahmatullah Alayhi* on the way and gain his permission to leave.

---

[278] Kulla, Kurti and Chowki Mung
[279] Chowki Mung
[280] Yasin Kalan
[281] Darya Sharif
[282] Gujarat, Kathaywar
[283] Chak No: 60, Sahiwal

In the brief meeting that I had with him (the previous night), I felt that Qibla Alam *Rahmatullah Alayhi* was a good and pious person. I met Qibla Alam *Rahmatullah Alayhi* as he was coming back from Mirpur.[284] I sought his permission to leave, he instructed me to face the direction of the *qibla* and focus on *la ilaha ill lallah* and empty my heart of all other things and inform him of the first thought that came to my heart. The first thing that came to my heart was 'dead in the hands of the living', *murda be dast-e zinda*. So I informed Qibla Alam *Rahmatullah Alayhi* and he instructed me to go back to Checheyan Sharif. As instructed I stayed a further few days. When I bid farewell to Qibla Alam *Rahmatullah Alayhi* at the appointed area, he embraced me and told me to avoid Mirpur.[285] As soon Qibla Alam *Rahmatullah Alayhi* bid farewell I was overwhelmed by grief and I could not stop crying. Wherever I looked I would see the image of Qibla Alam *Rahmatullah Alayhi*, I arrived in Sahiwal in this state. This feeling of longing for Qibla Alam *Rahmatullah Alayhi* kept increasing and I was forced to visit Checheyan Sharif again and this became my regular practice.

On my third visit I requested Qibla Alam *Rahmatullah Alayhi* for spiritual attention. As a result he very kindly taught me the teachings of the Mujaddidiyya path and finally gave me authorisation. Following this I was always in touch with him. I also benefitted from some senior *Sangis* such as Mawlana Ghulam Nabi from Bār and Khwaja Muhammad Akbar Ali *Rahmatullah Alayhima.*"

Mawlana Abd al-Khaliq narrates that Qibla Alam *Rahmatullah Alayhima* had instructed him to read the *khatam* of Hadrat Mujaddid *Rahmatullah Alayhi* after *asr*. "One day as I was reading the *khatam* in a quiet corner of the mosque, Qibla Alam *Rahmatullah Alayhi* was also inside the mosque and a person came and mentioned some court case to him. The thought came to my heart that matters of the world were being discussed inside the mosque. At that moment Qibla Alam *Rahmatullah Alayhi* said to the person, "Maulvi Sahib will be thinking to himself that worldly discussion is taking place in the mosque, what can we do, after all we are worldly people." When I heard this I was greatly embarrassed.

It has been mentioned earlier that once, Mawlana Abd al-Khaliq's body touched Qibla Alam *Rahmatullah Alayhi* as he was looking at a book and that part of his body began to cry out with 'Allah', 'Allah'. After mentioning the above incident

[284] Nala Khad
[285] Via Balaho Gallah, Kharri and avoid Jhelum and catch the train from Sara'in Alamgir

Mawlana Abd al-Khaliq *Rahmatullah Alayhi* stated, "No one should be under the allusion that we were impressed by miracles as in our view this is not proof of sainthood. The proof of sainthood is complete following of the Prophet. Let alone miss a *Sunnah,* we never saw Qibla Alam *Rahmatullah Alayhi* miss a desirable act. It was this perfection that attracted us to Qibla Alam *Rahmatullah Alayhi.*" Mawlana Abd al-Khaliq *Rahmatullah Alayhi* was a good calligrapher and examples of his writings on the theme of spiritually are preserved in Khanqah-e Sultaniyya.

19) **Sardar Diwan Ali Khan** (d.1943) *Rahmatullah Alayhi*

Sardar Diwan Ali Khan lived in Kulla and belonged to the Sadduzai' Pathan tribe. This tribe mostly resides in the Pūnch District or in the western part of Kotli. The people from this tribe have performed well in all walks of life, and in the past when education and employment was not common this tribe preferred to do military service. The deputy of Qibla Alam, Miyan Muhammad Alam *Rahmatullah Alayhima* migrated to the Kulla area. Subsequently Qibla Alam *Rahmatullah Alayhi* visited Kulla on numerous occasions and so this area benefitted from his presence.

Sardar Diwan Ali Khan was the *numberdar* (tax collector) of Kulla. He had a bad temper and would get into a rage over the slightest thing. Due to his temper he would create friction. The whole area knew of his bad temper, and therefore tried not to upset him. The Suddzai' tribe is renowned for its volatile temper and added to the position of tax collector made things worse for Sardar Sahib.

It is related that once Qibla Alam *Rahmatullah Alayhi* was in Kulla and Miyan Fadal Ilahi and Miyan Muhammad Alam *Rahmatullah Alayhima,* informed Sardar Sahib and expressed their desire that he attend the gathering. As Sardar Sahib was more interested in arguments and disputes he was not eager to attend the spiritual gathering. He pointed to his chest and said, "This is locked and nothing has any impact upon it, so what is the benefit of attending the gathering." When Qibla Alam *Rahmatullah Alayhi* went out to make *wudu*, some *Sangi* mentioned what Sardar Sahib had said. Qibla Alam *Rahmatullah Alayhi* did not comment however he enquired whether Sardar Sahib was married or a bachelor. Qibla Alam *Rahmatullah Alayhi* was informed that Sardar Sahib had two wives and was the father of girls but had no son. Qibla Alam *Rahmatullah Alayhi* remarked, "If it was not for the fear of Shari'ah he would roam in the jungles."

Soon something strange took place and Qibla Alam's focus began to bear fruit. Sardar Sahib's heart and mind was unlocked, which he had thought impossible. Sardar Sahib became a follower of Qibla Alam *Rahmatullah Alayhi*. As he entered the spiritual path all his previous negative characteristics were gradually removed. He followed the spiritual path with complete devotion and dedication and as a result he was given authorisation. Afterwards it was his practice that whenever Qibla Alam visited the region Sardar Sahib *Rahmatullah Alayhima* would come to pay his respects. His manner of visiting Qibla Alam *Rahmatullah Alayhi* was both unique and bold; as soon he would arrive he would touch Qibla Alam's feet and then wipe his hands over his face and then sit silently at the back of the gathering. He would not eat food from anyone's house and at meal times he would go home come and back later. He would stay with Qibla Alam *Rahmatullah Alayhi* until *asr* time then touch his feet and seek permission to leave.

Hadrat Sahib narrates, "Once I stayed at the home of Sardar Sahib with Qibla Alam *Rahmatullah Alayhima*. Afterwards I stayed at his house on numerous occasions. After the demise of Qibla Alam my main reason of going to Kulla was to visit Sufi Faujdar Khan *Rahmatullah Alayhima* who was posted at a nearby customs checkpoint. Sardar Sahib was a very close friend of Sufi Faujdar Khan *Rahmatullah Alayhima*. Apart from being *Sangis* both were deputies of Qibla Alam *Rahmatullah Alayhim*. Once I visited Sardar Sahib's home with Qibla Alam *Rahmatullah Alayhima*. In honour of the visit he presented Qibla Alam *Rahmatullah Alayhi* with a very beautiful buffalo but he refused. Sardar Sahib folded his hands and with a grieving voice humbly requested Qibla Alam *Rahmatullah Alayhima* "By not accepting the gift you have only increased this wretched person's misfortune." Seeing his state of despair Qibla Alam *Rahmatullah Alayhi* was obliged to accept his gift. This buffalo remained at Checheyan Sharif for many years."

Sardar Sahib *Rahmatullah Alayhi* was totally absorbed in his master and was always preoccupied in matters that would please him: sometimes he would personally carry beds or bedding many miles to present as a gift to Qibla Alam *Rahmatullah Alayhi*. Regarding his love for his master, Hadrat Sahib narrates, "After the demise of Qibla Alam *Rahmatullah Alayhi*, I was staying at the house of Raja Karim Dad[286] and Sardar Sahib *Rahmatullah Alayhi* came to meet me. At the time he was very old and when were we alone he requested that, "I am a servant of Qibla Alam *Rahmatullah Alayhi* and as such, love demands that you grant me permission to kiss the

---

[286] Manor

soles of your feet." Hadrat Sahib recalls, "I was shocked at his request and pleaded with him and reminded him of his senior age and rank." Once Kalu Khan invited Sardar Sahib *Rahmatullah Alayhi* to a gathering held in honour of a Shaykh. Sardar Sahib *Rahmatullah Alayhi* recalls, "I sat in that gathering for a few moments but the memory of Qibla Alam *Rahmatullah Alayhi* made me restless and I began to cry and I went home in that state as I remembered each meeting with him."

In the beginning Sardar Sahib *Rahmatullah Alayhi* was very temperamental and was an opponent of the spiritual path, being always drawn towards mischief. But after his link with the complete master, the positive side of his nature emerged. Subsequently he would be engaged in remembrance all the time. He allocated a special room in his house for worship and according to one narration he did seclusion for two months, all of these efforts were in order to purify his ego.

Sardar Sahib used to read all the *waza'if* that Qibla Alam *Rahmatullah Alayhima* had instructed him. His daily practices consisted of *dhikr* of 'Allah', 'Allah', *tahajjud*, *ishraq* and *awwabin*. Hadrat Sahib states that, "I had the opportunity to stay at Sardar Sahib's home and he used to read the Panjabi *shajarah tariqat* with such great passion and devotion, that during the recitation his long tresses would sway from one side to the other. When Sardar Sahib would reach the point where Qibla Alam *Rahmatullah Alayhima* was mentioned, he would shout *ill lallah* with such a force that often his cap would fall off his head.

Sardar Sahib *Rahmatullah Alayhi* used to read the *Dalail al-Khayrat* and in the copy that was in his use, the Monday section was worn out whereas the rest of the week was unused. This indicates that perhaps he was only instructed to read the Monday section. Sardar Sahib *Rahmatullah Alayhi* did not have a male heir and had two daughters. However his brother died and left two sons; Jan Muhammad and Wali Dad and a widow behind. When Qibla Alam *Rahmatullah Alayhi* visited Kulla he went to Sardar Sahib's home to express his condolence. A *Sangi* informed Qibla Alam that Sardar Sahib *Rahmatullah Alayhima* had become old and did not have a son. Unexpectedly Qibla Alam *Rahmatullah Alayhi* remarked, "Sardar Sahib should marry his daughters to his nephews and marry his brother's widow." The *Sangis* were puzzled by this suggestion but Sardar Sahib was such a devotee of his master that he could not refuse the order of Qibla Alam *Rahmatullah Alayhima*. Sardar Sahib *Rahmatullah Alayhi* did as he was commanded and Allah granted him a son named

Muhammad Sarwar, who kept a link with Hadrat Sahib. Muhammad Sarwar has also passed away.

Sardar Sahib's body was slim like his son Muhammad Sarwar. He had a light complexion, hair down to his shoulders, a wide forehead, and was of medium height. He dressed in a long shirt and *dhoti* and wore a five pointed cap. He passed away on 18th April 1943 in his ancestral village, Kulla and was buried near his house. His grave is made with bricks and the headstone is made of marble.

20) **Mawlana Hajji Baqa Muhammad** (d.1976) *Rahmatullah Alayhi*

His noble father was called Maulvi Ghulam Ali *Rahmatullah Alayhi*. Mawlana Hajji Baqa Muhammad *Rahmatullah Alayhi* was from the learned Qureshi Hashmi family and propagating Islam has been the main feature of this family. Wherever the family settled it took an active interest in promoting Islam. In the beginning the family lived in a village in Gujjar Khan [287] A mosque from the Mughal Emperor Akbar's period still stands in that area. The passion for religion led one branch of the family to migrate to the state of Jammu and Kashmir and settle in Kotli.[288] Later some members of the family moved to the nearby village of Nakka Kurti and Mawlana Baqa Muhammad *Rahmatullah Alayhi* belonged to this branch of the family. One pious member of the family named Hafiz Muhammad Zahid *Rahmatullah Alayhi*, is buried in the Ghawthiyya mosque.[289]

According to the family tradition Mawlana Baqa Muhammad *Rahmatullah Alayhi* began his education at home. For further studies he went to Qadi Nadir Ali *Rahmatullah Alayhi*.[290] Mawlana Baqa Muhammad *Rahmatullah Alayhi* recalls, "Qadi Nadir Ali *Rahmatullah Alayhi* was an expert in various sciences and had a deep understanding of matters." In particular he specialised in the art of calligraphy and measurement. Mawlana Baqa Muhammad *Rahmatullah Alayhi* learned calligraphy from him as well. Mawlana Baqa Muhammad *Rahmatullah Alayhi* relates, "The whole area was in the grip of poverty. The people were dying for a morsel of food." Due to the lack of finances he had to leave his kind teacher Qadi Nadir Ali *Rahmatullah Alayhi*. Mawlana Baqa Muhammad *Rahmatullah Alayhi* often related the following incident that would

---

[287] Suy'ian Hafizain
[288] Dhok Mohra, next to Kurti
[289] Baliyah
[290] Potha Bungash

bring tears to his eyes, "Once we were collecting bread from various houses when a dog bit my leg and the scar remained with me for the rest of my life."

Afterwards Mawlana Baqa Muhammad *Rahmatullah Alayhi* went to study in Gujjar Khan[291] and completed his studies there. His teacher was a very learned person and Mawlana Baqa Muhammad *Rahmatullah Alayhi* was proud of his teacher's vast knowledge.

Mawlana Baqa Muhammad *Rahmatullah Alayhi* had great interest in farming and alongside his duties as *imam* and orator he performed farming duties. He held a prominent post in the Anjuman-e Islamiyya, in the State of Jammu and Kashmir. He was gifted in both matters of *din* and *dunya*.

Mawlana Baqa Muhammad's meeting with Qibla Alam *Rahmatullah Alayhi* happened in this manner. He was performing his duties on behalf of the Anjuman-e Islamiyya in the Underhill area. One day he performed his *dhur* prayers in the mosque[292] and by a coincidence met Sain Muhammad Hasan *Zulfain Wallay Rahmatullah Alayhi*. Mawlana Baqa Muhammad was very impressed the way Sain Muhammad Hasan *Rahmatullah Alayhims* performed his prayer and enquired who his master was. Sain Muhammad Hasan explained that he was a follower of Qibla Alam *Rahmatullah Alayhima* who happened to be visiting the Underhill area.[293] Mawlana Baqa Muhammad *Rahmatullah Alayhi* states that, "Although Sain Muhammad Hasan *Rahmatullah Alayhi* was illiterate, he left me speechless. In answer to my query, "Whatever your master had instructed to you to read tell me so I could read it as well," Sain Muhammad Hasan *Rahmatullah Alayhi* replied, "If a patient is cured by a physician's remedy he does not became a physician himself. The best thing he can do is to direct the patient seeking a cure towards the physician."

By divine coincidence the next day Mawlana Baqa Muhammad met Qibla Alam *Rahmatullah Alayhima* in the Amb mosque. Subsequently Mawlana Baqa Muhammad became devoted to Qibla Alam *Rahmatullah Alayhima* and stayed with him. When Qibla Alam travelled, Mawlana Baqa Muhammad *Rahmatullah Alayhima* would

---

[291] Majutha
[292] Kandor
[293] And could be found either in Samlotha, Amb or Chinar

182

carry the box of his master's books. Gradually Qibla Alam trained Mawlana Baqa Muhammad *Rahmatullah Alayhima* and gave him authorisation.[294]

During the summer season the people would travel from these settlements to find fresh pastures for their livestock. The *Sangis* would gather there and make abundant *dhikr* of Allah. Mawlana Hajji Baqa Muhammad *Rahmatullah Alayhi* had a beautiful voice and when he sang poems his audience would be in ecstasy.

Mawlana Hajji Baqa Muhammad's daily practice consisted of 4 units of *tahajjud,* two units of *wudu* prayer, 4 units of *ishraq* and 4 units of *awwabin.* In addition he read a quarter *para* of the Holy Qur'an, *Dalail al-Khayrat* (daily section), *Hizb al-Azam* (daily section), *durud mustaghas, Awrad-e Fathiyya, dua'-e Suryani, Qasida Ghawthiyya, Chel Kaf* and the *Hizb al-Bahr.* He tried to read the written *wazifa* between *fajr* and *ishraq.* He recited *durud tunajjina* 313 times, *khatam-e khawajgan* and *khatam* of Hadrat Mujaddid *Rahmatullah Alayhi* before *fajr.* He would do the breathing *dhikr* of *la ilaha illallah* 500 times every day and *dhikr* of 'Allah' as well.

Mawlana Hajji Baqa Muhammad narrates that, "Qibla Alam *Rahmatullah Alayhima* instructed me, "Maulvi Sahib, lead the prayers." We Maulvi people jump at such an opportunity. So I led the prayer for a few days and tried my best to pronounce the words correctly and perform the postures with care. However after a few days Qibla Alam *Rahmatullah Alayhi* said, "Maulvi Sahib, I shall recite the Holy Qur'an and you listen." I knew that this was a subtle way of correcting my mistakes." Similarly, Qibla Alam showed Mawlana Hajji Baqa Muhammad *Rahmatullah Alayhima* how to tie the *dhoti* properly.

Mawlana Hajji Baqa Muhammad *Rahmatullah Alayhi* passed away in his village on 15th August 1976 and was buried next to the mosque. Due to the extension of the University Mosque, his grave was relocated nearby and a tomb was built over it. One of his loyal followers, Mir Baz known as Sain Baja who was buried next to him has also been relocated towards his feet outside the shrine at the western side.

---

[294] He had followers in Saran, Baglyaz, Chandimorr, and Dhara Mohra in occupied Kashmir. In addition he had a large following in the rural community of Tehsil Mehnder

Mawlana Hajji Baqa Muhammad's love for his master's family can be witnessed by the following incident. Mai Sharfain was keen to get Hadrat Sahib married and mentioned the matter to Qibla Alam *Rahmatullah Alayhi*, who instructed her to ask Hadrat Sahib's grandmother. When Hadrat Sahib's grandmother was asked she said, "Ask Hajji Baqa Muhammad."

Finally when Mawlana Hajji Baqa Muhammad *Rahmatullah Alayhi* was contacted about the matter he replied, "The wishes of this family is an obligation upon me however the present situation is that I have two daughters; the eldest I have promised to my sister and with regards to the youngest I had the intention to give her to my nephew. However I have not expressed this desire of mine nor have I given my word in this matter. If my children can be accepted for my master's family then that is a great fortune, I am willing to give my daughter." So at the request of Mai Sharfain the matter was agreed. Mawlana Hajji Baqa Muhammad *Rahmatullah Alayhi* was leaving for Bombay and left a message for his mother that, "If someone comes from my master's family with the proposal for my daughter then accept it with gratitude." Therefore Miyan Fath Muhammad and Baba Faqir Pothiyya *Rahmatullah Alayhima* came from Checheyan Sharif with the engagement dress.

Later when Qibla Alam *Rahmatullah Alayhi* visited this area, he enquired, "Where is our daughter?" He then stroked the girl's head. Subsequently Mawlana Hajji Baqa Muhammad *Rahmatullah Alayhi* became the father-in-law of Hadrat Sahib and the grandfather of Hajji Pir Sahib. On his way to Bombay Mawlana Hajji Baqa Muhammad visited the shrine of Sain Tawwakal Shah *Rahmatullah Alayhima* in Ambala, he relates, "When I meditated at the shrine I saw Sain Sahib, he was in the state of *ihram* and it seemed as if he had recently had a haircut."

Mawlana Hajji Baqa Muhammad *Rahmatullah Alayhi* was of medium height and slim stature. He had a brown complexion, long hair and for some time he used to dye his hair but later used henna. He wore a *shalwar* and *qamis* and wore a cap but often wore a green turban on top of his cap.

Mawlana Hajji Baqa Muhammad's family had traditionally written poetry and he was a good poet of the Panjabi language. He could compose poems spontaneously, and his poems strung the pearls of consul and guidance together. His eldest son Sahibzada Muhammad Yusuf was also a good poet. Both father and son would compose poems in their correspondence. Some people would take advantage of this ability of Mawlana Hajji Baqa Muhammad *Rahmatullah Alayhi,*and would ask him to write letters in poetry to their far off relatives. He principally wrote didactic poetry which was very evocative and hence very effective.

Mawlana Hajji Baqa Muhammad took great interest in the first shrine of Qibla Alam *Rahmatullah Alayhima* and during those days he published a poster for his mosque in Nakka Kurti, and made the following Farsi couplet the subject of his discussion:

> *Pai'-e ma lang ast wa manzil bas ba'id,*
> *Dast-e ma kuta wa khirma bar nakhil.*

Our feet are crippled and the destination far away,
Our hands are short and the dates are on the palm tree.

With some alteration to the famous couplet attributed to Khwaja Gharib Nawaz Chishti Ajmeri *Rahmatullah Alayhi,* he chose this couplet for Qibla Alam's shrine.

> *Naqisain ra pir-e kamil, salikanh ra rahnuma,*
> *Faiz bahksh-e ganj-e mahkhfi qibla sultan-e ma.*

The perfect guide of the incompetent and the guide of the seekers,
The bestower of hidden treasures is our master.

The list of some of the followers of Mawlana Hajji Baqa Muhammad includes: Sain Muhammad Ashraf who was the personal attendant of both Qibla Alam and Hadrat Sahib *Rahmatullah Alayhim.* He is buried at the Khidri mosque. Hajji Sakhi Walayat[295] *Rahmatullah Alayhi,* who was a wealthy merchant, Mir Baz, Mullah Lala and Nur Muhammad known as Nura, these three brothers and Mullah Lala in particular recited the Holy Qur'an well. In addition, his followers included Qadi Allah Ditta[296] and Mir Muhammad[297] and so forth.

---

[295] Chajla,Mehnder
[296] Chajla
[297] Checheyan Bandiyanh

185

For some time after Qibla Alam's demise Hajji Mawlana Baqa Muhammad *Rahmatullah Alayhima* guided seekers of the path, gave them *waza'if* and amulets. He performed exorcisms and as result the people who were possessed were cured by him. In addition for a short time, he performed the duty of *imam* in the army.

Mawlana Hajji Baqa Muhammad *Rahmatullah Alayhi* wrote a book called *Tohfa-e Sultaniyya* that was published in 1993. The story behind its publication has been mentioned earlier. From the book one can assess Mawlana Hajji Baqa Muhammad's knowledge of spirituality, love and devotion for Qibla Alam *Rahmatullah Alayhima* and his ability as an author.

Mawlana Hajji Baqa Muhammad *Rahmatullah Alayhi* had two sons: Muhammad Yusuf and Muhammad Manzur, the youngest of which has died. Mawlana Hajji Baqa Muhammad *Rahmatullah Alayhi* married twice and from his second wife he only had one daughter, Sa'dat Sultana and from his first wife he had two daughters, the eldest was married to Sufi Abd al-Qadir, son of Miyan Ghulam Nabi and she has passed away. His second daughter was married to Hadrat Sahib and she passed away on 6/7 August at midnight in 1997 and is buried in Khanqah-e Sultaniyya, Jhelum.

21) **Khwaja Muhammad Akbar Ali** (1889-1971) *Rahmatullah Alayhi*

He was born on 18th Ramadan al-Mubarak 1314, AH corresponding to 21st February 1889/ Pahgan 1953 Bikrami.[298] His father's name was Khwaja Muhammad Shahbaz Sultan Qadiri *Rahmatullah Alayhi*. It is said that he was an expert in the knowledge of *jufar* (astronomy) and had predicted even before his son's birth that he would have a bright future.

Initially Khwaja Muhammad Akbar Ali *Rahmatullah Alayhi* was recruited in the army in the Signal Corps. Afterwards he worked in the customs division. He was very handsome, well dressed and loved cleanliness. He was interested in spiritual matters from the beginning and sought a master for spiritual discipline. He became a follower of Sayyid Muhammad Jafar Ali Shah, the custodian of Shah Dula Gujarati *Rahmatullah Alayhima* in the Naqshbandiyya path. According to Muhammad Sadiq Qasuri in his appendix to the *Tazkira-e Mashaiykh Naqshbandiyya* by Allama Nur Bakhsh Tawwakali, "Sufi (Khwaja)

---

[298] Kala Ban, Kotli, Tehsil Rajouri

Muhammad Akbar Ali had authorisation from his master and at the time of his death, Sayyid Muhammad Jafar Ali Shah *Rahmatullah Alayhima* had instructed his followers to consult him for further training and development."

One of Qibla Alam's trusted *Sangis,* Sufi Faujdar Khan worked in the customs department and through this job he met and became familiar with Khwaja Muhammad Akbar Ali *Rahmatullah Alayhim.* Both were great devotees of their respective masters and consequently became close friends. Sufi Faujdar Khan had heard Qibla Alam *Rahmatullah Alayhima* mention the prayer mat made of lion's skin and thought that perhaps he desired it. In reality Qibla Alam *Rahmatullah Alayhi* had no desire other than Allah. Once Sufi Faujdar Khan was posted[299] and he found out that Khwaja Muhammad Akbar Ali *Rahmatullah Alayhima,* had a prayer mat made of tiger's skin. So he contacted Khwaja Muhammad Akbar Ali and requested the prayer mat for Qibla Alam *Rahmatullah Alayhima,* but he apologised and stated that he could not give it as he wanted to present it to his master Sayyid Muhammad Jafar Ali Shah *Rahmatullah Alayhi.*

Khwaja Muhammad Akbar Ali *Rahmatullah Alayhi* relates that, "Following this incident I saw a dream about Checheyan Sharif and the desire grew in my heart to visit Qibla Alam *Rahmatullah Alayhi.* One day I set off with my servant Salāh Muhammad with the prayer mat to visit Checheyan Sharif. When I reached Checheyan Sharif I left the prayer mat outside and went to meet Qibla Alam *Rahmatullah Alayhi,* who enquired, "Where is the prayer mat?," So I took the prayer mat to Qibla Alam *Rahmatullah Alayhi.* Later I requested Qibla Alam *Rahmatullah Alayhi* to grant me his spiritual attention and blessings. Qibla Alam *Rahmatullah Alayhi* replied, "First of all go and offer your *Fatiha* for your master as he has passed away." Khwaja Muhammad Akbar Ali *Rahmatullah Alayhi* states that he did not know that his master had passed away. Later Qibla Alam *Rahmatullah Alayhi* accepted me on the path and trained me. I was then granted authorisation."

Whatever exercises or *waza'if* Qibla Alam gave to Khwaja Muhammad Akbar Ali *Rahmatullah Alayhima* he recorded it in his diary. The original diary is in the possession of his family, however a photocopy is preserved in the Khanqah-e Sultaniyya. The prayer mat that Khwaja Muhammad Akbar Ali *Rahmatullah Alayhi* gave as a gift was also kept at the Khanqah-e Sultaniyya but over time it was cut into pieces and given to people so nothing remains from it.

---

[299] Paghawari Gali

When Qibla Alam *Rahmatullah Alayhi* granted him authorisation, he advised Khwaja Muhammad Akbar Ali *Rahmatullah Alayhi* to guide followers for six months in the State of Jammu and Kashmir, and six months in the Panjab. Khwaja Muhammad Akbar Ali *Rahmatullah Alayhi* followed this instruction to his dying day and so he had thousands of followers in both Kashmir and the Panjab.

Hadrat Sahib narrates, "When Qibla Alam *Rahmatullah Alayhi* granted authorisation to Khwaja Muhammad Akbar Ali, he instructed Maulvi Fadal Ahmad *Rahmatullah Alayhima*, "Take your *pir* to the Panjab." Maulvi Fadal Ahmad *Rahmatullah Alayhi* replied, "There are many learned and pious people in the Panjab and the people laugh at the Kashmiri language." Qibla Alam *Rahmatullah Alayhi* replied, "It is not your task to chase people, only deal with those people who come to seek your guidance." So Maulvi Fadal Ahmad set off with his master Khwaja Muhammad Akbar Ali and according to custom Qibla Alam *Rahmatullah Alayhim* came to the acacia tree to bid farewell to them. Qibla Alam *Rahmatullah Alayhi* said, "Shahbaz (Falcon) go to the Panjab, deputy after deputy and deputy after deputy." It is a coincidence that Khwaja Muhammad Akbar Ali's father is named Shahbaz as well.

The people of Kashmir referred to Khwaja Muhammad Akbar Ali *Rahmatullah Alayhi* as *'Sain'* and the people of Panjab as *'Kashmir Wallay Pir'*, however Qibla Alam *Rahmatullah Alayhi* called him 'Maulvi Sahib'. Qibla Alam's farewell words came true and Khwaja Muhammad Akbar Ali *Rahmatullah Alayhima* became very popular in the Panjab region. Some of his deputies in the Panjab include:

Maulvi Fadal Din,[300] Maulvi Fadal Din,[301] Maulvi Fadal Ahmad[302], Hafiz Ibrahim,[303] Maulvi Sayd Ahmad Yasin,[304] Babu Muhammad Nazir, Lahore and Faqir Shah Harni in occupied Kashmir *Rahmatullah Alayhim*. In the appendix of *Tazkira-e Mashaiykh Naqshbandiyya*, 45 deputies of Khwaja Muhammad Akbar Ali *Rahmatullah Alayhi* are mentioned. The appendix in the book covers Khwaja Muhammad Akbar Ali's religious and spiritual knowledge aas well as national contributions.

---

[300] Chak: 73
[301] Chak 45
[302] Khuthora
[303] Khuthora
[304] Kalan

Due to the partition in 1947 Khwaja Muhammad Akbar Ali *Rahmatullah Alayhi* had to migrate from his ancestral home.[305] His authorised deputy Maulvi Fadal Ahmad came to take him to Narowal but Khwaja Muhammad Akbar Ali *Rahmatullah Alayhima*, considered it important to assess the situation before moving there. After Maulvi Fadal Ahmad had made the necessary arrangements Khwaja Muhammad Akbar Ali *Rahmatullah Alayhima* moved to Narowal.

One of the reasons why Narowal was chosen is that it had modern facilities such as schools, hospital and a railway station. For six months Sufi Ahmad Din *Rahmatullah Alayhi* played host to Khwaja Muhammad Akbar Ali's group which was a very courageous thing to do at that critical time. During such times of chaos, to show hospitality could only be possible if the relationship was based on extreme love and affection. Afterwards, a house was allocated to Khwaja Muhammad Akbar Ali *Rahmatullah Alayhi* in Narowal for him to reside. This particular house once belonged to a Hindu station master. On the insistence of the *Sangis* Hadrat Sahib visited Narowal during that period. Khwaja Muhammad Akbar Ali would celebrate the *urs* ceremony of Qibla Alam *Rahmatullah Alayhima* in his home village, however due to migration it was decided to continue the ceremony in Narowal and so Hadrat Sahib was invited to attend. During this period Mufti Muhammad Amin Sahib from Faisalabad became acquainted with Hadrat Sahib.

Khwaja Muhammad Akbar Ali had presented a woollen shirt as a gift to Qibla Alam *Rahmatullah Alayhima* which he wore for some time. This woollen shirt was then hung up on a hook. Afterwards Hadrat Qibla Mai Sahiba *Rahmatullah Alayha* gave that shirt to Khwaja Muhammad Akbar Ali *Rahmatullah Alayhi* as a souvenir. During the partition in 1947 Khwaja Muhammad Akbar Ali *Rahmatullah Alayhi* carried that shirt on his head and protected it with his life. The shirt is now preserved by his family in Pakpattan Sharif.

Khwaja Muhammad Akbar Ali used to state about Qibla Alam *Rahmatullah Alayhima*, "That he was like a vintage wine; whoever came near him became intoxicated. Many of his intoxicated lovers roam in the Bannu area but he himself remained sober."

After staying in Narowal for some time, Khwaja Muhammad Akbar Ali *Rahmatullah Alayhi* permanently moved to Pakpattan Sharif, where he built a

---

[305] Via Kotli and Behari

religious institute called Dar al-Ulum Naqshbandiyya Ridiwiyya. He passed away on Wednesday 24th November 1971/ 5th Sha'ban 1391 AH at 11 a.m. and was buried next to the mosque.

According to Hadrat Sahib, Khwaja Muhammad Akbar Ali *Rahmatullah Alayhi* sometimes used to write Panjabi poetry. One of his authorised deputies Maulvi Fadal Din[306] *Rahmatullah Alayhi* was also a Panjabi poet, one of his poems is entitled *Sayf al-Rahman* (The Sword of the Merciful) which was a critique on defective *pirs*. Maulvi Fadal Din was a teacher and he used to accompany Khwaja Muhammad Akbar Ali *Rahmatullah Alayhima* on his tours. There was so much love and affection between the two that once, after the holidays Maulvi Fadal Din *Rahmatullah Alayhi* returned to teach at his religious school, and Khwaja Muhammad Akbar Ali felt lonely and depressed and so composed some affectionate verses and sent them to Maulvi Fadal Din *Rahmatullah Alayhima*. On the other hand Maulvi Fadal Din also greatly missed his master and quickly came to visit Khwaja Muhammad Akbar Ali *Rahmatullah Alayhima*. The verses Khwaja Muhammad Akbar Ali *Rahmatullah Alayhi* composed are as follows:

Alf ah jani, lahi' hijr kani, mera sada musafira rah'ya ho,
Teray bahj na aram jandari nunh, moriain wag mohar mai'ya ho.

Come, o beloved, my constant companion as separation is painful,
Without you there is no rest for me, come back, o beloved.

Fadal rabb rasul de tangh so'ni, zulf naznein cheel sap'iya ho,
Jib qasida wasl pala jaldi, meri jindari, sahkt gabara'i ah ho.

By the grace of Allah and His Prophet ﷺ untie your beautiful tresses, o beloved,
Come and quickly quench the thirst as my life in is great torment.

Khwaja Muhammad Akbar Ali's account of Hajj is not without interest. It is related that one of his devotees had Khwaja Sahib's passport made with an old photograph of him, but did not know Khwaja Sahib's father's name. The devotee wisely wrote Qibla Alam's name in the father's column as in reality the master is a spiritual father. All of this was done without Khwaja Sahib's knowledge, as the devotee feared that he might refuse. When the

---

[306] Chak No: 45

passport was made and presented to Khwaja Sahib *Rahmatullah Alayhi* and when he saw that Qibla Alam's name was written instead of his father's, he remained silent. After performing Hajj, Khwaja Sahib *Rahmatullah Alayhi* described the situation thus, "The prayers have become short and due to laziness the *Sunnah* and *nafila* have been ignored."

Khwaja Sahib *Rahmatullah Alayhi* was a very handsome, well dressed young man and dignity shone from his face. Once as he was travelling from Kokkhar to Narowal, some Sikhs saw him and were so impressed by his spirituality that they came and kissed his feet out of respect.

According to Khwaja Sahib's own account his daily practices consisted of: 8 units of *tahajjud*, in each unit he would recite *sura Ya-Sin* up to the *mubin* verse and in the last unit he would complete the whole chapter. He prayed two units' of *wudu*, *ishraq* and *awwabin*. After *tahajjud* he would read the *khatam* of Hadrat Mujaddid *Rahmatullah Alayhi*. In addition he would read *la ilaha illallah* with the breath, *durud tunajjina* and *durud hazra* 3,313 times. *Ya hayyu ya quyyum birahmatika astaghith* 500 times and *ism-e zat* 25,000 times daily. He would perform each meditation for the whole week and after *dhur* prayer he would read the written *wazifa* which included *Dalail al-Khayrat* daily section, *Hizb al-Azam*, *durud mustaghas*, *shajarah tariqat* and a quarter *para* of the Holy Qur'an.

Khwaja Sahib *Rahmatullah Alayhi* had two sons, Abu al-Tahir Muhammad Naqshband and Abu al-Hasan Faqir Muhammad *Rahmatullah Alayhima*. Sahibzada Muhammad Naqshband *Rahmatullah Alayhi* passed away on 10th April 2004/ 19th Safar 1445 AH and Sahibzada Faqir Muhammad *Rahmatullah Alayhi* passed away on 18th February 2004.

22) Sufi Faujdar Khan (d.1960) *Rahmatullah Alayhi*

He belonged to the Ghakkar tribe who ruled this region for centuries. However due to the defeat of the Ghakkars at the hands of the Sikhs, the tribe lost its prestige.[307] The Rajgan of this area[308] were respected and seen as the allies of the Sikh rulers, hence they were granted this area as a gift. One of his

---

[307] Subsequently the tribe was scattered in such places as Malot, Thub Rajgan, Khattar and Chalayar
[308] Chalayar

ancestors of Sufi Faujdar Khan *Rahmatullah Alayhi* later moved to Kotli.[309] Afterwards the family bought some land in the Pūnch province.[310] Sufi Faujdar Khan *Rahmatullah Alayhi* was strong and had a good physique. He was a wrestler but he never took it up as a profession. He would exercise a lot and took great care of his body. He would state, "Without exercise the body becomes lazy and a lazy body is of no use to anyone."

Maulvi Muhammad Akbar from Gujjar Khan was the teacher of Sufi Faujdar Khan *Rahmatullah Alayhima*, and he often used to pray for and also request prayers for his teacher. No information is available about his other teachers. He worked in the Pūnch customs department and as a result worked at all the checkpoints in the state.[311] The court case that took place during his employment has been mentioned earlier.

Sufi Faujdar Khan met Qibla Alam via Miyan Fath Muhammad *Rahmatullah Alayhim*. Sufi Faujdar Khan met Miyan Fath Muhammad *Rahmatullah Alayhima* in his village[312] and became his follower. He took the spiritual exercises from him and gained authorisation. Consequently he became attached to Qibla Alam *Rahmatullah Alayhi* and gained a special position of trust.

Sufi Faujdar Khan's firm belief and enthusiasm for the spiritual exercises can be attested by a number of sources. He took great care to read his *wazifa* in private. As a result sometimes he would go into the jungle or sit on his own. He states, "Once I was reading the *ayat karima* and the passion for Allah kept increasing. I suddenly got up and went outside where I saw a tree, and in this spiritual state I read the *ayat karima* and pointed a finger towards the tree, nothing happened and I went back inside. When I went outside the next morning I saw the tree had been cut and it transpired that my neighbour had done it, when I questioned him he replied, "I just felt the urge to chop the tree down."

Sufi Faujdar Khan *Rahmatullah Alayhi* explains another of his experiences. "Once I was posted at a checkpoint and according to my routine I was doing the *dhikr* of *ism-e zat* and I could visualise Allah in white on my subtle centres. And sometimes during the *dhikr* I would become so absorbed as if I was a horse

---

[309] Qamroti
[310] Jandrot
[311] Chachen, Kulla, Paghawari Gali, Balula and Sangyut
[312] Qamroti

ready to fly off. When the spiritual power appeared in the higher subtle centre then I would fly upwards and if it appeared in the lower subtle centre I would fly upside down. I would attend the gathering of the saints and I would be instructed to stand to the right and Qibla Alam *Rahmatullah Alayhi* would be there as well. One day I was making *dhikr* and one of the companions was cooking food. A few minutes later he came inside and informed me that there was no butter for cooking. He mentioned that there was some butter that had been confiscated in the storeroom, and asked my permission to use it and I gave him permission. When I ate that food all of my subtle centres became black and I lost all spirituality and I was not allowed to enter the gathering of the saints. I cried and pleaded for forgiveness and finally one day Qibla Alam *Rahmatullah Alayhi* said, "O the Ones who stand on the right, stand on the left."

It was Sufi Faujdar Khan's practice to help the *Sangis* improve themselves. If a *Sangi* was lazy in practicing his *wazifa*, he would explain to him that, "Our way is the Shari'ah, so be steadfast upon it. Even if you are steadfast upon the prayers there is hope of salvation. Do not be misguided by the pleasures of the world, remember the Hereafter." He would occupy himself in constant remembrance and had complete faith in its blessing. During times of difficulty he would gain comfort from the remembrance of Allah and would consistently perform *dhikr* for many months and years. He would encourage the *Sangis* to make *dhikr* during the difficult periods, and sometimes would join them in *dhikr*.

The incident of Kalu and Makhni is of this nature. Kalu was a poor person and Makhni was a beautiful woman. One person of her family who had influence with the authorities had Makhni kidnapped and moved to another state. Kalu was devastated and so Sufi Faujdar Khan *Rahmatullah Alayhi* began to read a *wazifa* to recover Makhni. This practice continued for a long time and Sufi Faujdar Khan *Rahmatullah Alayhi* said, "It is not possible that the *wazifa* would not show its effect." Finally one day Makhni came to Kalu of her own will and so his tribe gave him support out of tribal honour, despite the fact that his opponents had support from the authorities they were unsuccessful. Sufi Faujdar Khan *Rahmatullah Alayhi* mentioned what he read to Hadrat Sahib: *Bismilla hir rama nirhim ya hayyu ya qayyum ya dal jalal wal-ikram bi-haqq-e la ilaha illa anta subhanka inni kuntu minzalimin.* He read this *wazifa* thousands of times daily until he succeeded.

Hadrat Sahib states, "Sufi Faujdar Khan *Rahmatullah Alayhi* read this *wazifa* to me and said, "With Qibla Alam's permission I hand this over to you as he had granted me permission to read it." In addition Sufi Faujdar Khan *Rahmatullah Alayhi* informed me that *Ghunyatul Talibin,* mentions its virtues that the minister of Hadrat Sulayman named Asif ibn Barkhiya practised this supplication. It is with this that he brought the throne of the Queen of Sheba in the blink of an eye.

Sufi Faujdar Khan *Rahmatullah Alayhi* used to recite *sura Ya-Sīn* abundantly and so he possessed great spiritual power. For example once a person came who had severe arthritis in his hands and could not move his fingers, according to Sufi Faujdar Khan *Rahmatullah Alayhi* himself, "I focused on Qibla Alam *Rahmatullah Alayhi* and blew upon him and by Divine grace he was cured. Indeed he could even milk buffaloes after that." The news of this incident spread quickly in the local area and as a result Sufi Faujdar Khan *Rahmatullah Alayhi* had to move.[313]

Hadrat Sahib narrates that, "After the demise of Qibla Alam *Rahmatullah Alayhi* I went to visit Khwaja Muhammad Akbar Ali in his village, Sufi Faujdar Khan *Rahmatullah Alayhima* was also there, both of them expressed their desire to renew their *bay'a* and in support mentioned that the followers of Hadrat Mujaddid *Rahmatullah Alayhi* renewed their *bay'a* with his son Khwaja Muhammad Masum *Rahmatullah Alayhi.* Therefore according to the wishes of these deputies of Qibla Alam *Rahmatullah Alayhi* their *bay'a* was renewed."

Many miracles are attributed to Sufi Faujdar Khan *Rahmatullah Alayhi* and there are some accounts narrated by himself that have been mentioned earlier. Nevertheless there is no denying the fact that he performed many miracles. Many people became his followers including Kaka Khan[314]. Sufi Faujdar Khan *Rahmatullah Alayhi* performed seclusion[315] and the people of the Malik tribe greatly revered him.

Sufi Faujdar Khan *Rahmatullah Alayhi* passed away on 19th October 1960 at early dawn in his village.[316] Hadrat Sahib was in the village on the day and went to visit him and both were sat on the bed. Muhammad Zaman narrates, "Hadrat Sahib took my hand and placed it in my father's hands and he took my hand and

---

[313] Shadra
[314] Sangot
[315] Darhal Malikain
[316] Jandrot

placed it Hadrat Sahib's hands. Then Hadrat Sahib said, "Let Muhammad Zaman come with me and God willing I shall send him home by twelve o'clock from Kalu's home." After walking for some distance Hadrat Sahib told the other *Sangis* to go back and held my shoulder and said, "Explain to Sufi Sahib that we shall bury you in Kotli and ask him to grant us permission from his relatives." When I gave the message to my father he said to Subedar Neyk Muhammad, "Go and request Hadrat Sahib to pass through the mountains as quickly as possible." Sufi Faujdar Khan *Rahmatullah Alayhi* died at *sehri* time and his funeral was held in his village after *dhur* and after *asr*[317] and at midnight his body was sent to Kotli. In Kotli Hadrat Sahib personally led his funeral prayer, and the grave had been prepared so he was laid to rest at the basement of Jami'a al-Firdous. Later Sain Muhammad Ashraf *Rahmatullah Alayhi* was buried next to him. Presently both Sufi Faujdar Khan and Sain Muhammad Ashraf have been transferred to the Khidri mosque,[318] where Sain Muhammad Halim *Rahmatullah Alayhima* from Amb is also buried.

23) Sayyid Ghawth Ali Shah (d.1937) *Rahmatullah Alayhi*

He was a very noble and pious person. He was well known for piety in the area and belonged to a religious family who guided people.[319] He was a devout follower and deputy of Qibla Alam *Rahmatullah Alayhi*. Many people received guidance from him.[320] The Dholli family[321] in the Pūnch district were also amongst his followers. Two of his *Sangis* from Jhelum named Muhammad and Chan are worthy of mention. Although both were illiterate they had good manners and understood situations well, they spoke appropriately and silenced their opponents.

In those days a *pir* used to visit Jhelum called 'Pashuri pir' who was accompanied by a group of singers. Once Muhammad spoke to some of the followers of 'Pashuri pir' and said, "Remain followers of your *pir* but also visit our master so that you might pray regularly." Some jealous people twisted these simple words of Muhammad and told 'Pashuri pir' that he was trying to convert his followers. The jealous people enticed 'Pashuri pir' and he was enraged and

---

[317] Qamroti
[318] Gulpur
[319] Behari,Dadyal
[320] He had followers Jhelum: Baga Sai'nla, Kotala and the surrounding areas
[321] Batl

sent for Muhammad and shouted at him, "Is Ghawth Ali your mother's husband, is he your sister's husband, *Ghawth Ali teri manh na khasam hai, teri behain na khasam hai?*" Muhammad used wisdom and said, "Yes indeed Ghawth Ali Shah is my *khasam* (master) and thereby master of my brothers, sisters and my children but not in the manner you speak of as you are polluting your tongue by saying what you said, the rest is up to you, think what you want. All I said to your followers was you keep your *pir* but associate with our master so that you may become regular *namazis*." And the nobility of Sayyid Ghawth Ali Shah *Rahmatullah Alayhi* was such that when both he and 'Pashuri pir' were in Jhelum at the same time he said to his *Sangis*, "You can gladly go to the gatherings of 'Pashuri pir'," and told Muhammad, "You have been have you not?" Muhammad replied, "My heart is not content on visiting him but if it is an order that it is different." Then Muhammad explained his viewpoint, "Even if there is a dim light the moth gives his life for the lamp but he does not go towards the fire."

After Sayyid Ghawth Ali Shah *Rahmatullah Alayhi*, his son Pir Muhammad Shah became his authorised deputy. He kept in touch with Darbar Sharif via letters and his letters very always were interesting. The main builder in Darbar Sharif, Muhammad Sharif was a sincere follower of Shah Sahib, and had great love for his master. Muhammad Sharif played an important part in the building of the grand mosque [322] and his loyalty and dedication for Darbar Sharif is unique. Sayyid Ghawth Ali Shah *Rahmatullah Alayhi* passed away on 28th Cheayth 1995 Bikrami.

24) Qadi Karam Ali Khan *Rahmatullah Alayhi*

He belonged to the Kalowatra tribe.[323] Miyan Abd al-Karim *Rahmatullah Alayhi* also belonged to the same area and both were very pious people.[324] Qadi Karam Ali *Rahmatullah Alayhi* was well versed in matters of jurisprudence. Both were followers of Hadrat Khwaja Ghulam Muhyi al-Din *Chardey Wallay Pir* *Rahmatullah Alayhi* from Bawali Sharif. After the demise of their master both became followers of Qibla Alam *Rahmatullah Alayhi* and completed their training under him in the Mujaddidiyya path and were given authorisation. Both stayed in touch with Darbar Sharif. Further information about them could not be found.

---

[322] Behari
[323] Lam Rajuah,Banah,Kotli
[324] Banah,Pakhrani

25) Sayyid Baqar Shah

He is well known for his piety.[325] Even in his old age, he has a good sense of humour and charms anyone who meets him. Hadrat Sahib states that Sayyid Baqar Shah narrated to me, "There was a lot of talk about Qibla Alam's spirituality in our area, as there were many followers of his authorised deputy, Miyan Fath Muhammad *Rahmatullah Alayhi*. Through Miyan Fath Muhammad I gained a desire to meet Qibla Alam *Rahmatullah Alayhima*. Subsequently about ten Sayyids went to Checheyan Sharif and requested *bay'a* from Qibla Alam *Rahmatullah Alayhi*. He replied, "You are Sayyids and the Shaykh in Golra Sharif is also a Sayyid therefore you should take *bay'a* from him." Upon hearing this I and my companion Sayyid Muhammad Shah began to cry and thus Qibla Alam *Rahmatullah Alayhi* took pity upon us, and gave us both *bay'a* and taught us some spiritual exercises."

When Sufi Faujdar Khan *Rahmatullah Alayhi* was working as a customs officer at the check post[326] Hadrat Sahib went to visit him. Whilst he was there he saw the exorcist Sain Baga Ali encouraging Sayyid Baqar Shah to sit in seclusion and promised him that he would be able to control Jinns and spirits. When the news of this incident reached the *Sangis* they were worried and tried to warn Sayyid Baqar Shah that this act was not permissible in the Naqshbandiyya path. In order to save him from the clutches of the exorcist Sufi Faujdar Khan *Rahmatullah Alayhi* instructed Sayyid Baqar Shah to do seclusion inside the mosque. Sufi Faujdar Khan *Rahmatullah Alayhi* taught the method of *dhikr* to Sayyid Baqar Shah and granted him authorisation. When Sayyid Baqar Shah completed his seclusion the *Sangis* helped him financially. All of these efforts were made to merely save Sayyid Baqar Shah from the un-Islamic practice of exorcism.

Sayyid Baqar Shah has a nice voice and even in his old age there is still magic in it and people gain pleasure from it. He used to give sermons as well. When the group of *Sangis* led by Sayyid Baqar Shah used to recite poetry before their departure from Qibla Alam's shrine, it would bring tears to the listener's eyes. The poem is as follows;

> *Sah'il nunh amid lagi pakki mehl hosi dilbar da',*
> The Beggar is very hopeful that he shall see the beloved.

---

[325] He lives in Tehsil Nekyal in Fathpur
[326] Paghawari Gali

Due to old age it is not possible for Sayyid Baqar Shah to travel to Darbar Sharif. However he sends messages via Sain Shah Sahib who works in the *Awqaf* (Endowment) Department. Amongst Sayyid Baqar Shah's followers are Sain Farda,[327] Sain Kalu and others.

26) **Miyan Hashmat Ali** (1875-1951) *Rahmatullah Alayhi*

His noble father was called Fadal Din *Rahmatullah Alayhi* known as *Sain Littain Wallay.*[328] He was born around 1875 in Mirpur.[329] He belonged to the Arain tribe (Koka). He passed away at the age of 76 in 1951. His grave[330] is near the shrine of Sakhi Sarkar *Rahmatullah Alayhi* and this area is three miles from the city.[331] He had a nomadic nature.[332] He was the only son of his father and had two sisters both of whom have died and are buried in Kotli.[333]

Miyan Sahib *Rahmatullah Alayhi* had read the Holy Qur'an and spent most of his life teaching the Qur'an as the *imam* of the mosque. Originally he was a follower of the elder brother of Pir Aftab Husayn Shah in Kotli, Hadrat Ahmad Shah *Rahmatullah Alayhi* and later became a devotee of Qibla Alam *Rahmatullah Alayhi*. Whenever Qibla Alam *Rahmatullah Alayhi* visited Mirpur,[334] Miyan Sahib *Rahmatullah Alayhi* would often stay with him and consequently he adopted his characteristics. It could not be confirmed if Miyan Sahib *Rahmatullah Alayhi* actually took *bay'a* from Qibla Alam *Rahmatullah Alayhi*. Miyan Sahib *Rahmatullah Alayhi* was about 5ft 6 inches tall and was of medium build, had a long nose and a long and bushy beard. He had a light complexion, and normally wore a *qamis*, *dhoti* and a turban. He would dye his clothes with bark from the acacia tree. Miyan Sahib *Rahmatullah Alayhi* did not like idle talk. He would encourage people to make *dhikr* and warned them about the fear of God and retribution. His *waza'if* included *Qasida Burda Sharif*, *Qasida Ghawthiyya*, *Qasida Rumi*, *durud taj* and *du'a suryani*.

---

[327] Dabsi
[328] Bunna Bagh
[329] Fathpur Jabr
[330] Plakhar Bunna Bagh
[331] Kallar Sayyidain
[332] From Mirpur he moved to Plakhar, Kahouta, Rawalpindi and then to Bunna post office Dhok Khlot
[333] Mandi
[334] Fathpur Jabr

27) Sain Abd al-Halim Larrwi *Rahmatullah Alayhi*

His ancestral home was in Kashmir.[335] It is said that he was a close relative of the famous spiritual master Ji Sahib *Rahmatullah Alayhi*. He sought spirituality and set off to find a complete master. In those days Qibla Alam *Rahmatullah Alayhi* was visiting the Kotli region and was visiting the relatives of his personal attendant, Hajji Sain Muhammad Ashraf *Rahmatullah Alayhi*. By coincidence Sain Abd al-Halim reached this area and was going past it, when suddenly Qibla Alam *Rahmatullah Alayhima* came out of the house to perform *wudu*. Qibla Alam *Rahmatullah Alayhi* saw that he was a stranger, called him and during the conversation it emerged that he was the seeker and Qibla Alam *Rahmatullah Alayhi* was the sought. Ji Sahib *Rahmatullah Alayhi* had a good opinion of Qibla Alam *Rahmatullah Alayhi* as mentioned earlier. And perhaps such words of praise increased the desire in the heart of Sain Abd al-Halim to visit Qibla Alam *Rahmatullah Alayhima*.

Sain Abd al-Halim became a follower of Qibla Alam *Rahmatullah Alayhima*, completed his spiritual training and was given authorisation. He had a large following in occupied Kashmir. His followers also include Maulvi Amir Ali[336] and some relatives of Miyan Sattar Muhammad *Rahmatullah Alayhi*.[337] Sain Abd al-Halim and Miyan Sattar Muhammad *Rahmatullah Alayhima* were best friends. Miyan Sattar Muhammad had two sons, Muhammad Sadiq and Abd al-Haqq and Sain Abd al-Halim *Rahmatullah Alayhima* had only one son Muhammad Ismail known as Kalu and a daughter called Salima who was married to Muhammad Sadiq. Both Kalu and Abd al-Haqq went to study religious studies at under Hafiz Muhkam Din *Rahmatullah Alayhi*. Abd al-Haqq spent the rest of his life with his teacher and Kalu went back to Kashmir after the partition in 1947. The family were traditionally shepherds and Kalu chose this profession. Sometime later Sain Abd al-Halim *Rahmatullah Alayhi* also went back to occupied Kashmir, and thus contact with Darbar Sharif could not be maintained.

The daughter of Sain Abd al-Halim *Rahmatullah Alayhi*, Salima was left in Amb with her husband Muhammad Sadiq. She would enquire from the shepherds if they knew anything about her father and brother. In order to please her, the shepherds would make up tales about her father and brother. The grandson of Ji Sahib *Rahmatullah Alayhi*, Miyan Muhammad Bashir was a member of

---

[335] Wangat Pargana Larr
[336] Noble father of Hafiz Fadal Karim, the personal attendant of Hadrat Sahib
[337] Also in Thanpal and Rajur

the Assembly in Occupied Kashmir. When he visited Pakistan due to their family links, Salima would enquire from him about the whereabouts of her father and brother but he did not pay any attention to this matter. Due to the lack of contact between occupied and independent Kashmir there were many tragedies of this nature.

Hadrat Sahib greatly desired to know the whereabouts of Sain Abd al-Halim one of the loyal *Sangis* and the authorised deputy of Qibla Alam *Rahmatullah Alayhima*, but due to lack of contact there was no progress. Once Hadrat Sahib went to visit Sirhind Sharif in India and there met a person called Muhammad Nazir, who held an important position in the Law department in Occupied Kashmir. In order to perform his duties he had to go to both Jammu and Srinagar and when the matter of Sain Abd al-Halim *Rahmatullah Alayhi* was mentioned to him, he promised to provide information. When Muhammad Nazir could not find suitable transportation, he set off on his own towards that area[338] in extremely difficult circumstances. There he met prominent scholars like Mawlana Abd al-Rashid and Sufi Abd al-Karim. So Muhammad Nazir paid respect at the shrine of Ji Sahib *Rahmatullah Alayhi* of Larr and read *Fatiha* there. He also visited the graves Mai Sahiba and Miyan Nizam al-Din *Rahmatullah Alayhima* who are also buried there. But no one knew where Sain Abd al-Halim *Rahmatullah Alayhi* was buried. Someone pointed out a grave in the local cemetery but due to the snow it was not possible to verify whose grave it was. So Muhammad Nazir left the matter for a future visit and wrote the details of his findings to Hadrat Sahib. In addition he mentioned that Sain Kalu had died.[339]

The mystery surrounding the whereabouts of Sain Abd al-Halim *Rahmatullah Alayhi* and Kalu finally became clear on 31st January 1990, when Kalu obtained a visa to visit Azad Kashmir. He came to Darbar Sharif and explained that as long as his father was healthy he travelled and provided spiritual guidance to the people but when he became ill he stayed with him. Sain Kalu narrated that, "Our tribe moved year on the 12th of Bisakh the shepherds head off to the valley.[340] We have made a bridge and we used to take my late father on a horse, he used to stay in the small mosque.[341] One year on 12th of Bisakh

---

[338] Wangat
[339] Rajouri
[340] Wangat to Sandarban, situated between Veri Pattan and Aknur
[341] Sandarban

we set off and arrived at the village.[342] My father said, "Do not go forward or else you shall have to return." Then he placed his hand on a rock and said, "Place this as a headstone." Then he remarked, "There is a mosque and fountain here." The *imam* Sahib led the *asr* prayer then my father had a bath and dressed himself and continued his devotional practices. Then he began to pray *maghrib* and in the third unit he remained in prostration. After the prayer we found out that he had passed away. I spread a blanket and laid him upon it and all night people recited the Holy Qur'an and other shepherds joined us as well. The *imam* of the mosque, Muhammad Shafi Sahib led the funeral prayer in which many prominent people took part. We buried him with wooden planks. And as for his relics only his thick rosary, long shirt and needle remain as all other things have been distributed." This was the authentic account by a son of his noble father.

In light of this information the *Sangis* [343] were advised by Hadrat Sahib, to visit Sain Abd Al-Halim's grave and hold *khatam* there. Sain Kalu has since died and his son came to visit Hadrat Sahib. He would have stayed in touch with Darbar Sharif but due to the freedom movement, the Hindu authorities have made life for Muslims unbearable in this region. Presently all forms of correspondence are suspended. Salima often kept in touch with Hadrat Sahib, but now both she and her husband have died.

When Sain Abd al-Halim *Rahmatullah Alayhi* lived in Amb, he related, "One evening I wanted to cross the river Pūnch with my son and daughter. There was no boat and there were high tides in the river. The crossing was unfamiliar to us and there was no one there to guide us. Night was approaching and where I wanted to cross was not the normal place and was dangerous. At that moment my son said, "Look the old man is pointing to cross from there." When I looked it was Qibla Alam *Rahmatullah Alayhi* indicating where it was safe to cross the river. Heeding his advice we crossed the river and he disappeared. This incident took place a few years after Qibla Alam's demise.

It was the dearest wish of Hadrat Sahib to bring the body of Sain Abd al-Halim Larrwi *Rahmatullah Alayhi* from occupied Kashmir to Azad Kashmir. In 1990 reliable information was obtained about his grave and ever since this matter was under consideration. By Divine grace this hurdle was removed in 2006. From Occupied Kashmir Mawlana Abd al-Ghani and other *Sangis* were entrusted with

---

[342] Banghai, situated between Rajouri Tana Mandi and Shadra
[343] Mehnder and Rajouri

this task, and in Azad Kashmir it was the duty of Hafiz Abd al-Rahim to receive the body. In order to find an appropriate time to transfer the body both parties spent four to six weeks making arrangements. Finally on 9th September 2006 at 3 pm. the body was handed over to Hafiz Abd al-Rahim in Azad Kashmir, the whole process was done in secrecy and the same night between *maghrib* and *isha* the body arrived at Gulhar Sharif. It was safely placed in one of the rooms, and preparations began to bury the body in the Khidri mosque.

On 10th September 2006 at 4.30 pm, Ustad Ghulam Husayn Sahib, Hafiz Fadal Karim Sahib, Professor Akbar Dad Sahib, Muhammad Maqsud (the builder) and Hajji Muhammad Masud Sahib took the body and set off for the Khidri mosque, they arrived there at 5 pm and the body was safely placed in the northern part of the mosque and the door locked. *Asr* was prayed in congregation then the process of burial began. In the vicinity of this mosque three sincere *Sangis* of Qibla Alam *Rahmatullah Alayhi* are already buried; Sufi Faujdar Khan, Sain Muhammad Halim, Sain Muhammad Ashraf and Sain Abd al-Halim Larrwi's grave was made towards the feet of Sain Muhammad Halim *Rahmatullah Alayhim*. The burial process was completed by 7 pm. Then on every Thursday a gathering was held to send the merit to his soul, these gatherings were led by Hadrat Sahibzada Hajji Pir Sahib. On 8th October 2006 the gravestone was erected. And on 2nd November a large gathering was organised in which around 100 teachers, 300 students and many other *Sangis* attended the event and Hadrat Sahibzada Hajji Pir Sahib made the final supplication.

Sain Abd al-Halim *Rahmatullah Alayhi* passed away on 28th Bisakh and the year is not known. In order to find out the exact year of his demise Mawlana Abd al-Ghani was contacted in Occupied Kashmir, this is an extract from his letter. "His funeral was led by Qadi Muhammad Shafi the *imam* of the mosque[344]. His wife Khatun Begum guided us to the grave. Further information shall take more time as I have spoken in detail to Mawlana Ghulam Rasul Sahib. He further stated that Sain Abd al-Halim's grandson was on his travels[345] and would arrive soon and he shall write after the meeting him." As yet no reliable information has emerged. Near the Khidri mosque, in a village[346] lives one of the followers of Sain Abd al-Halim *Rahmatullah Alayhi* called Amir Ali Sahib who is

---

[344] Phangai'
[345] Sandarban
[346] Arna

the father of Hafiz Fadal Karim Sahib. Despite his old age he often visits the shrine of his master.

Translator's Note

The translation of *Tazkira-e Sultaniyya* ends here, however it is befitting to conclude this book by providing a summary of Qibla Alam's only son and successor Hadrat Sahib *Rahmatullāh Alayhima*. We now turn our focus to Hadrat Sahib *Rahmatullāh Alayhi* who passed away before the *Tazkira-e Sultaniyya* was published. The following section on Hadrat Sahib *Rahmatullāh Alayhi* was written in Urdu by a number of *Sangis,* and was read on his annual ceremony that took place at the Khanqah-e Fathiyya on 31st December 2009.

Chapter Four

Hadrat Sahib (1921-2008) *Rahmatullah Alayhi*

Introduction

This branch (al-Bakri al-Siddiqi) originally ruled Yemen and left its governance in order to spread the *din*. This love for the *din* and knowledge brought them out of the Arabian Peninsula and into Iran, Hindustan and finally Kashmir. Rasul Allah ﷺ said, *"When Allah loves a person, He sends for Jibril and commands him: Indeed, I love such and such a person; you should also love him, so Jibril loves him as well. Then Jibril proclaims in the heavens that Allah loves such and such a person; you should also love him. Then the residents of the heavens love him as well. Then his love is sent down to the earth (the world)"* (*Narrated by Bukhari, Muslim, Tirmidhi, and Musnad Ahmad*).

The theme of Hadith Sharif mentioned above beautifully manifests itself in the person of Hadrat Sahib *Rahmatullah Alayhi*. His fame has not only spread in Azad Kashmir and Pakistan but also in Arabia and non-Arab lands. The hand of nature (Allah) carved him like a precious diamond and from whichever angle one observes one sees a new colour and a new shape. His physical appearance, life, speech, character, movements, habits, virtues and manners, indeed, whichever aspect one observes, one cries out: "His every action pulls the heartstrings." The Divine Will operates in mysterious ways and creates reasons to bring about its purpose. It was the Divine Will that appointed Hadrat Sahib *Rahmatullah Alayhi* to turn Kotli into a centre of guidance. Through Hadrat Sahib *Rahmatullah Alayhi* the people of Kotli were taken out of the darkness and in to the light, and for this favour they can never thank Allah enough. Due to Hadrat Sahib's efforts every home in this area became familiar with the *din*.

Family Background

Some of our friends do not know the lineage of Hadrat Sahib *Rahmatullah Alayhi* and for their information a summary of his ancestors is provided. Hadrat Khwaja Muhammad Sadiq *Rahmatullah Alayhi* known as 'Hadrat Sahib' is of pure Arab ancestry, and a descendent of Sayyiduna Abu Bakr Siddiq's ﷺ eldest son Hadrat Abd al-Rahman ؓ. His genealogy links him with Sayyiduna Abu Bakr Siddiq ﷺ through 38 generations. This branch of the family was always interested in knowledge and spreading the *din*. Seven generations after Sayyiduna Abu Bakr Siddiq 🕮, his descendent, Shaykh Ahmad bin Mahmud *Rahmatullah Alayhi* became the ruler of Yemen. His fourth successor, Shaykh Kamal al-Din Muhammad Yemeni *Rahmatullah Alayhi* whose students include Shaykh Baha al-Din Zakariyya Multani *Rahmatullah Alayhi*, left his rule in Yemen and settled in Madinah Sharif and for fifty years taught Hadith Sharif in the neighbourhood of the Prophet 🕮. He was later appointed as the Qadi of Sistan in Iran. This position was occupied by his descendents for the next six generations.

The Arrival of His Great Ancestor to the Indo-Pak Subcontinent

Hadrat Qadi Qiwam al-Din bin Husam al-Din was the first ancestor of Hadrat Sahib *Rahmatullah Alayhima* to enter Hindustan. He was the seventeenth descendent of Sayyiduna Abu Bakr Siddiq 🕮 and the sixth descendent of Shaykh Kamal al-Din Muhammad Yemeni *Rahmatullah Alayhi*. In 700 AH/1300 CE at the request of the Tughluq Sultans he arrived with his nephews in Delhi. Prior to his arrival in Delhi, he was the *qadi* of Jjnayr in Sistan in the kingdom of Iran. In Delhi he received *khilafat* from Shaykh Nizam al-Din Awliya *Rahmatullah Alayhi*. The King of the time appointed him as the *qadi* (judge) and sent him to Rohtak.[347] He and his wife Ayn al-Badr bint Qadi Sultan Muhammad Surkh Dhu al-Qarni *Rahmatullah Alayhima* are buried in the fort in Rohtak. This fort was constructed by the Yemeni masters under the supervision of Qadi Sultan Muhammad Surkh Dhu al-Qarni *Rahmatullah Alayhi*. Until 1947 his descendents lived in the village[348] in their regal forts (due to the al-Bakri al-Siddiqi family this area was named Mehm Sharif). These forts are mentioned by Abu al-Fadl in his book *A'ain-e Akbari* (p.922-1003).

The Family's Contributions and Achievements

"Some members of this family held prominent posts under the Pathan Sultans of Delhi and the Mughal Emperors. In addition, the family played an important role in the conversion and the transformation of the Rajputs."[349] (*The Imperial Coronation, Delhi Darbar.*[350] During the Muslim rule this al-Bakri al-Siddiqi branch continually occupied places of knowledge, honour, spirituality

---

[347] Haryana District located seventy kilometres north west of Delhi
[348] Mehm, thirty kilometres from Rohtak
[349] Hisar, Rohtak, Karnal and Gurgoan
[350] Printed in Madras, (1911) p: *381*

and leadership. The family held the post of the local *qadi*, *mufti* (authority on religious rulings), *muhtasib* (inspector), *amir-e adl* (chief justice), *khatib* (orator) of Friday and *eid* prayers. In addition they had held high offices in both civil and military ranks at a national level. They also contributed greatly in the fields of literature, education and propagating Islam in the surrounding districts of Delhi.[351] Furthermore they played an important part in the conversion and guidance of Hindu Jats and Rajputs and some other tribes to Islam.

The Period of Tribulation

A few years after the British East India Company took full control of Hindustan, they changed the administrate language and the system of governance, consequently the function of the *qadi* and *mufti* was terminated. In accordance with section five of the Third Act of 1838, all of their land grants were confiscated and the office holders (*qadi* and *mufti*) were made redundant. As for their role in the Battle of Independence in 1857, this family was branded the leaders of the rebels and subsequently fourteen prominent members of the family were martyred. Their homes were dug two feet deep in order to find weapons, and consequently numerous relics and artefacts that had been in the family's possession for centuries were stolen by the soldiers. The walls of their fort were demolished. Despite all these destructions, the government was not able to stop the religious efforts of this family as it continued to teach and spread Islam. During the British Raj the financial situation of the family was adverse. Although a few were wealthy, most were at the mercy of local petty rulers. During the 138 years of the British Raj this family's recognition was in the field of knowledge and nobility.

According to the 1880 Census of the Rohtak District, there were just eighteen Christians from the indigenous population and half of the fourteen per cent of the Muslim population, comprised of people whose ancestors had recently converted to Islam. The historical achievement of the al-Bakri al-Siddiqi family of the Rohtak District, was that they prevented people from being converted to Christianity despite the fact that they (Christians) were openly supported by the British government. Due to the efforts of this family one european officer stationed at Delhi converted to Islam and thousands of Jats, Rajputs, Kai'sath, Jogis and so forth also embraced Islam.

---

[351]Rohtak, Gurgoan, Hisar and Karnal

During the British Raj the writers from this family made valuable contributions in the field of Urdu literature; composing and translating works on Sufism, Jurisprudence, Medicine, Critique, History, Biographies, Biography of the Prophet ﷺ, Law, Philosophy, Ethics, Politics, Astronomy, Municipal administration, Logic, Literature, Morphology, Syntax, Dictionaries, Comparative Religions and so forth. The contributions of the family were mentioned in the report of the Delhi Darbar held in 1911. "This family has occupied prominent offices generation after generation for many centuries. Some members of this family simultaneously held key posts such as Judge, Chief Justice, Inspector, *mufti*, Custodian and Orator." For one family to hold prominent posts for five centuries clearly suggests that this family possessed qualities such as knowledge, wisdom and administrative skills. In the field of politics the family played an important part in the independence movement of India and Pakistan. During the partition of 1947 one tenth of the Muslim population of Rohtak was martyred and the rest were forced to flee to Pakistan. Presently most of the descendents of Qadi Qiwam al-Din Rohtaki *Rahmatullah Alayhi* are settled in Pakistan.

The Arrival of a Beloved Son of the al-Bakri al-Siddiqi Family to the State of Jammu and Kashmir

The ruler of Mirpur, Sultan Fath Muhammad Khan Ghakkar received the title of (Sultan) from the Mughal Emperor Awrangzaib Alamgir *Rahmatullah Alayhima*. He founded the area called Fathpur[352] (1051 AH/1640 CE). He had the history of the Ghakkars written entitled: *Tarikh Fath Khani,* which contained authentic accounts of the period. It was on his request that Hadrat Qadi Fath Allah Qadiri Shattari Rohtaki *Rahmatullah Alayhi* came to Mirpur as the Chief Judge and settled there. In this way the service for Islam led this al-Bakri al-Siddiqi branch from Makkah Sharif, Madinah Sharif, Yemen, Sistan (Iran), Hindustan and finally to Mirpur.

Sultan Fath Muhammad Khan Ghakkar *Rahmatullah Alayhi* was a very pious and God fearing person. He gave his daughter in marriage to Hadrat Qadi Fath Allah *Rahmatullah Alayhi*, who subsequently moved from Rohtak to Mirpur where he built the city's first mosque. He was travelling to Delhi and whilst en route he

---

[352] Ruled Chalayar and Kotli

died on 16th October 1677 in an area[353] in Panipat. His body was brought back to Mirpur with a royal escort and laid to rest in the family cemetery. This spiritual centre (shrine) remained intact until the onslaught of the Sikhs. When the Sikhs took control of Mirpur this family suffered persecution like other Muslims. After the Sikh occupation of the state, some surviving members of the family which included the great-great grandfather of Hadrat Sahib, Qadi Muhammad Akbar Ali *Rahmatullah Alayhima* moved to a village called Checheyan Sharif, north west of Mirpur.

In 1967 this area became submerged under the Mangla Lake and so the family had to migrate once again. One branch of the family led by Hadrat Sahib *Rahmatullah Alayhi* moved to Kaladeo (Khanqah-e Sultaniyya), Jhelum, whilst other members of the family moved to Dina.[354] Nowadays Hadrat Sahib's family is settled in two places: Kaladeo Sharif, (Khanqah-e Sultaniyya) Jhelum and Gulhar Sharif (Khanqah-e Fathiyya) Kotli, Azad Kashmir. Both of these centres provide spiritual guidance for needy people. The shrine of Hadrat Qadi Fath Allah Qadiri Shattari *Rahmatullah Alayhi* remained a place of pilgrimage until the construction of the Mangla Dam, following which it became submerged. This situation remained for the next eighteen years. Subsequently, for the convenience of pilgrims, on Friday 8th February 1985 his blessed body was moved to Jami'a al-Firdous[355] and this became his third place of burial.

The Blessed Birth

Hadrat Sahib *Rahmatullah Alayhi* was born in Checheyan Sharif near Fathpur. According to reliable sources his birth took place on 25th December 1921 on Friday/Saturday night at dawn.

Glad Tidings about His Birth

Once, Qibla Alam was meditating according to his normal practice at the grave of his father Qadi Muhammad Rukn Alam *Rahmatullah Alayhima* in the family cemetery. In his state of total absorption he saw his father emerge with a child in his hands, he placed the child in Qibla Alam's lap and said, "Take Muhammad

---

[353] Dar Samalaka
[354] Chitarparhi
[355] Gulhar Sharif, Kotli, Azad Jammu and Kashmir

Sadiq." This glad tiding remained a secret but an incident occurred which forced it to be revealed. At the age of six Hadrat Sahib *Rahmatullah Alayhi* was enrolled under the name Muhammad Sadiq *Rahmatullah Alayhi* at the primary school in Ladar. It is human nature to like new things and so when Hadrat Sahib *Rahmatullah Alayhi* heard the names of his fellow pupils he felt his name should be changed. A request was put forward to Qibla Alam *Rahmatullah Alayhi* and he declined it saying, "My beloved father chose this name for you and I would not dare to change it."

Once when Sufi Faujdar Khan visited Checheyan Sharif, Qibla Alam *Rahmatullah Alayhima* said to him, "A very honourable guest shall arrive soon." He enquired, "Will we have the opportunity to see him?" Qibla Alam *Rahmatullah Alayhima* replied, "Yes, many times." Qibla Alam *Rahmatullah Alayhi* stated that the guest would be called Muhammad Sadiq. Six months later Sufi Faujdar Khan went to congratulate Qibla Alam *Rahmatullah Alayhima* (on the birth of a son). After the *asr* prayer, Qibla Alam said to Sufi Faujdar Khan *Rahmatullah Alayhima*, "The great personality whose arrival we had mentioned is here, let's go and see him." He then took Sufi Faujdar Khan downstairs where Qibla Mai Sahiba *Rahmatullah Alayha* lived. Qibla Alam *Rahmatullah Alayhi* went inside the room and brought a baby in his hands and said, "This is the person we had mentioned to you." When Sufi Faujdar Khan *Rahmatullah Alayhi* saw the face of the baby he observed, "Whatever Qibla Alam *Rahmatullah Alayhi* had mentioned about him was evident in the child's face."

Bay'a and Authorisation

Due to Qibla Alam's spiritual concentration (*tawajjuh*), Hadrat Sahib *Rahmatullah Alayhima* attained all the necessary qualities required for spiritual development. He took *bay'a* from Qibla Alam *Rahmatullah Alayhi* in his childhood and was given the necessary *waza'if* to read. Apart from the training at home, Qibla Alam *Rahmatullah Alayhi* used to take him on journeys and train him accordingly. In this way the foundation of the Path was laid, which would later lead to perfection. Qibla Alam *Rahmatullah Alayhi* granted him permission and authorisation in his own lifetime.

Hadrat Sahib *Rahmatullah Alayhi* became an orphan at the age of twelve years and four months and fourteen days hence his noble mother Qibla Mai Sahiba *Rahmatullah Alayha* who was an institution by herself, played a pivotal role in his spiritual development. After the demise of his noble father his nurture and development came under his mother's supervision, who guided him for fifty years. Hadrat Sahib *Rahmatullah Alayhi* acknowledged that whatever he had achieved after his father's demise was due to the *tawajjuh* of his noble mother. Some sincere and senior *Sangis* of Qibla Alam such as Sufi Faujdar Khan and Miyan Sattar Muhammad *Rahmatullah Alayhima*, also assisted Hadrat Sahib's spiritual development. Due to his piety and exceptional spiritual struggles (*mujahidat*), Hadrat Sahib *Rahmatullah Alayhi* attained the highest rank in *taqwa* and the station of the beloved.

Education

As far as religious education was concerned Hadrat Sahib *Rahmatullah Alayhi* inherited a love for knowledge from his ancestors. According to the family custom his education began at home at an early age. His first teacher was his father who taught him the basic tenets of Islam. As for the conventional education he was enrolled at the primary school in Ladar, where the head teacher was Chaudary Nawab al-Din[356]. Hadrat Sahib *Rahmatullah Alayhi* studied there until the fourth grade (in those days the primary education was up to fourth grade). Qibla Alam *Rahmatullah Alayhi* would wait outside the village to receive him at the end of the school day. For further education he was enrolled in the Government High School in Old Mirpur.

Hadrat Sahib *Rahmatullah Alayhi* mentioned that one of his teachers was a Hindu called Budh Raj who used to teach English. Whilst Hadrat Sahib *Rahmatullah Alayhi* was in the sixth grade his father passed away and thus his school education ended. Outwardly it would seem that it was the demise of Qibla Alam *Rahmatullah Alayhi* which put an end to his school education but in reality destiny had planned something else from him.

Sometime later he studied books on Farsi with Hakim Miyan Muhammad Sahib[357] *Rahmatullah Alayhi*. Afterwards he began his studies with the leading scholar of the time Hadrat Mawlana Muhammad Abd Allah *Rahmatullah Alayhi* of Ladar, who according to some had mastered fourteen and according to others twenty six different sciences. He had travelled on foot to *Haramain Sharifain*

---

[356] Tahtahi Kasgumma
[357] Agro

(Makkah and Madinah Sharif), in order to gain knowledge. He studied with the leading scholars of the time such as Shaykh Mawlana Nur Ahmad[358] *Rahmatullah Alayhi* He studied the leading books on Arabic syntax; *Sharh Jami, Mullah Abd al-Ghafur.* During this time he also benefitted spiritually from Hadrat Hajji Pir Imdad Allah Muhajir Makki, who granted him his shoes and clothes before Mawlana Abd Allah *Rahmatullah Alayhima* left Makkah Sharif.

With the permission of leading masters, Mawlana Abd Allah *Rahmatullah Alayhi* landed in Bombay and spent five months there. Finally from Bombay he arrived in Delhi, there was a mosque[359] where a leading scholar of Hadith and principles of Hadith called Allama Abd al-Karim Panjabi *Rahmatullah Alayhi,* distributed oceans of knowledge to students. With Allama Abd al-Karim Panjabi *Rahmatullah Alayhi,* he studied Hadith and leading works on Logic and Philosophy such as *Salm al-Ulum, Mullah Hasan, Hamd Allah, Mir Zahid, Sadra, Shamas Bazigha* and so forth. He spent three years in Delhi and completed his studies. When he returned to his native village in Ladar, the local people including his relatives did not recognize him. However, when he went to the local mosque and gave *adhan* in his distinctive voice, people began to gather around him. It was then the people realised that the person giving *adhan* in such an emotional voice was none other than Mawlana Abd Allah *Rahmatullah Alayhi,* who had spent ten years studying away from home in Makkah and Madinah Sharif, and Delhi and had now returned as a fully qualified scholar.

This lengthy account suggests that Hadrat Sahib's studies linked him with the leading Sufis and scholars of his time. Hadrat Sahib *Rahmatullah Alayhi* gained religious knowledge and understanding of the Holy Qur'an from Mawlana Abd Allah *Rahmatullah Alayhi* and with further prolific study, he became so well versed in these sciences that the leading jurists, transmitters of Hadith and religious judges were amazed at the depth of knowledge he possessed and would accept his verdicts without reservation.

Passion for Mosques

Allah Almighty says: "The mosques of Allah shall be visited and maintained by such as believe in Allah and the Last Day" (9:18). Rasul Allah ﷺ

---

[358] Originally from Pakhal, he settled and taught in Makkah Sharif
[359] Tilyawarr

211

said, "He who builds a mosque for Allah, Allah would build for him (a house) in Paradise like it," (*Narrated by Bukhari, Muslim, Tirmidhi, Ibn Majah and Musnad Ahmad*). Abu Sa'id al-Khudri ﷺ reports that the Prophet ﷺ said, "If you see a man frequenting the mosque, then testify that he has faith, as Allah states: "The mosques of Allah shall be visited and maintained by such as believe in Allah and the Last Day," (*Narrated by Tirmidhi, Ibn Majah and Darimi*).

Hadrat Sahib *Rahmatullah Alayhi* used the mosque as the centre of guidance. Nowadays hundreds of mosques are run under the supervision of Khanqah-e Fathiyya. These mosques are dedicated only to the remembrance of Allah and matters of dispute are avoided. Some of these mosques have educational faculties where thousands of students learn knowledge. Hundreds of graduates from these faculties are now employed as *a'ima* (prayer leaders) and orators in Azad Kashmir, Pakistan and England.

In addition, amongst the graduates there are hundreds of *Huffaz,* both male and female. Some students from these faculties have obtained Law degrees and are now employed in various posts throughout the country. Due to the spiritual links with Hadrat Sahib *Rahmatullah Alayhi,* thousands of people's lives have been transformed and their characteristics and habits have changed for the better. This is a silent movement which aims to change people's lives for the better, without the aid of electronic media or propagation. Presently, at least three hundred mosques are managed by Khanqah-e Fathiyya: these mosques are located in Panjab, North West Frontier, Azad Kashmir, Bangladesh and Britain. All of these mosques are run by Divine Providence. Every project is based on an inspiration and reflects God's providence.

Rasul Allah ﷺ personally took part in the construction of the Masjid an-Nabawwi Sharif; as a labourer and builder. Although his companions begged him not to do such hard work he continued his duty. Eyewitness accounts suggest that our Hadrat Sahib *Rahmatullah Alayhi* carried out this *Sunnah* during the building of the mosque.[360] He used to carry heavy stones from the stream and recite *sura Ya-Sīn* on them until the mosque was completed. It was around 1960 that Hadrat Sahib *Rahmatullah Alayhi* used to carry stones from the stream for the

---

[360] Kurti Bangla

mosque.[361] Hadrat Sahib *Rahmatullah Alayhi* also worked in levelling the ground in the Ashab-e Rada area. He used to carry the tray and pulled the cart.

Although Hadrat Sahib *Rahmatullah Alayhi* built hundreds of mosque, he never consulted an engineer or an architect. He would remain in his chamber and make plans for these mosques on a piece of paper (pencil drawings), and give instructions on how to build them. He would guide the builders from the foundation, the construction and to the placing of the light on top of the dome. In the early days, he would often personally inspect the construction work.

Each mosque has its unique beauty and design. His passion for mosques does not need an introduction as one can view his work and designs in village after village, which attract the attention of passerbys. Some experts in the building trade have marvelled at these mosques and wondered how a simple and humble Darwish, who normally stayed in his chamber, could produce works of such design, beauty and strength. Hadrat Sahib *Rahmatullah Alayhi* was a naturally gifted architect and a specialist draughtsman the like of whom is difficult to find.

Some Aspects of His Blessed Life

Allah Almighty says, "Behold! Verily on the friends of Allah there is no fear, nor shall they grieve; those who believe and (constantly) guard against evil; for them are glad tidings, in the life of the present and in the Hereafter."(10: 62-63) On the authority of Abu Hurairah ؓ who said, "The Messenger of Allah ﷺ said, "Allah the Almighty has said, "Whosoever shows enmity to a friend of Mine, I shall be at war with him. My servant does not draw near to Me with anything more loved by Me than the religious duties I have imposed upon him, and My servant continues to draw near to Me with supererogatory works so that I shall love him. When I love him I am his hearing with which he hears, his seeing with which he sees, his hand with which he strikes, and his foot with which he walks. Were he to ask [something] of Me, I would surely give it to him and were he to ask Me for refuge, I would surely grant him it," (*Narrated by Bukhari*).

---

[361] Rajur

213

Allama Taftazani *Rahmatullah Alayhi* writes, "A *wali* (saint) is that perfect believer, who knows God, and is constantly engaged in worship, keeps away from all kinds of sins and avoids all types of lust and pleasure," (*Sharh al-Maqāsid*). Hafiz Ibn Hajr Asqalani *Rahmatullah Alayhi* asserts, "By *wali* it means a person who has knowledge and is constantly engaged in sincere worship," (*Fath al-Bari Sharh al-Bukhari*).

Hadrat Sahib *Rahmatullah Alayhi* is the epitome of the pious generations; he lived according to the practices of these people and his noble ancestors. No aspect of his life was outside the boundaries of Shari'ah, and in every matter he followed the path of the pious. He did not accept the modern changes and lived his life according to the way of the *salaf as-salihin*: simplicity, integrity, and complete trust in God were his main characteristics. His life was so simple that despite modern luxuries, he stayed in the mosque and lived in the chamber. He was the epitome of humility. His simplicity and beautiful characteristics are worthy of praise. He used to give *bay'a* to people and guide them and considered it an honour to serve the *Sangis*. His good manners were exceptional and as a human, he always treated people equally regardless of their age, gender, caste, poverty or wealth. He did not give any importance to the common division of high and low caste. However, he would respect people due their piety and religious observance. Allah Almighty had adorned him with perfect knowledge and great spiritual splendour.

Hadrat Sahib's way of life was based on the noble Sunnah of the Prophet ﷺ. Hence his characteristics were exceptional: sincerity, self-denial, piety, trust in God, patience, thankfulness, humility, modesty, knowledge, simplicity, hospitality, lack of interest both in the world and worldly people, concern for the Hereafter, hatred for wastefulness, value for time, following the difficult rulings, and the negation of the self. Which beautiful characteristics can one mention that he did not possess? Above all *dhikr* and contemplation, passion for worship and mosques reached its peak in his personality.

Hadrat Sahib *Rahmatullah Alayhi* ate little as his life was completely devoted to worship and hardship. Eating was not the purpose of life, but a means to gain strength to perform the acts of worship according to the Shari'ah and avoid lethargy. He had no particular preference for any type of food, he would eat whatever was available and considered it a blessing from Allah. He lived in this transitory world for eighty seven years and six days. From the age of puberty he always performed the prayer in congregation, and also read *tahajjud* and other optional prayers on a regular basis. He was so absorbed in the remembrance of Allah that it became his second nature and so he would be engaged in *dhikr* effortlessly. He used to take special care of prayer and ablution to such an extent, that he would not miss any liked act.

In his private chamber Hadrat Sahib *Rahmatullah Alayhi* would briefly meet the people who were going abroad and after enquiring of their circumstances, he would give them some advice and bid them farewell. He would advise them, "This world shall end and to dedicate one's whole life to it and to forget the hereafter is a great loss, it would be wise if one were to use this temporary life to gain salvation in the hereafter. Provision is in the hands of Allah, He increases or decreases it and to seek lawful livelihood is an obligation, but one must not get so pre-occupied in the world that one neglects one's duties to Allah and to one's fellow human beings. Wherever a person lives, his preference should be to put his faith over *dunya*. In the foreign countries there are many avenues that are available to commit sins but one must avoid them."

At the end of the meeting Hadrat Sahib *Rahmatullah Alayhi* would say, "There is a relationship of religious brotherhood between you and us." Sincerity is the basis for every pious action. On this topic Hadrat Sahib *Rahmatullah Alayhi* said, "An act done with sincerity even if little is like mountains and without sincerity, even mountains of good deeds are like a pile of wood that can be raised to the ground in an instant by a display of show." Once Hadrat Sahib *Rahmatullah Alayhi* advised a *Sangi* as he was about to leave, "Sincerity is a big thing and any step taken with it is never wasted, reward is with Allah, the world is temporary. Everything in the world shall perish except for those moments that are spent in the remembrance of Allah, they will last forever." He advised another *Sangi*, "Allah Almighty values sincerity, any work that is done sincerely to please Him is filled with blessings."

The Prophet ﷺ said, "Amongst Allah's creation some people are created to fulfil people's needs and hence people shall seek their needs from them. These people shall be protected from Allah's punishment." (*Narrated by Tabarani in al-Kabir and also by Abu Na'im and Qadai'i and it is considered Hasan*). Abd Allah ibn Umar ﷺ narrates that the Prophet ﷺ said, "Due to the blessing of a pious person Allah Almighty shall protect a hundred houses in his neighbourhood and remove difficulties from a hundred houses." Then Ibn Umar

🌸 recited the verse: "And did not Allah check one set of people by means of another, the earth would indeed be full of mischief," (2:251) (*Narrated by Ibn Jarir*).

Thuban 🌸 narrates the Prophet 🌸 said, "Seven people shall always remain amongst you due to whom you will be helped and due to whom you are given rain and it is due to them that you receive provisions until the matter of Allah takes place (Day of Judgement)," (*Narrated by Tabarani*). Ubada ibn Samit 🌸 narrates that Prophet 🌸 said, "There are thirty *Abdals* (Substitutes) in my *ummah* and due to their blessing you are given provisions, rain and receive help," (*Narrated by Tabarani*). Anas 🌸 relates that the Prophet 🌸 said, "The earth will never lack forty men similar to the Friend of the Merciful [Prophet Ibrahim], and through them people receive rain and are given help. None of them dies except Allah substitutes another in his place." (*Narrated by Tabarani, Mu'jam al-Awsat, its chain is Hasan and also narrated in the Mujama az-Zawaid vol 10:62*).

When people would come to Hadrat Sahib *Rahmatullah Alayhi* seeking help he would say, "I shall pray for you and you should pray for me." Most people's experiences suggests that their problems would be resolved but when they mentioned this to Hadrat Sahib *Rahmatullah Alayhi* he would respond, "I am a humble servant and worry about my own salvation. There were many great people in the *silsila* (spiritual chain), and due to the blessings of one of them this matter has been resolved."

Hadrat Sahib's life was very simple and reminded one of the first generation of Muslims; the same simplicity, the same humility and modesty and all other qualities were exemplified in him and to give preference to one quality over another is pointless. For example, consider the feature of hospitality; He spent his whole life practicing this. Whoever came, whatever food was available was served. On a daily basis hundreds of people ate from his table spread: friends, foes, colleagues and strangers were fed without discrimination. Despite this generosity nobody ever heard him say that he had done a favour to anyone. Indeed, he had instructed the *Sangis* that since Gulhar Sharif (Khanqah-e Fathiyya) was located at a crossing, all kinds of people came there, and they should be looked after regardless of their background and food should be served to them and accommodation provided for their stay at night according to the requirements of the weather. Throughout his life he provided shelter for the needy and whoever was in need came to him, and his/her needs were met. Every type of person would benefit from his company and did not feel like a stranger. Seeing his kindness, everyone felt that they were dearest to him.

Such people shall be granted high ranks on the Day of Judgement, regarding which the Prophet said, "Surely, amongst the slaves of God, are those whom prophets and martyrs will envy." The companions asked, "O Messenger of God 鷺, who are they; inform us so that we may love them." Upon their request the Prophet 鷺 said, "They are such a community that although they have no property (transaction) and kinship between themselves, they love each other. Their faces are full of light. They are on pulpits of light. They continue not to fear when the public fears. They do not grieve when the public grieves." The Prophet 鷺 then recited the verse: "Know well that the friends (saintly servants) of God, they will have no fear, nor will they grieve," (*Narrated by Abu Dawud, Tirmidhi and by Bah'aiqi in Shua'b al-Iman*).

The Prophet 鷺 said, "Some people shall rise from their graves and their faces will be full of light and they will be seated upon thrones of rubies and people shall be envious of their lofty rank, these people will neither be prophets or martyrs." One Bedouin enquired, "Who will these people be and how shall we recognize them." The Prophet 鷺 replied, "They shall be people who love one another for Allah's sake," (*Narrated by Tabarani).* The Prophet 鷺 said, "Allah will say on the Day of Resurrection, "Where are those who love one another through My glory? Today I shall give them shade in My shade," (*Narrated by Muslim*). Love for such people leads to the pleasure of Allah and salvation in the hereafter. May Allah grant us love for the pious people. Abd Allah ibn Masud 鷺 narrates that a person asked the Prophet 鷺, "A person loves a pious person but does not perform acts like him." The Prophet 鷺 said, "It does not matter as a person shall be with whom he loves," (*Narrated by Bukhari*).

History testifies that for the past four centuries the al-Bakri al-Siddqi family has made great contributions in raising religious awareness amongst people, and reforming the society. The main feature of this family's religious service has been that everything was done solely for Allah's pleasure. May Allah keep this dedication for the Faith alive in Hadrat Sahib's family, and may they devote all their energies in the cause of Islam. *Amin.*

Whoever wishes to read the *khatam* of Hadrat Sahib *Rahmatullah Alayhi* for blessings is hereby given permission. In order to receive full benefit, read the *khatam* sitting on your knees with complete respect.

1. *Durud Sharif*   (100 times)
2. فَاللّٰهُ خَيْرٌ حَافِظًا ۖ وَهُوَ أَرْحَمُ الرَّاحِمِينَ (500 times)
3. *Durud Sharif*   (100 times)

Send the merit (*sawab*) of this to Hadrat Sahib *Rahmatullah Alayhi* and ask Allah to fulfil your needs for his sake. *"Our duty is merely to convey."*

Life: Summary

Hadrat Sahib *Rahmatullah Alayhi* was the living embodiment of the Qura'nic verse: "Say, indeed my prayers, sacrifices; life and death are only for the Lord of the worlds (6:162)." His days and nights were occupied with the constant remembrance of Allah and he strongly recommended that the people do the same. His love for the Holy Qur'an is well known as he spent his whole life spreading the teaching of Allah's book. His life revolved around the blessed Sunnah of the Prophet 🕮 and was dedicated to its propagation. Following the Prophet's example, the mosque played a pivotal role in his life and teachings. Using the mosque as his headquarters he guided people who had lost their way, helped the weak, the orphans and the needy. Yet he never attributed any greatness to himself and always kept away from controversy. He never used any honorific titles for himself and would always simply sign his birth name. He stated: **"I am helpless as a chick without wings, indeed I am merely a lump of flesh**, *Main chirri nain behche nein tarah hanh jis nain par nein nikleye, main luth-teh ne luth hanh.*" He never approved of any one heaping praise on him whether in private or public as in his view this is the age of extremes and such things should be avoided, as no one is safe until he has achieved his salvation. Lavish praises only provide fodder for the ego and leads the person into a false sense of security. To state that Hadrat Sahib *Rahmatullah Alayhi* lived a simple life is an understatement. His life was based on the following tradition of the Prophet 🕮:

"كُنْ فِي الدُّنْيَا كَأَنَّكَ غَرِيبٌ أَوْ عَابِرُ سَبِيلٍ"

Be in the world as though you were a stranger or a wayfarer,

(*Narrated by Bukhari*)

"In order to guide the people on the Noble Path (Naqshbandiyya Mujaddidiyya) this humble servant's two sons, Hafiz Muhammad Abd al-Wahid Sahib (Janab Qibla Hajji Pir Sahib) and Hafiz Muhammad Zahid Sahib (Janab Sahibzada Sahib) are present. *Masha Allah* both are learned, noble, pious and have been authorised. *Insha Allah* they are capable of providing exceptional guidance for the *Sangis*. May Allah Almighty keep them on the path of their predecessors and accept them for the service of the *din*. The present period is a time of waywardness and confusion as the Devil has laid his trap everywhere. Only by the grace of Allah and constant vigilance can a person safeguard himself. The *Sangis* are requested to constantly pray for them," (*Maqalāt*, 2006:234).

Blessed Cloak Granted by Bawali Sharif

Blessed Cap

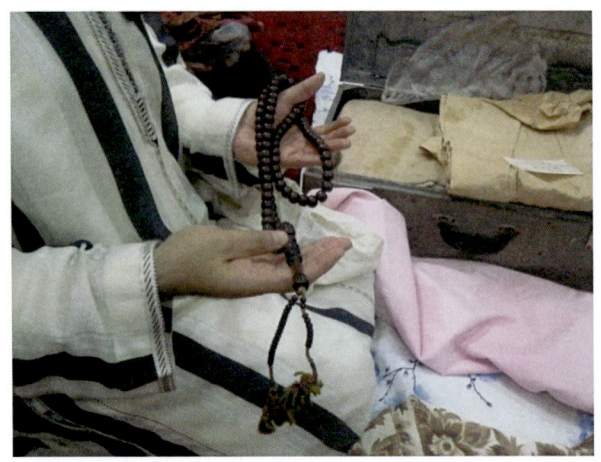

Blessed Rosary

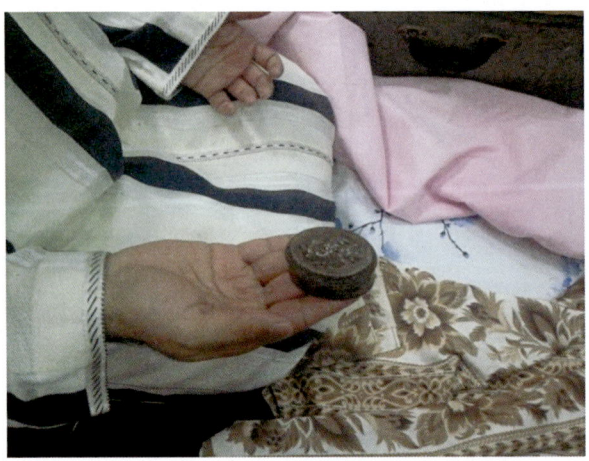

Mysterious Silver Object

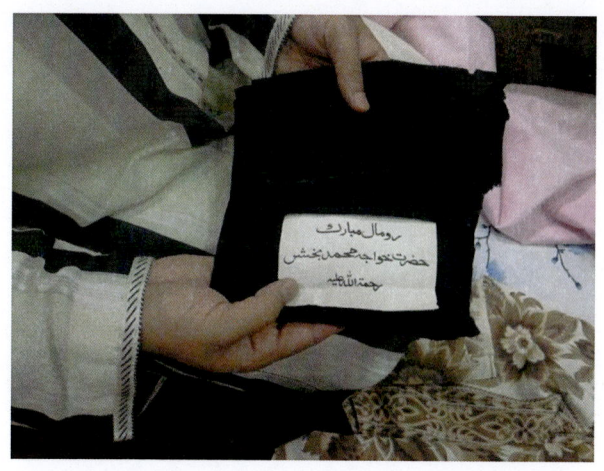

Blessed Scarf of Khwaja Muhammad Bakhsh *Rahmatullah Alayhi*

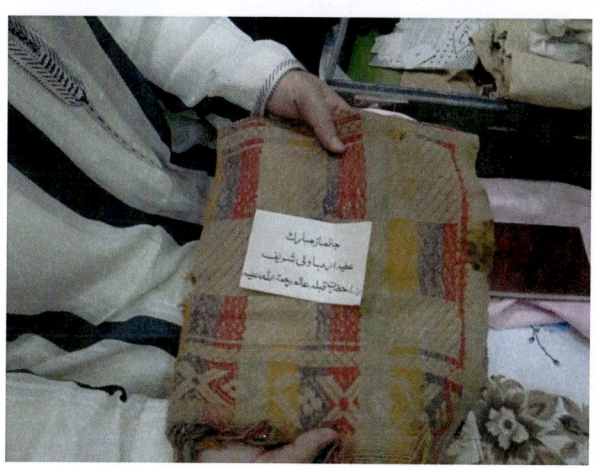

Prayer Mat Granted by Bawali Sharif

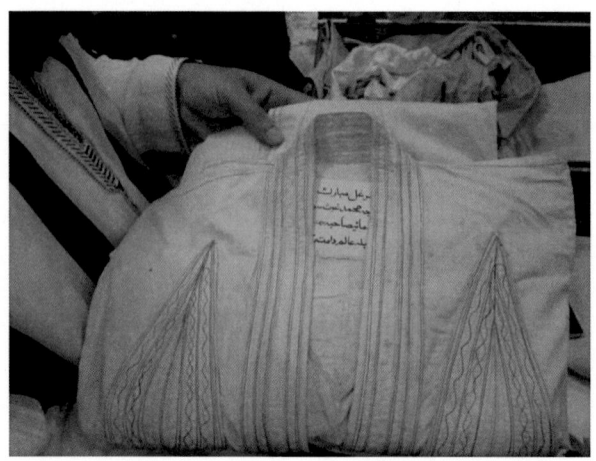

Cloak Granted by Bawali Sharif

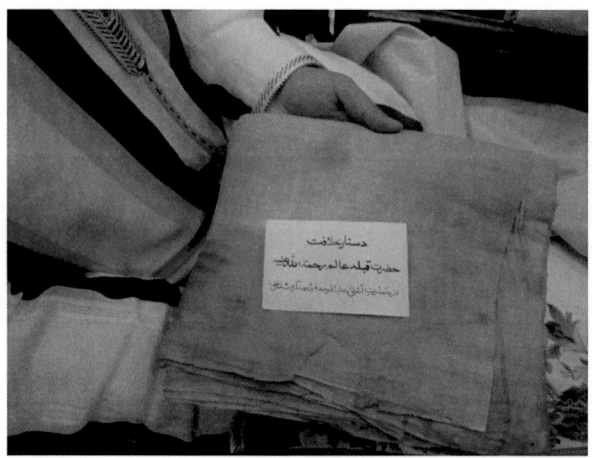

Authorisation from Khwaja Hafiz Muhammad Hayat *Rahmatullah Alayhi*

Signature of Qibla Alam *Rahmatullah Alayhi*